Learn React Hooks

Build and refactor modern React.js applications using Hooks

Daniel Bugl

BIRMINGHAM - MUMBAI

Learn React Hooks

Copyright © 2019 Packt Publishing

Commissioning Editor: Pavan Ramchandani
Acquisition Editor: Heramb Bhavsar
Content Development Editor: Keagan Carneiro
Senior Editor: Mohammed Yusuf Imaratwale
Technical Editor: Suwarna Patil
Copy Editor: Safis Editing
Project Coordinator: Manthan Patel
Proofreader: Safis Editing
Indexer: Pratik Shirodkar
Production Designer: Aparna Bhagat

First published: October 2019

Production reference: 1181019

Published by Packt Publishing Ltd.
Livery Place
35 Livery Street
Birmingham
B3 2PB, UK.

ISBN 978-1-83864-144-3

www.packt.com

To my family and friends for supporting me during the creation of this book.

To my father, who has supported me throughout my whole life.

To my co-founder, Georg Schelkshorn, who runs an amazing company with me. Thank you for taking care of business while I was writing this book.

To my amazing girlfriend, Junxian Wang, for improving my life in many ways, for making me more productive, and for always taking care of me. I love you so much.

Without you, all of this would not have been possible.

– Daniel Bugl

Packt.com

Subscribe to our online digital library for full access to over 7,000 books and videos, as well as industry leading tools to help you plan your personal development and advance your career. For more information, please visit our website.

Why subscribe?

- Spend less time learning and more time coding with practical eBooks and Videos from over 4,000 industry professionals

- Improve your learning with Skill Plans built especially for you

- Get a free eBook or video every month

- Fully searchable for easy access to vital information

- Copy and paste, print, and bookmark content

Did you know that Packt offers eBook versions of every book published, with PDF and ePub files available? You can upgrade to the eBook version at www.packt.com and as a print book customer, you are entitled to a discount on the eBook copy. Get in touch with us at customercare@packtpub.com for more details.

At www.packt.com, you can also read a collection of free technical articles, sign up for a range of free newsletters, and receive exclusive discounts and offers on Packt books and eBooks.

Foreword

When Hooks were initially released, I was excited, but also skeptical. Being able to rely only on functions was fantastic. On the other hand, Hooks such as `useEffect` required the whole React community to rethink how to approach managing side effects.

Hooks made it very easy to handle the most commonplace things, such as rendering and managing state. For such things, most of the time, you can get away with not actually knowing that much about Hooks. Still, now and then, you will need to handle more complex requirements and this requires you to have a deep understanding of when to apply which Hook.

In his book, Daniel starts from the very beginning. Anyone with a basic understanding of React can get started with it. Even so, this book goes very deep and even someone experienced with Hooks will most likely learn something new since Daniel also touches on design decisions and shows basic implementations of the presented concepts. Also, while he covers the theory well, each chapter has plenty of hands-on examples.

Nik Graf
ReactVienna organizer
ReasonConf organizer

About Nik Graf

Nik Graf initiated the ReactVienna Meetup in 2015. He has created several open source projects, including DraftJs plugins, Polished, and Belle, which all featured at Stripe's Open-Source Retreat in 2016. As a consultant/freelancer, he supports multiple companies with their frontend architecture using React and GraphQL. In addition to that, he produces video courses, which can be found on his personal website: `https://www.nikgraf.com`.

When React Hooks were released, Nik created a searchable collection of community-created Hooks at `https://nikgraf.github.io/react-hooks/`.

Contributors

About the author

Daniel Bugl is a developer, product designer, and entrepreneur focusing on web technologies. He has a Bachelor of Science degree in business informatics and information systems and is now studying data science at the Vienna University of Technology (TU Wien). He is a contributor to many open source projects and a member of the React community. He also founded and runs his own hardware/software start-up, TouchLay, which helps other companies present their products and services. At his company, he constantly works with web technologies, particularly making use of React and React Hooks.

I want to thank the people involved in the production of this book, my co-founder, Georg Schelkshorn; my family and friends; and my girlfriend, Junxian Wang.

About the reviewers

Farzad YousefZadeh is a self-taught senior software engineer and an international conference speaker with an academic background in aerospace engineering and astrophysics. He lives in Finland with his wife and their cat. He mainly works with JavaScript and TypeScript on different platforms, but he is most passionate about client-side applications, thriving to solve UI development challenges by studying revolutionary approaches. He is fascinated by tooling around with development experience and automation. He is an active member of the open source community by constantly contributing to OSS, public technical speaking, and volunteering in free educational programs.

Kirill Ezhemenskii is an experienced software engineer, a frontend and mobile developer, a solution architect, and the CTO at a healthcare company. He's a functional programming advocate and an expert in the React stack, GraphQL, and TypeScript. He's also a React native mentor.

Packt is searching for authors like you

If you're interested in becoming an author for Packt, please visit `authors.packtpub.com` and apply today. We have worked with thousands of developers and tech professionals, just like you, to help them share their insight with the global tech community. You can make a general application, apply for a specific hot topic that we are recruiting an author for, or submit your own idea.

Table of Contents

Preface

React is a JavaScript library for building efficient and extensible web applications. React is developed by Facebook and is used in many large-scale web applications, such as Facebook, Instagram, Netflix, and WhatsApp Web.

React Hooks were introduced in the React 16.8 release and solve many common problems with React projects. Hooks make components less complex, more concise, and easier to read and refactor. Furthermore, they make many React features much easier to use and understand, and we avoid having to use wrapper components.

This book is the definitive guide to learning React Hooks. You are going to learn all the facets of React Hooks for managing state and effects in React components, as well as using other React features, such as context, via Hooks. With practical examples, you are going to learn how to develop large-scale and efficient applications with code that is extensible and easy to understand.

The book also delves into advanced concepts, such as using Hooks in combination with libraries like Redux and MobX. Furthermore, you are going to learn when and how existing projects can be efficiently migrated to React Hooks.

Who this book is for

The book is intended for web developers at any level of expertise with JavaScript and the React framework. The book will also cater to developers who have been migrating to React for its advanced feature set and capabilities.

What this book covers

Chapter 1, *Introducing React and React Hooks*, covers the fundamental principles of React and React Hooks, what they are and why to use them. We then learn about the functionality of Hooks by introducing the State Hook as an alternative to React state in class components. Finally, we introduce the kinds of Hooks React provides and introduce a couple of Hooks that we are going to learn about throughout the book.

Chapter 2, *Using the State Hook*, explains how Hooks work in depth by reimplementing the useState Hook. By doing so, we find out that there are certain limitations of Hooks. We are then going to compare our reimplementation of a Hook with real Hooks. Furthermore, we introduce alternative Hook APIs and discuss the problems they have. Finally, we learn how to solve common problems with Hooks, such as conditional Hooks and Hooks in loops.

Chapter 3, *Writing Your First Application with React Hooks*, takes what we learned from the first two chapters and puts it into practice by developing a blog application using React Hooks, specifically the State Hook. In this chapter, we also learn how to structure React projects in a way that scales well.

Chapter 4, *Using the Reducer and Effect Hooks*, moves on from learning about the simple State Hook and using it in practice. We are going to learn about the other two main Hooks predefined by the React library: the Reducer and Effect Hooks. We first learn when we should use a Reducer Hook instead of a State Hook. Then we learn how to turn our existing State Hook into a Reducer Hook to get an idea of the concept. Finally, we learn how to use Effect Hooks for more advanced functionality.

Chapter 5, *Implementing React Context*, explains React context and how it can be used in our application. Then we implement React context in our blog application to provide theming functionality and global state using Context Hooks.

Chapter 6, *Implementing Requests and React Suspense*, covers requesting resources from a server with Hooks using an Effect Hook and a State or Reducer Hook. Then we learn how to use React.memo to prevent unnecessary component re-renders. Finally, we learn about React Suspense, which can be used to defer rendering until a condition is met, also called lazy loading.

Chapter 7, *Using Hooks for Routing*, explains how to use Hooks to implement routing in our blog application. We learn about Navi, a routing library for React that makes use of Hooks and Suspense. We start by implementing pages in our application, then define routes, and finally move on to implementing routing Hooks.

Chapter 8, *Using Community Hooks*, explains that the React community has already developed various libraries that make use of Hooks. In this chapter, we learn about implementing various Hooks from the community, as well as where to find more of them. We first learn about the input handling Hook. Next, we learn how to replace React life cycle methods with Hooks. Then, we learn about various useful Hooks and responsive design with Hooks. Furthermore, we learn how to implement undo/redo functionality using Hooks. Finally, we learn where to find other Hooks provided by the community.

Chapter 9, *Rules of Hooks*, covers the rules of Hooks. Having a grasp on the rules of Hooks is very important for building our own Hooks, which we are going to do in the next chapter. We also learn about the limitations of Hooks in depth and discover what we need to watch out for. Finally, we learn how to enforce the rules of Hooks using a linter.

Chapter 10, *Building Your Own Hooks*, moves on from the basic concepts of Hooks. We are now going to build our own Hooks. We start by extracting a custom Hook from an existing function of our blog application, and then we learn how to use our custom Hook. Next, we learn about passing information between Hooks. Finally, we learn about the React Hooks API and additional Hooks we can use to build our own Hooks. At the end of this chapter, our application will be fully powered by Hooks!

Chapter 11, *Migrating from React Class Components*, covers state handling with React class components. We start by implementing a simple ToDo application with class components. Then, we learn how to migrate an existing project using class components to a Hook-based implementation. Finally, we learn about the trade-offs of using class components versus Hooks and a strategy to efficiently migrate existing projects.

Chapter 12, *Redux and Hooks*, explains state handling with Redux. We start by migrating our existing ToDo application to Redux, and then we learn how to use Redux with Hooks. Furthermore, we learn how to migrate an existing Redux application to Hooks. Finally, we learn about the trade-offs of using Redux.

Chapter 13, *MobX and Hooks*, covers state handling with MobX. We start by migrating our existing ToDo application to MobX. Then we learn how to use MobX with Hooks. Furthermore, we learn how to migrate an existing MobX application to Hooks. Finally, we learn about the trade-offs of using MobX.

To get the most out of this book

We assume that you have already worked with React in some way, although this book should be understandable for complete beginners of React as well.

Please note that it is highly recommended that you write the code on your own. Do not simply run the code examples that are provided. It is important to write the code yourself in order to learn and understand it properly. However, if you run into any issues, you can always refer to the code example.

Download the example code files

You can download the example code files for this book from your account at `www.packt.com`. If you purchased this book elsewhere, you can visit `www.packtpub.com/support` and register to have the files emailed directly to you.

You can download the code files by following these steps:

1. Log in or register at `www.packt.com`.
2. Select the **Support** tab.
3. Click on **Code Downloads**.
4. Enter the name of the book in the **Search** box and follow the onscreen instructions.

Once the file is downloaded, please make sure that you unzip or extract the folder using the latest version of:

- WinRAR/7-Zip for Windows
- Zipeg/iZip/UnRarX for Mac
- 7-Zip/PeaZip for Linux

The code bundle for the book is also hosted on GitHub at `https://github.com/PacktPublishing/Learn-React-Hooks`. In case there's an update to the code, it will be updated on the existing GitHub repository.

We also have other code bundles from our rich catalog of books and videos available at `https://github.com/PacktPublishing/`. Check them out!

Download the color images

We also provide a PDF file that has color images of the screenshots/diagrams used in this book. You can download it here: `https://static.packt-cdn.com/downloads/9781838641443_ColorImages.pdf`.

Code in Action

Visit the following link to check out videos of the code being run:

`http://bit.ly/2Mm9yoC`

Conventions used

There are a number of text conventions used throughout this book.

CodeInText: Indicates code words in text, folder names, filenames, file extensions, pathnames, dummy URLs, and user input. Here is an example: "JavaScript classes provide a render method, which returns the user interface (usually via JSX)."

A block of code is set as follows:

```
class Example extends React.Component {
```

When we wish to draw your attention to a particular part of a code block, the relevant lines or items are set in bold:

```
constructor (props) {
    super(props)
    this.state = { name: '' }
    this.handleChange = this.handleChange.bind(this)
}
```

Any command-line input or output is written as follows:

```
> npm run-script build
```

Bold: Indicates a new term, an important word, or words that you see onscreen. Here is an example: " Throughout this chapter, we are also going to learn about **JSX**, and new JavaScript features that have been introduced in **ES6**, up to **ES2018**."

In blocks of code, we use bold formatting to highlight changes in the code. Usually, we highlight new code using bold. If specified, we might also indicate which parts of code should be deleted by using bold formatting.

 Warnings or important notes appear like this.

 Tips and tricks appear like this.

Get in touch

Feedback from our readers is always welcome.

General feedback: If you have questions about any aspect of this book, mention the book title in the subject of your message and email us at customercare@packtpub.com.

Errata: Although we have taken every care to ensure the accuracy of our content, mistakes do happen. If you have found a mistake in this book, we would be grateful if you would report this to us. Please visit www.packtpub.com/support/errata, selecting your book, clicking on the Errata Submission Form link, and entering the details.

Piracy: If you come across any illegal copies of our works in any form on the Internet, we would be grateful if you would provide us with the location address or website name. Please contact us at copyright@packt.com with a link to the material.

If you are interested in becoming an author: If there is a topic that you have expertise in and you are interested in either writing or contributing to a book, please visit authors.packtpub.com.

Reviews

Please leave a review. Once you have read and used this book, why not leave a review on the site that you purchased it from? Potential readers can then see and use your unbiased opinion to make purchase decisions, we at Packt can understand what you think about our products, and our authors can see your feedback on their book. Thank you!

For more information about Packt, please visit packt.com.

Section 1: Introduction to Hooks

In the first part of the book, we will introduce and cover the basics of React and React Hooks, including why and how to use them. Following this, we will use our knowledge gained in a practical setting, to create a blog application using React Hooks.

In this section, we will cover the following chapters:

- Chapter 1, *Introducing React and React Hooks*
- Chapter 2, *Using the State Hook*
- Chapter 3, *Writing Your First Application with React Hooks*

Introducing React and React Hooks

React is a JavaScript library that can be used to build efficient and extensible web applications. React was developed by Facebook, and is used in many large-scale web applications, such as Facebook, Instagram, Netflix, and WhatsApp Web.

In this book, we are going to learn how to build complex and efficient user interfaces with React, while keeping the code simple and extensible. Using the new paradigm of React Hooks, we can greatly simplify dealing with state management and side effects in web applications, ensuring the potential for growing and extending the application later on. We are also going to learn about **React context** and **React Suspense**, as well as how they can be used with Hooks. Afterward, we are going to learn how to integrate **Redux** and **MobX** with React Hooks. Finally, we are going to learn how to migrate from existing React class components, Redux, and MobX web applications, to React Hooks.

In the first chapter of this book, we are going to learn about the fundamental principles of React and React Hooks. We start by learning what React and React Hooks are, and why we should use them. Then, we move on to learn about the functionality of Hooks. Finally, we give an introduction to the kinds of Hooks that are provided by React, and a couple of Hooks that we are going to learn about throughout the book. By learning the fundamentals of React and React Hooks, we will be better able to understand the concepts that will be introduced in this book.

The following topics will be covered in this chapter:

- Learning about the fundamental principles of React
- Motivating the need for React Hooks
- Getting started with React Hooks
- Giving an overview of various Hooks

Technical requirements

A fairly recent version of Node.js should already be installed (v11.12.0, or higher). The npm package manager for Node.js also needs to be installed.

The code for this chapter can be found on the GitHub repository: https://github.com/ PacktPublishing/Learn-React-Hooks/tree/master/Chapter01.

Check out the following video to see the code in action:

http://bit.ly/2Mm9yoC

Please note that it is highly recommended that you write the code on your own. Do not simply run the code examples that were previously provided. It is important to write the code yourself in order to learn and understand it properly. However, if you run into any issues, you can always refer to the code example.

Now, let's get started with the chapter.

Principles of React

Before we start learning about React Hooks, we are going to learn about the three fundamental principles of React. These principles allow us to easily write scalable web applications. The fundamental principles are important to know, as they will help us to understand how and why Hooks fit into the React ecosystem.

React is based on three fundamental principles:

- **Declarative**: Instead of telling React how to do things, we tell it what we want it to do. As a result, we can easily design our applications and React will efficiently update and render just the right components when the data changes. For example, the following code, which duplicates strings in an array is imperative, which is the opposite of declarative:

```
const input = ['a', 'b', 'c']
let result = []
for (let i = 0; i < input.length; i++) {
    result.push(input[i] + input[i])
}
console.log(result) // prints: [ 'aa', 'bb', 'cc' ]
```

As we can see, in imperative code, we need to tell the computer exactly what to do, step by step. However, with declarative code, we can simply tell the computer what we want, as follows:

```
const input = ['a', 'b', 'c']
let result = input.map(str => str + str)
console.log(result) // prints: [ 'aa', 'bb', 'cc' ]
```

In the previous declarative code, we tell the computer that we want to map each element of the input array from str to str + str. As we can see, declarative code is much more concise.

- **Component-based**: React encapsulates components that manage their own state and views, and then allows us to compose them in order to create complex user interfaces.
- **Learn once, write anywhere**: React does not make assumptions about your technology stack, and tries to ensure that you can develop apps without rewriting existing code as much as possible.

We just mentioned that React is component-based. In React, there are two types of components:

- **Function components**: JavaScript functions that take the props as an argument, and return the user interface (usually via JSX)
- **Class components**: JavaScript classes that provide a render method, which returns the user interface (usually via JSX)

While function components are easier to define and understand, class components were needed to deal with state, contexts, and many more of React's advanced features. However, with React Hooks, we can deal with React's advanced features without needing a class component!

Motivation for using React Hooks

React's three fundamental principles make it easy to write code, encapsulate components, and share code across multiple platforms. Instead of reinventing the wheel, React always tries to make use of existing JavaScript features as much as possible. As a result, we are going to learn software design patterns that will be applicable in many more cases than just designing user interfaces.

React always strives to make the developer experience as smooth as possible, while ensuring that it is kept performant enough, without the developer having to worry too much about how to optimize performance. However, throughout the years of using React, a couple of problems have been identified.

Let's take a look at these problems in detail in the following sections.

Confusing classes

In the past, we had to use class components with special functions called life cycle methods, such as `componentDidUpdate`, and special state-handling methods, such as `this.setState`, in order to deal with state changes. React classes, and especially the `this` context, which is a JavaScript object, are hard to read and understand for both humans and machines.

`this` is a special keyword in JavaScript that always refers to the object that it belongs to:

- In a method, `this` refers to the class object (instance of the class).
- In an event handler, `this` refers to the element that received the event.
- In a function or when standing alone, `this` refers to the global object. For example, in a browser, the global object is the `Window` object.
- In strict mode, `this` is `undefined` in a function.
- Additionally, methods such as `call()` and `apply()` can change the object that `this` refers to, so it can refer to any object.

For humans, classes are hard because `this` always refers to different things, so sometimes (for example, in event handlers) we need to manually rebind it to the class object. For machines, classes are hard, because the machines do not know which methods in a class will be called, and how `this` will be modified, making it hard to optimize performance and remove unused code.

Furthermore, classes sometimes require us to write code in multiple places at once. For example, if we want to fetch data when the component renders, or the data updates, we need to do this using two methods: once in `componentDidMount`, and once in `componentDidUpdate`.

To give an example, let's define a class component that fetches data from an **Application Programming Interface (API)**:

1. First, we define our class component by extending the `React.Component` class:

    ```
    class Example extends React.Component {
    ```

2. Then, we define the `componentDidMount` life cycle method, where we pull data from an API:

    ```
    componentDidMount () {
        fetch(`http://my.api/${this.props.name}`)
            .then(...)
    }
    ```

3. However, we also need to define the `componentDidUpdate` life cycle method in case the `name` prop changes. Additionally, we need to add a manual check here, in order to ensure that we only re-fetch data if the `name` prop changed, and not when other props change:

    ```
    componentDidUpdate (prevProps) {
        if (this.props.name !== prevProps.name) {
            fetch(`http://my.api/${this.props.name}`)
                .then(...)
        }
    }
    ```

4. To make our code less repetitive, we could define a separate method called `fetchData`, in order to fetch our data, as follows:

    ```
    fetchData () {
        fetch(`http://my.api/${this.props.name}`)
            .then(...)
    }
    ```

5. Then, we could call the method in `componentDidMount` and `componentDidUpdate`:

    ```
    componentDidMount () {
        this.fetchData()
    }

    componentDidUpdate (prevProps) {
        if (this.props.name !== prevProps.name) {
            this.fetchData()
    ```

```
      }
    }
```

However, even then we still need to call `fetchData` in two places. Whenever we update arguments that are passed to the method, we need to update them in two places, which makes this pattern very prone to errors and future bugs.

Wrapper hell

Before Hooks, if we wanted to encapsulate state management logic, we had to use higher-order components and render props. For example, we create a React component that uses contexts to deal with user authentication as follows:

1. We start by importing the `authenticateUser` function in order to wrap our component with the context, and the `AuthenticationContext` component in order to access the context:

```
import authenticateUser, { AuthenticationContext } from
'./auth'
```

2. Then, we define our `App` component, where we make use of the `AuthenticationContext.Consumer` component and the `user` render prop:

```
const App = () => (
    <AuthenticationContext.Consumer>
        {user =>
```

3. Now, we display different texts depending on whether the user is logged in or not:

```
user ? `${user} logged in` : 'not logged in'
```

Here, we used two JavaScript concepts:

- A ternary operator, which is an inline version of the `if` conditional. It looks as follows: `ifThisIsTrue ? returnThis : otherwiseReturnThis`.
- A template string, which can be used to insert variables into a string. It is defined with backticks (`` ` ``) instead of normal single quotes (`'`). Variables can be inserted via the `${variableName}` syntax. We can also use any JavaScript expressions within the `${}` brackets, for example, `${someValue + 1}`.

4. Finally, we export our component after wrapping it with the `authenticateUser` context:

```
        }
    </AuthenticationContext.Consumer>
)

export default authenticateUser(App)
```

In the previous example, we used the higher-order `authenticateUser` component to add authentication logic to our existing component. We then used `AuthenticationContext.Consumer` to inject the `user` object into our component through its render props.

As you can imagine, using many contexts will result in a large tree with many sub-trees, also called **wrapper hell**. For example, when we want to use three contexts, the wrapper hell looks as follows:

```
<AuthenticationContext.Consumer>
    {user => (
        <LanguageContext.Consumer>
            {language => (
                <StatusContext.Consumer>
                    {status => (
                        ...
                    )}
                </StatusContext.Consumer>
            )}
        </LanguageContext.Consumer>
    )}
</AuthenticationContext.Consumer>
```

This is not very easy to read or write, and it is also prone to errors if we need to change something later on. Furthermore, the wrapper hell makes debugging hard, because we need to look at a large component tree, with many components just acting as wrappers.

Hooks to the rescue!

React Hooks are based on the same fundamental principles as React. They try to encapsulate state management by using existing JavaScript features. As a result, we do not need to learn and understand specialized React features anymore; we can simply tap into our existing JavaScript knowledge in order to use Hooks.

Using Hooks, we can solve all the previously mentioned problems. We do not need to use class components anymore, because Hooks are simply functions that can be called in function components. We also do not need to use higher-order components and render props for contexts anymore, because we can simply use a Context Hook to get the data that we need. Furthermore, Hooks allow us to reuse stateful logic between components, without creating higher-order components.

For example, the aforementioned problems with life cycle methods could be solved using Hooks, as follows:

```
function Example ({ name }) {
    useEffect(() => {
        fetch(`http://my.api/${this.props.name}`)
            .then(...)
    }, [ name ])
    // ...
}
```

The Effect Hook that was implemented here will automatically trigger when the component mounts, and whenever the `name` prop changes.

Furthermore, the wrapper hell that was mentioned earlier could also be solved using Hooks, as follows:

```
const user = useContext(AuthenticationContext)
const language = useContext(LanguageContext)
const status = useContext(StatusContext)
```

Now that we know which problems Hooks can solve, let's get started using Hooks in practice!

Getting started with React Hooks

As we can see, React Hooks solve many problems, especially of larger web applications. Hooks were added in React 16.8, and they allow us to use state, and various other React features, without writing a class. In this section, we are going to start out by initializing a project with `create-react-app`, then we will define a class component, and finally we will write the same component as a function component using Hooks. By the end of this section, we will have talked about the advantages of Hooks, and how we would go about migrating to a Hook-based solution.

Initializing a project with create-react-app

To initialize a React project, we can use the `create-react-app` tool, which sets up the environment for React development, including the following:

- Babel, so that we can use the JSX and ES6 syntaxes
- It even includes language extras beyond ES6, such as the object spread operator, which we are going to make use of later
- Additionally, we could even use TypeScript and Flow syntax

Furthermore, `create-react-app` sets up the following:

- Autoprefixed **Cascading Style Sheets** (**CSS**), so that we do not need browser-specific prefixes such as `-webkit`
- A fast interactive unit test runner with code coverage reporting
- A live development server, which warns us about common mistakes
- A build script, which bundles JavaScript, CSS, and images for production, including hashes and sourcemaps
- An offline-first service worker and a web app manifest to meet all criteria of a **Progressive Web App** (**PWA**)
- Hassle-free updates for all the tools that have been previously listed

As we can see, the `create-react-app` tool makes React development a lot easier for us. It is the perfect tool for us to use in order to learn about React, as well as for deploying React applications in production.

Creating a new project

In order to set up a new project, we run the following command, which creates a new directory named `<app-name>`:

```
> npx create-react-app <app-name>
```

If you prefer using the `yarn` package manager, you can run `yarn create react-app <app-name>` instead.

We are now going to create a new project using `create-react-app`. Run the following command to create a new React project for the first example of the first chapter:

```
> npx create-react-app chapter1_1
```

Now that we have initialized our project, let's move on to starting the project.

Starting a project

In order to start a project in development mode, we have to run the `npm start` command. Run the following command:

```
> npm start
```

Now, we can access our project by opening `http://localhost:3000` in our browser:

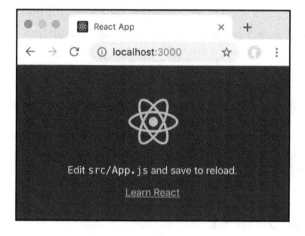

Our first React app!

As we can see, with `create-react-app`, it is quite easy to set up a new React project!

Deploying a project

To build a project for production deployments, we simply run the `build` script:

1. Run the following command to build the project for production deployment:

    ```
    > npm run-script build
    ```

Using yarn, we can simply run `yarn build`. Actually, we can run any package script that does not conflict with the name of an internal `yarn` command in this way: `yarn <script-name>`, instead of `npm run-script <script-name>`.

2. We can then serve our static build folder with a web server, or by using the `serve` tool. First, we have to install it:

   > **npm install -g serve**

3. Then, we can run the `serve` command, as follows:

   > **serve -s build**

 The `-s` flag of the `serve` command rewrites all not-found requests to `index.html`, allowing for client-side routing.

Now, we can access the same app by opening `http://localhost:5000` in our browser. Please note that the `serve` tool does not automatically open the page in your browser.

After learning about `create-react-app`, we are now going to write our first component with React.

Starting with a class component

First, we start out with a traditional React class component, which lets us enter a name, which we then display in our app.

Setting up the project

As mentioned before, we are going to use `create-react-app` to initialize our project. If you have not done so already, run the following command now:

> **npx create-react-app chapter1_1**

Next we are going to define our app as a class component.

Defining the class component

We first write our app as a traditional class component, as follows:

1. First, we remove all code from the `src/App.js` file.

2. Next, in `src/App.js`, we import React:

   ```
   import React from 'react'
   ```

3. We then start defining our own class component—`MyName`:

   ```
   class MyName extends React.Component {
   ```

4. Next, we have to define a `constructor` method, where we set the initial `state` object, which will be an empty string. Here, we also need to make sure to call `super(props)`, in order to let the `React.Component` constructor know about the `props` object:

   ```
   constructor (props) {
       super(props)
       this.state = { name: '' }
   }
   ```

5. Now, we define a method to set the `name` variable, by using `this.setState`. As we will be using this method to handle input from a text field, we need to use `evt.target.value` to get the value from the input field:

   ```
   handleChange (evt) {
       this.setState({ name: evt.target.value })
   }
   ```

6. Then, we define the `render` method, where we are going to display an input field and the name:

   ```
   render () {
   ```

7. To get the `name` variable from the `this.state` object, we are going to use destructuring:

   ```
   const { name } = this.state
   ```

   The previous statement is the equivalent of doing the following:

   ```
   const name = this.state.name
   ```

8. Then, we display the currently entered `name` state variable:

```
return (
    <div>
        <h1>My name is: {name}</h1>
```

9. We display an `input` field, passing the handler method to it:

```
            <input type="text" value={name}
    onChange={this.handleChange} />
            </div>
        )
    }
}
```

10. Finally, we export our class component:

```
export default MyName
```

If we were to run this code now, we would get the following error when entering text, because passing the handler method to `onChange` changes the `this` context:

Uncaught TypeError: Cannot read property 'setState' of undefined

11. So, now we need to adjust the `constructor` method and rebind the `this` context of our handler method to the class:

```
constructor (props) {
    super(props)
    this.state = { name: '' }
    this.handleChange = this.handleChange.bind(this)
}
```

 There is the possibility of using arrow functions as class methods, to avoid having to re-bind the `this` context. However, to use this feature we need to install the Babel compiler plugin, `@babel/plugin-proposal-class-properties`, as it is not a released JavaScript feature yet.

Finally, our component works! As you can see, there is a lot of code required to get state handling to work properly with class components. We also had to rebind the `this` context, because otherwise our handler method would not work. This is not very intuitive, and is easy to miss while developing, resulting in an annoying developer experience.

Example code

The example code can be found in the `Chapter01/chapter1_1` folder.

Just run `npm install` in order to install all dependencies, and `npm start` to start the application; then visit `http://localhost:3000` in your browser (if it did not open automatically).

Using Hooks instead

After using a traditional class component to write our app, we are going to write the same app using Hooks. As before, our app is going to let us enter a name, which we then display in our app.

 Please note that it is only possible to use Hooks in React function components. You cannot use Hooks in a React class component!

We now start by setting up the project.

Setting up the project

Again, we use `create-react-app` to set up our project:

```
> npx create-react-app chapter1_2
```

Let's get started with defining a function component using Hooks now.

Defining the function component

Now, we define the same component as a function component:

1. First, we remove all code from the `src/App.js` file.
2. Next, in `src/App.js`, we import React, and the `useState` Hook:

```
import React, { useState } from 'react'
```

3. We start with the function definition. In our case, we do not pass any arguments, because our component does not have any props:

```
function MyName () {
```

The next step would be to get the `name` variable from the component state. However, we cannot use `this.state` in function components. We have already learned that Hooks are just JavaScript functions, but what does that really mean? It means that we can simply use Hooks from function components, just like any other JavaScript function!

To use state via Hooks, we call `useState()` with our initial state as the argument. This function returns an array with two elements:

- The current state
- A setter function to set the state

4. We can use destructuring to store these two elements in separate variables, as follows:

```
const [ name, setName ] = useState('')
```

The previous code is equivalent to the following:

```
const nameHook = useState('')
const name = nameHook[0]
const setName = nameHook[1]
```

5. Now, we define the input handler function, where we make use of the `setName` setter function:

```
function handleChange (evt) {
    setName(evt.target.value)
}
```

 As we are not dealing with classes now, there is no need to rebind `this` anymore!

6. Finally, we render our user interface by returning it from the function. Then, we export the function component:

```
return (
    <div>
        <h1>My name is: {name}</h1>
        <input type="text" value={name}
onChange={handleChange} />
    </div>
    )
}

export default MyName
```

And that's it—we have successfully used Hooks for the first time! As you can see, the `useState` Hook is a drop-in replacement for `this.state` and `this.setState`.

Let's run our app by executing `npm start`, and opening `http://localhost:3000` in our browser:

Our first React app with Hooks

After implementing the same app with a class component and a function component, let's compare the solutions.

Example code

The example code can be found in the `Chapter01/chapter1_2` folder.

Just run `npm install` in order to install all dependencies, and `npm start` to start the application; then visit `http://localhost:3000` in your browser (if it did not open automatically).

Comparing the solutions

Let's compare our two solutions, in order to see the differences between class components, and function components using Hooks.

Class component

The class component makes use of the `constructor` method in order to define state, and needs to rebind `this` in order to pass the handler method to the `input` field. The full class component code looks as follows:

```
import React from 'react'

class MyName extends React.Component {
    constructor (props) {
        super (props)
        this.state = { name: '' }

        this.handleChange = this.handleChange.bind(this)
    }

    handleChange (evt) {
        this.setState({ name: evt.target.value })
    }

    render () {
        const { name } = this.state
        return (
            <div>
                <h1>My name is: {name}</h1>
                <input type="text" value={name}
onChange={this.handleChange} />
            </div>
        )
    }
}

export default MyName
```

As we can see, the class component needs a lot of boilerplate code to initialize the `state` object and handler functions.

Now, let's take a look at the function component.

Function component with Hook

The function component makes use of the `useState` Hook instead, so we do not need to deal with `this` or a `constructor` method. The full function component code looks as follows:

```
import React, { useState } from 'react'

function MyName () {
    const [ name, setName ] = useState('')

    function handleChange (evt) {
        setName(evt.target.value)
    }

    return (
        <div>
            <h1>My name is: {name}</h1>
            <input type="text" value={name} onChange={handleChange} />
        </div>
    )
}

export default MyName
```

As we can see, Hooks make our code much more concise and easier to reason about. We do not need to worry about how things work internally anymore; we can simply use state, by accessing the `useState` function!

Advantages of Hooks

Let's remind ourselves about the first principle of React:

Declarative: Instead of telling React how to do things, we tell it what we want it to do. As a result, we can easily design our applications, and React will efficiently update and render just the right components when the data changes.

As we have learned in this chapter, Hooks allow us to write code that tells React what we want. With class components, however, we need to tell React how to do things. As a result, Hooks are much more declarative than class components, making them a better fit in the React ecosystem.

Hooks being declarative also means that React can do various optimizations on our code, since it is easier to analyze functions and function calls rather than classes and their complex `this` behavior. Furthermore, Hooks make it easier to abstract and share common stateful logic between components. By using Hooks, we can avoid render props and higher-order components.

We can see that Hooks not only make our code more concise, and are easier to reason about for developers, but they also make the code easier to optimize for React.

Migrating to Hooks

Now, you might be wondering: does that mean class components are deprecated, and we need to migrate everything to Hooks now? Of course not—Hooks are completely opt-in. You can try Hooks in some of your components without rewriting any of your other code. The React team also does not plan on removing class components at the moment.

There is no rush to migrate everything to Hooks right now. It is recommended that you gradually adopt Hooks in certain components where they will be most useful. For example, if you have many components that deal with similar logic, you can extract the logic to a Hook. You can also use function components with Hooks side by side with class components.

Furthermore, Hooks are 100% backward-compatible, and provide a direct API to all the React concepts that you already know about: **props**, **state**, **context**, **refs**, and **life cycle**. Furthermore, Hooks offer new ways to combine these concepts and encapsulate their logic in a much better way that does not lead to wrapper hell or similar problems. We are going to learn more about this later in the book.

The Hooks mindset

The main goal of Hooks is to decouple stateful logic from rendering logic. They allow us to define logic in separate functions and reuse them across multiple components. With Hooks, we do not need to change our component hierarchy in order to implement stateful logic. There is no need to define a separate component that provides the state logic to multiple components anymore, we can simply use a Hook instead!

However, Hooks require a completely different mindset from classic React development. We should not think about the life cycle of components anymore. Instead, we should think about data flow. For example, we can tell Hooks to trigger when certain props or values from other Hooks change. We are going to learn more about this concept in Chapter 4, *Using the Reducer and Effect Hooks*. We should also not split components based on life cycle anymore. Instead, we can use Hooks to deal with common functionalities, such as fetching data, or setting up a subscription.

Rules of Hooks

Hooks are very flexible. However, there are certain limitations to using Hooks, which we should always keep in mind:

- Hooks can only be used in function components, not in class components
- The order of Hook definitions matters, and needs to stay the same; thus, we cannot put Hooks in if conditionals, loops, or nested functions

We are going to discuss these limitations in more detail, as well as how to work around them, throughout this book.

Overview of various Hooks

As we learned in the previous section, Hooks provide a direct API to all React concepts. Furthermore, we can define our own Hooks in order to encapsulate logic without having to write a higher-order component, which causes a wrapper hell. In this section, we are going to give an overview of various Hooks, which we are going to learn about throughout the book.

Hooks provided by React

React already provides various Hooks for different functionalities. There are three basic Hooks, and a handful of additional Hooks.

Basic Hooks

Basic Hooks provide the most commonly needed functionalities in stateful React apps. They are as follows:

- `useState`
- `useEffect`
- `useContext`

Let's take a look at each of these in the following sections.

useState

We have already used this Hook. It returns a stateful value (`state`) and a setter function (`setState`) in order to update the value.

The `useState` Hook is used to deal with `state` in React. We can use it as follows:

```
import { useState } from 'react'

const [ state, setState ] = useState(initialState)
```

The `useState` Hook replaces `this.state` and `this.setState()`.

useEffect

This Hook works similarly to adding a function on `componentDidMount` and `componentDidUpdate`. Furthermore, the Effect Hook allows for returning a cleanup function from it, which works similarly to adding a function to `componentWillUnmount`.

The `useEffect` Hook is used to deal with effectful code, such as timers, subscriptions, requests, and so on. We can use it as follows:

```
import { useEffect } from 'react'

useEffect(didUpdate)
```

The `useEffect` Hook replaces the `componentDidMount`, `componentDidUpdate`, and `componentWillUnmount` methods.

useContext

This Hook accepts a context object and returns the current context value.

The useContext Hook is used to deal with context in React. We can use it as follows:

```
import { useContext } from 'react'

const value = useContext(MyContext)
```

The useContext Hook replaces context consumers.

Additional Hooks

Additional Hooks are either more generic variants of basic Hooks or are needed for certain edge cases. The additional Hooks we are going to look at are as follows:

- useRef
- useReducer
- useMemo
- useCallback
- useLayoutEffect
- useDebugValue

Let's dive deeper into these additional Hooks in the following sections.

useRef

This Hook returns a mutable ref object, where the .current property is initialized to the passed argument (initialValue). We can use it as follows:

```
import { useRef } from 'react'

const refContainer = useRef(initialValue)
```

The useRef Hook is used to deal with references to elements and components in React. We can set a reference by passing the ref prop to an element or a component, as follows:
<ComponentName ref={refContainer} />

useReducer

This Hook is an alternative to `useState`, and works similarly to the Redux library. We can use it as follows:

```
import { useReducer } from 'react'

const [ state, dispatch ] = useReducer(reducer, initialArg, init)
```

The `useReducer` Hook is used to deal with complex state logic.

useMemo

Memoization is an optimization technique where the result of a function call is cached, and is then returned when the same input occurs again. The `useMemo` Hook allows us to compute a value and memoize it. We can use it as follows:

```
import { useMemo } from 'react'

const memoizedValue = useMemo(() => computeExpensiveValue(a, b), [a, b])
```

The `useMemo` Hook is useful for optimization when we want to avoid re-executing expensive operations.

useCallback

This Hook allows us to pass an inline callback function, and an array of dependencies, and will return a memoized version of the callback function. We can use it as follows:

```
import { useCallback } from 'react'

const memoizedCallback = useCallback(
    () => {
        doSomething(a, b)
    },
    [a, b]
)
```

The `useCallback` Hook is useful when passing callbacks to optimized child components. It works similarly to the `useMemo` Hook, but for callback functions.

useLayoutEffect

This Hook is identical to useEffect, but it only fires after all **Document Object Model (DOM)** mutations. We can use it as follows:

```
import { useLayoutEffect } from 'react'

useLayoutEffect(didUpdate)
```

The useLayoutEffect Hook can be used to read information from the DOM.

 Use the useEffect Hook when possible, because useLayoutEffect will block visual updates and slow down your application.

Finally, we are going to take a look at the last Hook provided by React at the time of writing.

useDebugValue

This Hook can be used to display a label in React DevTools when creating custom Hooks. We can use it as follows:

```
import { useDebugValue } from 'react'

useDebugValue(value)
```

Make sure to use this Hook in custom Hooks to display the current state of your Hooks, as it will make it easier to debug them.

Community Hooks

In addition to all the Hooks that React provides, there are already plenty of libraries that have been published by the community. These libraries also provide Hooks. The Hooks we are going to look into are as follows:

- useInput
- useResource
- useDimensions
- Navigation Hooks

- Life cycle Hooks
- Timer Hooks

Let's see an overview of what these Hooks are in the following sections.

useInput

This Hook is used to easily implement input handling, and to synchronize the state of an `input` field with a variable. It can be used as follows:

```
import { useInput } from 'react-hookedup'

function App () {
    const { value, onChange } = useInput('')
    return <input value={value} onChange={onChange} />
}
```

As we can see, Hooks greatly simplify dealing with input fields in React.

useResource

This Hook can be used to implement asynchronous data loading via requests in our application. We can use it as follows:

```
import { useRequest } from 'react-request-hook'

const [profile, getProfile] = useResource(id => ({
    url: `/user/${id}`,
    method: 'GET'
}))
```

As we can see, using a special Hook for dealing with fetching data is quite simple.

Navigation Hooks

These Hooks are part of the Navi library, and are used to implement routing via Hooks in React. The Navi library provides many more routing-related Hooks. We are going to learn about routing via Hooks, in depth, later on in the book. We can use them as follows:

```
import { useCurrentRoute, useNavigation } from 'react-navi'

const { views, url, data, status } = useCurrentRoute()
const { navigate } = useNavigation()
```

As we can see, Hooks make routing much easier to deal with.

Life cycle Hooks

The `react-hookedup` library provides various Hooks, including all life cycle listeners for React.

 Please note that it is not recommended to think in terms of a component life cycle when developing with Hooks. These Hooks just provide a quick way to refactor existing components to Hooks. However, when developing new components, it is recommended that you think about data flow and dependencies, rather than life cycles.

Here, we list two of them, but the library actually provides many more Hooks, which we will learn about later on. We can use the Hooks provided by `react-hookedup` as follows:

```
import { useOnMount, useOnUnmount } from 'react-hookedup'

useOnMount(() => { ... })
useOnUnmount(() => { ... })
```

As we can see, Hooks can directly replace life cycle methods in class components.

Timer Hooks

The `react-hookedup` library also provides Hooks for `setInterval` and `setTimeout`. These work similarly to calling `setTimeout` or `setInterval` directly, but as a React Hook, which will persist between re-renders. If we directly defined timers in our function component without Hooks, we would be resetting the timer every time the component re-renders.

We can pass the time in milliseconds as a second argument. We can use them as follows:

```
import { useInterval, useTimeout } from 'react-hookedup'

useInterval(() => { ... }, 1000)
useTimeout(() => { ... }, 1000)
```

As we can see, Hooks greatly simplify how we deal with intervals and timeouts in React.

Other community Hooks

As you can imagine, there are many more Hooks that are provided by the community. We will learn about the previously mentioned community Hooks in depth, and various other community Hooks in `Chapter 8`: *Using Community Hooks*.

Summary

In this first chapter of the book, we started out by learning the fundamental principles of React and which types of components it provides. We then moved on to learning about common problems with class components, and using existing features of React, and how they break the fundamental principles. Next, we implemented a simple application using class components and function components with Hooks, in order to be able to compare the differences between the two solutions. As we found out, function components with Hooks are a much better fit for React's fundamental principles, as they do not suffer from the same problems as class components, and they make our code much more concise and easy to understand! Finally, we got our first glimpse of the various Hooks that we are going to learn about throughout this book. After this chapter, the basics of React and React Hooks are clear. We can now move on to more advanced concepts of Hooks.

In the next chapter, we are going to gain an in-depth knowledge of how the State Hook works, by reimplementing it from scratch. By doing so, we are going to get a grasp on how Hooks work internally, and what their limitations are. Afterward, we are going to create a small blog application using the State Hook!

Questions

To recap what we have learned in this chapter, try answering the following questions:

1. What are React's three fundamental principles?
2. What are the two types of components in React?
3. What are the problems with class components in React?
4. What is the problem of using higher-order components in React?

5. Which tool can we use to set up a React project, and what is the command that we need to run to use it?

6. What do we need to do if we get the following error with class components: *TypeError: undefined is not an object (evaluating 'this.setState')*?

7. How do we access and set React state using Hooks?

8. What are the advantages of using function components with Hooks, in comparison to class components?

9. Do we need to replace all class components with function components using Hooks when updating React?

10. What are the three basic Hooks that are provided by React?

Further reading

If you are interested in more information about the concepts that we have learned in this chapter, take a look at the following reading material:

- Create React App on GitHub: `https://github.com/facebook/create-react-app#create-react-app--`
- RFC for React Hooks: `https://github.com/reactjs/rfcs/blob/master/text/0068-react-hooks.md`
- Handling input with React: `https://reactjs.org/docs/forms.html`
- State and life cycle in React with class components: `https://reactjs.org/docs/state-and-lifecycle.html`
- Destructuring: `http://exploringjs.com/es6/ch_destructuring.html`
- Template strings: `https://developer.mozilla.org/en-US/docs/Web/JavaScript/Reference/Template_literals`
- Ternary operator: `https://developer.mozilla.org/en-US/docs/Web/JavaScript/Reference/Operators/Conditional_Operator`

Using the State Hook

2

Now that you've learned about the principles of React and had an introduction to Hooks, we are going to learn about the State Hook in depth. We will start by learning how the State Hook works internally by reimplementing it ourselves. Next, we learn about some of the limitations of Hooks, and why they exist. Then, we will learn about possible alternative Hook APIs and their associated problems. Finally, we learn how to solve the common problems that result from the limitations of Hooks. By the end of this chapter, we will know how to use the State Hook in order to implement stateful function components in React.

The following topics will be covered in this chapter:

- Reimplementing the `useState` Hook as a simple function, which accesses the global state
- Comparing our reimplementation to real React Hooks and learning about the differences
- Learning about possible alternative Hook APIs and their trade-offs
- Solving common problems resulting from the limitations of Hooks
- Solving problems with conditional Hooks

Technical requirements

A fairly recent version of Node.js should already be installed (v11.12.0 or higher). The `npm` package manager for Node.js also needs to be installed.

The code for this chapter can be found in the GitHub repository: `https://github.com/PacktPublishing/Learn-React-Hooks/tree/master/Chapter02`.

Check out the following video to see the code in action:

`http://bit.ly/2Mm9yoC`

Please note that it is highly recommended that you write the code on your own. Do not simply run the code examples that have been previously provided. It is important that you write the code yourself so that you learn and understand it properly. However, if you run into any issues, you can always refer to the code example.

Now, let's get started with the chapter.

Reimplementing the useState function

In order to get a better understanding of how Hooks work internally, we are going to reimplement the useState Hook from scratch. However, we are not going to implement it as an actual React Hook, but as a simple JavaScript function—just to get an idea of what Hooks are actually doing.

 Please note that this reimplementation is not exactly how React Hooks work internally. The actual implementation is similar, and thus, it has similar constraints. However, the real implementation is much more complicated than what we will be implementing here.

We are now going to start reimplementing the State Hook:

1. First, we copy the code from chapter1_2, where we are going to replace the current useState Hook with our own implementation.
2. Open src/App.js and remove the import of the Hook by removing the following line:

```
import React, { useState } from 'react'
```

Replace it with these lines of code:

```
import React from 'react'
import ReactDOM from 'react-dom'
```

 We are going to need ReactDOM in order to force rerendering of the component in our reimplementation of the useState Hook. If we used actual React Hooks, this would be dealt with internally.

3. Now, we define our own `useState` function. As we already know, the `useState` function takes the `initialState` as an argument:

```
function useState (initialState) {
```

4. Then, we define a value, where we will store our state. At first, this value will be set to `initialState`, which is passed as an argument to the function:

```
let value = initialState
```

5. Next, we define the `setState` function, where we will set the value to something different, and force the rerendering of our `MyName` component:

```
function setState (nextValue) {
    value = nextValue
    ReactDOM.render(<MyName />,
document.getElementById('root'))
    }
```

6. Finally, we return the `value` and the `setState` function as an array:

```
return [ value, setState ]
}
```

The reason why we use an array, and not an object, is that we usually want to rename the `value` and `setState` variables. Using an array makes it easy to rename the variables through destructuring:

```
const [ name, setName ] = useState('')
```

As we can see, Hooks are simple JavaScript functions that deal with side effects, such as setting a stateful value.

Our Hook function uses a closure to store the current value. The closure is an environment where variables exist and are stored. In our case, the function provides the closure, and the `value` variable is stored within that closure. The `setState` function is also defined within the same closure, which is why we can access the `value` variable within that function. Outside of the `useState` function, we cannot directly access the `value` variable unless we return it from the function.

Problems with our simple Hook implementation

If we run our Hook implementation now, we are going to notice that when our component rerenders, the state gets reset, so we cannot enter any text in the field. This is due to the reinitialization of the `value` variable every time our component gets rendered, which happens because we call `useState` each time we render the component.

In the upcoming sections, we are going to solve this problem by using a global variable and then turn the simple value into an array, allowing us to define multiple Hooks.

Using a global variable

As we have learned, the value is stored within the closure that is defined by the `useState` function. Every time the component rerenders, the closure is reinitialized, which means that our value will be reset. To solve this, we need to store the value in a global variable, outside of the function. That way, the `value` variable will be in the closure outside of the function, which means that when the function gets called again, the closure will not be reinitialized.

We can define a global variable as follows:

1. First, we add the following line (in bold) above the `useState` function definition:

   ```
   let value

   function useState (initialState) {
   ```

2. Then, we replace the first line in our function with the following code:

   ```
   if (typeof value === 'undefined') value = initialState
   ```

Now, our `useState` function uses the global `value` variable, instead of defining the `value` variable within its closure, so it will not be reinitialized when the function gets called again.

Defining multiple Hooks

Our Hook function works! However, if we wanted to add another Hook, we would run into another problem: all the Hooks write to the same global `value` variable!

Let's take a closer look at this problem by adding a second Hook to our component.

Adding multiple Hooks to our component

Let's say we want to create a second field for the last name of the user, as follows:

1. We start by creating a new Hook at the beginning of our function, after the current Hook:

   ```
   const [ name, setName ] = useState('')
   const [ lastName, setLastName ] = useState('')
   ```

2. Then, we define another `handleChange` function:

   ```
   function handleLastNameChange (evt) {
       setLastName(evt.target.value)
   }
   ```

3. Next, we place the `lastName` variable after the first name:

   ```
   <h1>My name is: {name} {lastName}</h1>
   ```

4. Finally, we add another `input` field:

   ```
   <input type="text" value={lastName}
   onChange={handleLastNameChange}
       />
   ```

When we try this out, we are going to notice that our reimplemented Hook function uses the same value for both states, so we are always changing both fields at once.

Implementing multiple Hooks

In order to implement multiple Hooks, instead of having a single global variable, we should have an array of Hook values.

We are now going to refactor the `value` variable to a `values` array so that we can define multiple Hooks:

1. Remove the following line of code:

   ```
   let value
   ```

   Replace it with the following code snippet:

   ```
   let values = []
   let currentHook = 0
   ```

2. Then, edit the first line of the useState function where we now initialize the value at the currentHook index of the values array:

```
if (typeof values[currentHook] === 'undefined')
    values[currentHook] = initialState
```

3. We also need to update the setter function, so that only the corresponding state value is updated. Here, we need to store the currentHook value in a separate hookIndex variable, because the currentHook value will change later. This ensures that a copy of the currentHook variable is created within the closure of the useState function. Otherwise, the useState function would access the currentHook variable from the outer closure, which gets modified with each call to useState:

```
let hookIndex = currentHook
function setState (nextValue) {
    values[hookIndex] = nextValue
    ReactDOM.render(<MyName />,
document.getElementById('root'))
    }
```

4. Edit the final line of the useState function, as follows:

```
return [ values[currentHook++], setState ]
```

Using values[currentHook++], we pass the current value of currentHook as an index to the values array, and then increase currentHook by one. This means that currentHook will be increased after returning from the function.

If we wanted to first increment a value and then use it, we could use the arr[++indexToBeIncremented] syntax, which first increments, and then passes the result to the array.

5. We still need to reset the currentHook counter when we start rendering our component. Add the following line (in bold) right after the component definition:

```
function Name () {
    currentHook = 0
```

Finally, our simple reimplementation of the `useState` Hook works! The following screenshot highlights this:

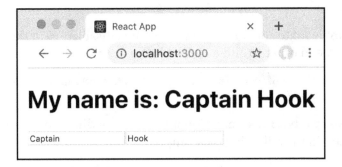

Our custom Hook reimplementation works

As we can see, using a global array to store our Hook values solved the problems that we had when defining multiple Hooks.

Example code

The example code for the simple Hook reimplementation can be found in the `Chapter02/chapter2_1` folder.

Just run `npm install` in order to install all the dependencies and `npm start` to start the application, and then visit `http://localhost:3000` in your browser (if it did not open automatically).

Can we define conditional Hooks?

What if we wanted to add a checkbox that toggles the use of the first name field?

Let's find out by implementing such a checkbox:

1. First, we add a new Hook in order to store the state of our checkbox:

   ```
   const [ enableFirstName, setEnableFirstName ] = useState(false)
   ```

2. Then, we define a handler function:

   ```
   function handleEnableChange (evt) {
       setEnableFirstName(!enableFirstName)
   }
   ```

3. Next, we render a checkbox:

```
<input type="checkbox" value={enableFirstName}
onChange={handleEnableChange} />
```

4. We do not want to show the first name if it is disabled. Edit the following existing line in order to add a check for the `enableFirstName` variable:

```
<h1>My name is: {enableFirstName ? name : ''}
{lastName}</h1>
```

5. Could we put the Hook definition into an `if` condition, or a ternary expression, like we are in the following code snippet?

```
const [ name, setName ] = enableFirstName
    ? useState('')
    : [ '', () => {} ]
```

6. The latest version of `react-scripts` actually throws an error when defining conditional Hooks, so we need to downgrade the library for this example, by running the following command:

```
> npm install --save react-scripts@^2.1.8
```

Here, we either use the Hook, or if the first name is disabled, we return the initial state and an empty setter function so that editing the input field will not work.

If we now try out this code, we are going to notice that editing the last name still works, but editing the first name does not work, which is what we wanted. As we can see in the following screenshot, only editing the last name works now:

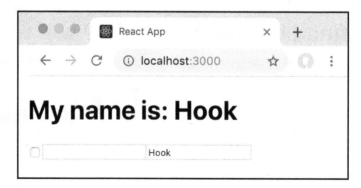

State of the app before checking the checkbox

When we click the checkbox, something strange happens:

- The checkbox is checked
- The first name input field is enabled
- The value of the last name field is now the value of the first name field

We can see the result of clicking the checkbox in the following screenshot:

State of the app after checking the checkbox

We can see that the last name state is now in the first name field. The values have been swapped because the order of Hooks matters. As we know from our implementation, we use the `currentHook` index in order to know where the state of each Hook is stored. However, when we insert an additional Hook in-between two existing Hooks, the order gets messed up.

Before checking the checkbox, the `values` array was as follows:

- `[false, '']`
- Hook order: `enableFirstName, lastName`

Then, we entered some text in the `lastName` field:

- `[false, 'Hook']`
- Hook order: `enableFirstName, lastName`

Next, we toggled the checkbox, which activated our new Hook:

- `[true, 'Hook', '']`
- Hook order: `enableFirstName, name, lastName`

As we can see, inserting a new Hook in-between two existing Hooks makes the `name` Hook steal the state from the next Hook (`lastName`) because it now has the same index that the `lastName` Hook previously had. Now, the `lastName` Hook does not have a value, which causes it to set the initial value (an empty string). As a result, toggling the checkbox puts the value of the `lastName` field into the `name` field.

Example code

The example code for the problem of the conditional Hook of our simple Hook reimplementation can be found in the `Chapter02/chapter2_2` folder.

Just run `npm install` in order to install all dependencies and `npm start` to start the application, and then visit `http://localhost:3000` in your browser (if it did not open automatically).

Comparing our reimplementation with real Hooks

Our simple Hook implementation already gives us an idea about how Hooks work internally. However, in reality, Hooks do not use global variables. Instead, they store state within the React component. They also deal with the Hook counter internally, so we do not need to manually reset the count in our function component. Furthermore, real Hooks automatically trigger rerenders of our component when the state changes. To be able to do this, however, Hooks need to be called from a React function component. React Hooks cannot be called outside of React, or inside React class components.

By reimplementing the `useState` Hook, we have learned a couple things:

- Hooks are simply functions that access React features
- Hooks deal with side effects that persist across rerenders
- The order of Hook definitions matters

The last point is especially important because it means that we cannot conditionally define Hooks. We should always have all the Hook definitions at the beginning of our function component, and never nest them within `if` or other constructs.

Here we have also learned the following:

- React Hooks need to be called inside React function components
- React Hooks cannot be defined conditionally, or in loops

We are now going to look at alternative Hook APIs that allow conditional Hooks.

Alternative Hook APIs

Sometimes, it would be nice to define Hooks conditionally or in loops, but why did the React team decide to implement Hooks like this? What are the alternatives? Let's go through a few of them.

Named Hooks

We could give each Hook a name and then store the Hooks in an object instead of an array. However, this would not make for a nice API, and we would also always have to think of coming up with unique names for Hooks:

```
// NOTE: Not the actual React Hook API
const [ name, setName ] = useState('nameHook', '')
```

Furthermore, what would happen when the conditional is set to `false`, or an item is removed from the loop? Would we clear the Hook state? If we do not clear the Hook state, we might be causing memory leaks.

Even if we solved all these problems, there would still be the problem of name collisions. If we, for example, create a custom Hook that makes use of the `useState` Hook, and call it `nameHook`, then we cannot call any other Hook `nameHook` in our component anymore, or we will cause a name collision. This is even the case for Hook names from libraries, so we need to make sure we avoid name collisions with Hooks that have been defined by libraries as well!

Hook factories

Alternatively, we could also create a Hook factory function, which uses `Symbol` internally, in order to give each Hook a unique key name:

```
function createUseState () {
    const keyName = Symbol()
```

```
    return function useState () {
        // ... use unique key name to handle hook state ...
    }
}
```

Then, we could use the factory function as follows:

```
// NOTE: Not the actual React Hook API
const useNameState = createUseState()

function MyName () {
    const [ name, setName ] = useNameState('')
    // ...
}
```

However, this means that we will need to instantiate each Hook twice: once outside of our component and once inside the function component. This creates more room for errors. For example, if we create two Hooks and copy and paste the boilerplate code, then we might make a mistake in the name of our Hook resulting from the factory function, or we might make a mistake when using the Hook inside the component.

This approach also makes it much harder to create custom Hooks, which forces us to write wrapper functions. Furthermore, it is harder to debug these wrapped functions than it is to debug a simple function.

Other alternatives

There were many proposed alternative APIs for React Hooks, but each of them suffered from similar problems: either making the API harder to use, harder to debug, or introducing the possibility of name collisions.

In the end, the React team decided that the simplest API was to keep track of Hooks by counting the order in which they are called. This approach comes with its own downsides, such as not being able to call Hooks conditionally or in loops. However, this approach makes it very easy for us to create custom Hooks, and it is simple to use and debug. We also do not need to worry about naming Hooks, name collisions, or writing wrapper functions. The final approach for Hooks lets us use Hooks just like any other function!

Solving common problems with Hooks

As we found out, implementing Hooks with the official API also has its own trade-offs and limitations. We are now going to learn how to overcome these common problems, which stem from the limitations of React Hooks.

We will take a look at solutions that can be used to overcome these two problems:

- Solving conditional Hooks
- Solving Hooks in loops

Solving conditional Hooks

So, how do we implement conditional Hooks? Instead of making the Hook conditional, we can always define the Hook and use it whenever we need it. If this is not an option, we need to split up our components, which is usually better anyway!

Always defining the Hook

For simple cases, such as the first and last name example that we had previously, we can just always keep the Hook defined, as follows:

```
const [ name, setName ] = useState('')
```

Always defining the Hook is usually a good solution for simple cases.

Splitting up components

Another way to solve conditional Hooks is to split up one component into multiple components and then conditionally render the components. For example, let's say we want to fetch user information from a database after the user logs in.

We cannot do the following, as using an `if` conditional could change the order of the Hooks:

```
function UserInfo ({ username }) {
    if (username) {
        const info = useFetchUserInfo(username)
        return <div>{info}</div>
    }
    return <div>Not logged in</div>
}
```

Instead, we have to create a separate component for when the user is logged in, as follows:

```
function LoggedInUserInfo ({ username }) {
    const info = useFetchUserInfo(username)
    return <div>{info}</div>
}

function UserInfo ({ username }) {
    if (username) {
        return <LoggedInUserInfo username={username} />
    }
    return <div>Not logged in</div>
}
```

Using two separate components for the non-logged in and logged in state makes sense anyway, because we want to stick to the principle of having one functionality per component. So, usually, not being able to have conditional Hooks is not much of a limitation if we stick to best practices.

Solving Hooks in loops

As for Hooks in loops, we can either use a single State Hook containing an array, or we can split up our components. For example, let's say we want to display all the users that are online.

Using an array

We could simply use an array that contains all `users`, as follows:

```
function OnlineUsers ({ users }) {
    const [ userInfos, setUserInfos ] = useState([])
    // ... fetch & keep userInfos up to date ...
    return (
        <div>
            {users.map(username => {
                const user = userInfos.find(u => u.username === username)
                return <UserInfo {...user} />
            })}
        </div>
    )
}
```

However, this might not always make sense. For example, we might not want to update the `user` state through the `OnlineUsers` component because we would have to select the correct `user` state from the array, and then modify the array. This might work, but it is quite tedious.

Splitting up components

A better solution would be to use the Hook in the `UserInfo` component instead. That way, we can keep the state for each user up to date, without having to deal with array logic:

```
function OnlineUsers ({ users }) {
    return (
        <div>
            {users.map(username => <UserInfo username={username} />)}
        </div>
    )
}

function UserInfo ({ username }) {
    const info = useFetchUserInfo(username)
    // ... keep user info up to date ...
    return <div>{info}</div>
}
```

As we can see, using one component for each functionality keeps our code simple and concise, and also avoids the limitations of React Hooks.

Solving problems with conditional Hooks

Now that we have learned about the different alternatives to conditional Hooks, we are going to solve the problem that we had in our small example project earlier. The simplest solution to this problem would be to always define the Hook, instead of conditionally defining it. In a simple project like this one, always defining the Hook makes the most sense.

Edit `src/App.js` and remove the following conditional Hook:

```
const [ name, setName ] = enableFirstName
    ? useState('')
    : [ '', () => {} ]
```

Replace it with a normal Hook, such as the following:

```
const [ name, setName ] = useState('')
```

Now, our example works fine! In more complex cases, it might not be feasible to always define the Hook. In that case, we would need to create a new component, define the Hook there, and then conditionally render the component.

Example code

The example code for the simple solution to the conditional Hooks problem can be found in the `Chapter02/chapter2_3` folder.

Just run `npm install` in order to install all dependencies and `npm start` to start the application, and then visit `http://localhost:3000` in your browser (if it did not open automatically).

Summary

In this chapter, we started out by reimplementing the `useState` function, by making use of global state and closures. We then learned that in order to implement multiple Hooks, we need to use a state array instead. By using a state array, however, we were forced to keep the order of Hooks consistent across function calls. This limitation made conditional Hooks and Hooks in loops impossible. We then learned about possible alternatives to the Hook API, their trade-offs, and why the final API was chosen. Finally, we learned how to solve the common problems that stem from the limitations of Hooks. We now have a solid understanding of the inner workings and limitations of Hooks. Furthermore, we learned about the State Hook in depth.

In the next chapter, we are going to create a blog application using the State Hook, and learn how to combine multiple Hooks.

Questions

To recap what we have learned in this chapter, try to answer the following questions:

1. What problems did we run into while developing our own reimplementation of the `useState` Hook? How did we solve these problems?
2. Why are conditional Hooks not possible in the React implementation of Hooks?
3. What are Hooks, and what do they deal with?
4. What do we need to watch out for when using Hooks?
5. What are the common problems of alternative API ideas for Hooks?
6. How do we implement conditional Hooks?
7. How do we implement Hooks in loops?

Further reading

If you are interested in finding out more about the concepts that we have learned in this chapter, take a look at the following reading material:

- More information on flaws of alternative Hook APIs: `https://overreacted.io/why-do-hooks-rely-on-call-order/`
- Official comment on alternative Hook APIs: `https://github.com/reactjs/rfcs/pull/68#issuecomment-439314884`
- Official documentation on why conditional Hooks do not work: `https://reactjs.org/docs/hooks-rules.html#explanation`

3
Writing Your First Application with React Hooks

After learning about the State Hook in depth, we are now going to make use of it by creating a blog application from scratch. Throughout this chapter, we are going to learn how to structure React apps in a way that scales well, how to use multiple Hooks, where to store state, and how to solve common use cases with Hooks. At the end of this chapter, we are going to have a basic blog application, where we can log in, register, and create posts.

The following topics will be covered in this chapter:

- Structuring React projects in a scalable way
- Implementing static React components from a mock-up
- Implementing stateful components with Hooks

Technical requirements

A fairly recent version of Node.js should already be installed (v11.12.0 or higher). The npm package manager for Node.js also needs to be installed.

The code for this chapter can be found in the GitHub repository: `https://github.com/PacktPublishing/Learn-React-Hooks/tree/master/Chapter03`.

Check out the following video to see the code in action:

`http://bit.ly/2Mm9yoC`

Please note that it is highly recommended that you write the code on your own. Do not simply run the previously provided code examples. It is important that you write the code yourself in order to be able to learn and understand properly. However, if you run into any issues, you can always refer to the code example.

Now, let's get started with the chapter.

Structuring React projects

After learning about the principles of React, how to use the `useState` Hook, and how Hooks work internally, we are now going to make use of the real `useState` Hook in order to develop a blog application. First, we are going to create a new project, and structure the folders in a way that will allow us to scale the project later on. Then, we are going to define the components that we are going to need in order to cover the basic features of a blog application. Finally, we are going to use Hooks to introduce state to our application! Throughout this chapter, we are also going to learn about **JSX**, and new JavaScript features that have been introduced in **ES6**, up to **ES2018**.

Folder structure

There are many ways that projects can be structured, and different structures can do well for different projects. Usually, we create a `src/` folder, and group our files there by features. Another popular way to structure projects is to group them by routes. For some projects, it might make sense to additionally separate by the kind of code, such as `src/api/` and `src/components/`. However, for our project, we are mainly going to focus on the **user interface** (**UI**). As a result, we are going to group our files by features in the `src/` folder.

 It is a good idea to start with a simple structure at first, and only nest more deeply when you actually need it. Do not spend too much time thinking about the file structure when starting a project, because usually, you do not know up front how files should be grouped.

Choosing the features

We first have to think about which features we are going to implement in our blog application. At the bare minimum, we want to implement the following features:

- Registering users
- Logging in/out
- Viewing a single post
- Creating a new post
- Listing posts

Now that we have chosen the features, let's come up with an initial folder structure.

Coming up with an initial structure

From our previous functionalities, we can abstract a couple of feature groups:

- User (registering, log in/log out)
- Post (creating, viewing, listing)

We could now just keep it very simple, and create all of the components in the src/ folder, without any nesting. However, since we already have quite a clear picture on the features that a blog application is going to need, we can come up with a simple folder structure now:

- src/
- src/user/
- src/post/

After defining the folder structure, we can move on to the component structure.

Component structure

The idea of components in React is to have each component deal with a single task or UI element. We should try to make components as fine-grained as possible, in order to be able to reuse code. If we find ourselves copying and pasting code from one component to another, it might be a good idea to create a new component, and reuse it in multiple other components.

Usually, when developing software, we start with a UI mock-up. For our blog application, a mock-up would look as follows:

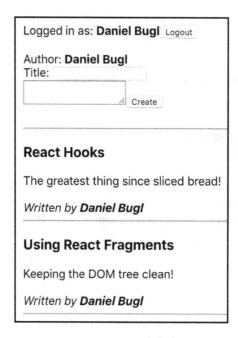

Initial mock-up of our blog application

When splitting components, we use the single responsibility principle, which states that every module should have responsibility over a single encapsulated part of the functionality.

In this mock-up, we can draw boxes around each component and subcomponent, and give them names. Keep in mind that each component should have exactly one responsibility. We start with the fundamental components that make up this app:

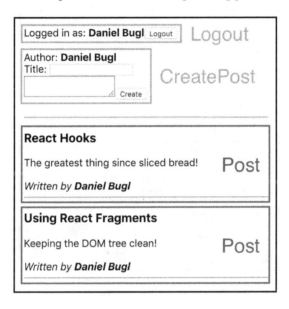

Defining the fundamental components from our mock-up

We defined a `Logout` component for the logout feature, a `CreatePost` component, which contains the form to create a new post, and a `Post` component to display the actual posts.

Now that we have defined our fundamental components, we are going to look at which components logically belong together, thereby forming a group. To do so, we now define the container components, which we need in order to group the components together:

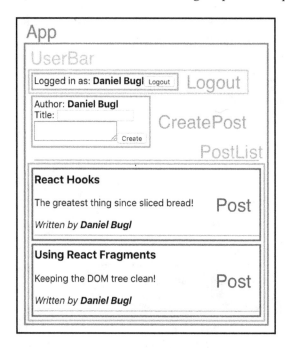

Defining the container components from our mock-up

We defined a `PostList` component in order to group posts together, then a `UserBar` component in order to deal with login/logout and registration. Finally, we defined an `App` component in order to group everything together, and define the structure of our app.

Now that we are done with structuring our React project, we can move on to implementing the static components.

Implementing static components

Before we start adding state via Hooks to our blog application, we are going to model the basic features of our application as static React components. Doing this means that we have to deal with the static view structure of our application.

It makes sense to deal with the static structure first, so as to avoid having to move dynamic code to different components later on. Furthermore, it is easier to deal only with **Hypertext Markup Language (HTML)** and CSS first—helping us to get started with projects quickly. Then, we can move on to implementing dynamic code and handling state.

Doing this step by step, instead of implementing everything at once, helps us to quickly get started with new projects without having to think about too much at once, and lets us avoid having to restructure projects later!

Setting up the project

We have already learned how to set up a new React project. As we have learned, we can use the `create-react-app` tool to easily initialize a new project. We are going to do so now:

1. First, we use `create-react-app` to initialize our project:

   > **npx create-react-app chapter3_1**

2. Then, we create folders for our features:

   - **Create folder**: `src/user/`
   - **Create folder**: `src/post/`

Now that our project structure is set up, we can start implementing components.

Implementing users

We are going to start with the simplest feature in terms of static components: implementing user-related functionality. As we have seen from our mock-up, we are going to need four components here:

- A `Login` component, which we are going to show when the user is not logged in yet
- A `Register` component, which we are also going to show when the user is not logged in yet
- A `Logout` component, which is going to be shown after the user is logged in
- A `UserBar` component, which will display the other components conditionally

We are going to start by defining the first three components, which are all stand-alone components. Lastly, we will define the `UserBar` component, because it depends on the other components being defined.

The Login component

First, we define the `Login` component, where we show two fields: a **Username** field, and a **Password** field. Furthermore, we show a **Login** button:

1. We start by creating a new file for our component: `src/user/Login.js`
2. In the newly created `src/user/Login.js` file, we import React:

   ```
   import React from 'react'
   ```

3. Then, we define our function component. For now, the `Login` component will not accept any props:

   ```
   export default function Login () {
   ```

4. Finally, we return the two fields and the **Login** button, via JSX. We also define a `form` container element to wrap them in. To avoid a page refresh when the form is submitted, we have to define an `onSubmit` handler and call `e.preventDefault()` on the event object:

   ```
   return (
       <form onSubmit={e => e.preventDefault()}>
           <label htmlFor="login-username">Username:</label>
           <input type="text" name="login-username" id="login-
   username" />
           <label htmlFor="login-password">Password:</label>
           <input type="password" name="login-password" id="login-
   password" />
           <input type="submit" value="Login" />
       </form>
   )
   }
   ```

Here, we are using an anonymous function to define the `onSubmit` handler. Anonymous functions are defined as follows, if they do not have any arguments: `() => { ... }`, instead of `function () { ... }`. With arguments, we could write `(arg1, arg2) => { ... }`, instead of `function (arg1, arg2) { ... }`. We can omit the `()` brackets if we only have a single argument. Additionally, we can omit the `{}` brackets if we only have a single statement in our function, like this: `e => e.preventDefault()`.

Using semantic HTML elements such as `<form>` and `<label>` make your app easier to navigate for people using accessibility assistance software, such as screen readers. Furthermore, when using semantic HTML, keyboard shortcuts, such as submitting forms by pressing the return key, automatically work.

Our `Login` component is implemented, and is now ready to be tested.

Testing out our component

Now that we have defined our first component, let's render it and see what it looks like:

1. First, we edit `src/App.js`, and remove all its contents.
2. Then, we start by importing `React` and the `Login` component:

```
import React from 'react'

import Login from './user/Login'
```

It is a good idea to group imports in blocks of code that belong together. In this case, we separate external imports, such as React, from local imports, such as our `Login` component, by adding an empty line in between. Doing so keeps our code readable, especially when we add more import statements later.

3. Finally, we define the `App` component, and return the `Login` component:

```
export default function App () {
    return <Login />
}
```

If we are only returning a single component, we can omit the brackets in the `return` statement. Instead of writing `return (<Login />)`, we can simply write `return <Login />`.

4. Open `http://localhost:3000` in your browser, and you should see the `Login` component being rendered. If you already had the page open in your browser, it should refresh automatically when you change the code:

The first component of our blog application: logging in by username and password

As we can see, the static `Login` component renders fine in React. We can now move on to the `Logout` component.

The Logout component

Next, we define the `Logout` component, which is going to display the currently logged in user, and a button to log out:

1. Create a new file: `src/user/Logout.js`
2. Import `React`, as follows:

```
import React from 'react'
```

3. This time, our function is going to take a `user` prop, which we are going to use to display the currently logged-in user:

```
export default function Logout ({ user }) {
```

Here we use destructuring in order to extract the `user` key from the `props` object. React passes all component props, in a single object, as the first argument to a function. Using destructuring on the first argument is similar to doing `const { user } = this.props` in a class component.

4. Finally, we return a text that shows the currently logged-in `user` and the **Logout** button:

```
return (
    <form onSubmit={e => e.preventDefault()}>
        Logged in as: <b>{user}</b>
        <input type="submit" value="Logout" />
```

```
            </form>
        )
    }
```

5. We can now replace the `Login` component with the `Logout` component in `src/App.js`, in order to see our newly defined component (do not forget to pass the `user` prop to it!):

```
import React from 'react'

import Logout from './user/Logout'

export default function App () {
    return <Logout user="Daniel Bugl" />
}
```

Now, the `Logout` component is defined, and we can move on to the `Register` component.

The Register component

The static `Register` component will be very similar to the `Login` component, with an additional field to repeat the password. You might get the idea to merge them into one component if they are so similar, and add a prop to toggle the **Repeat password** field. However, it is best to stick to the single responsibility principle, and to have each component deal with only one functionality. Later on, we are going to extend the static components with dynamic code, and then `Register` and `Login` will have vastly different code. As a result, we would need to split them up again later.

Nevertheless, let's start working on the code for the `Register` component:

1. We start by creating a new `src/user/Register.js` file, and copying the code from the `Login` component, as the static components are very similar, after all. Make sure to change the name of the component to `Register`:

```
import React from 'react'

export default function Register () {
    return (
        <form onSubmit={e => e.preventDefault()}>
            <label htmlFor="register-username">Username:</label>
            <input type="text" name="register-username"
id="register-username" />
            <label htmlFor="register-password">Password:</label>
            <input type="password" name="register-password"
id="register-password" />
```

2. Next, we add the **Repeat password** field, right below the **Password** field code:

```
        <label htmlFor="register-password-repeat">Repeat
password:</label>
        <input type="password" name="register-password-repeat"
id="register-password-repeat" />
```

3. Finally, we also change the value of the submit button to **Register**:

```
        <input type="submit" value="Register" />
    </form>
  )
}
```

4. Again, we can edit `src/App.js` in order to show our component, in a similar way to how we did with the `Login` component:

```
import React from 'react'

import Register from './user/Register'

export default function App () {
    return <Register />
}
```

As we can see, our `Register` component looks very similar to the `Login` component.

The UserBar component

Now it is time to put our user-related components together into a `UserBar` component. Here we are going to conditionally show either the `Login` and `Register` components, or the `Logout` component, depending on whether the user is already logged in or not.

Let's start implementing the `UserBar` component:

1. First, we create a new `src/user/UserBar.js` file, and import `React` as well as the three components that we defined:

```
import React from 'react'

import Login from './Login'
import Logout from './Logout'
import Register from './Register'
```

2. Next, we define our function component, and a value for the user. For now, we just save it in a static variable:

```
export default function UserBar () {
    const user = ''
```

3. Then, we check whether the user is logged in or not. If the user is logged in, we display the Logout component, and pass the user value to it:

```
if (user) {
    return <Logout user={user} />
```

4. Otherwise, we show the Login and Register components. Here, we can use React.Fragment instead of a <div> container element. This keeps our UI tree clean, as the components will simply be rendered side by side, instead of being wrapped in another element:

```
} else {
    return (
        <React.Fragment>
            <Login />
            <Register />
        </React.Fragment>
    )
}
}
```

5. Again, we edit src/App.js, and now we show our UserBar component:

```
import React from 'react'

import UserBar from './user/UserBar'

export default function App () {
    return <UserBar />
}
```

6. As we can see, it works! We now show both the `Login` and `Register` components:

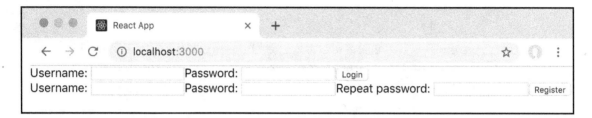

Our UserBar component, showing both the Login and Register components

7. Next, we can edit the `src/user/UserBar.js` file, and set the `user` value to a string:

```
const user = 'Daniel Bugl'
```

8. After doing so, our app now shows the `Logout` component:

Our app showing the Logout component after defining the user value

Later on in this chapter, we are going to add Hooks to our application, so that we can log in and have the state change dynamically without having to edit the code!

Example code

The example code for the user-related components can be found in the `Chapter03/chapter3_1` folder.

Just run `npm install` to install all dependencies, and `npm start` to start the application, then visit `http://localhost:3000` in your browser (if it did not open automatically).

Implementing posts

After implementing all the user-related components, we move on to implementing posts in our blog app. We are going to define the following components:

- A Post component to display a single post
- A CreatePost component for creating new posts
- A PostList component to show multiple posts

Let's get started implementing the post related components now.

The Post component

We have already thought about which elements a post has when creating the mock-up. A post should have a title, content, and an author (the user who wrote the post).

Let's implement the Post component now:

1. First, we create a new file: src/post/Post.js
2. Then, we import React, and define our function component, accepting three props: title, content, and author:

   ```
   import React from 'react'

   export default function Post ({ title, content, author }) {
   ```

3. Next, we render all props in a way that resembles the mock-up:

   ```
   return (
       <div>
           <h3>{title}</h3>
           <div>{content}</div>
           <br />
           <i>Written by <b>{author}</b></i>
       </div>
   )
   }
   ```

4. As always, we can test our component by editing the `src/App.js` file:

```
import React from 'react'

import Post from './post/Post'

export default function App () {
    return <Post title="React Hooks" content="The greatest thing
since sliced bread!" author="Daniel Bugl" />
}
```

Now, the static `Post` component has been implemented, and we can move on to the `CreatePost` component.

The CreatePost component

Next, we implement a form to allow for the creation of new posts. Here, we pass the `user` value as a prop to the component, as the author should always be the currently logged-in user. Then, we show the author, and provide an input field for the `title`, and a `<textarea>` element for the content of the blog post.

Let's implement the `CreatePost` component now:

1. Create a new file: `src/post/CreatePost.js`
2. Define the following component:

```
import React from 'react'

export default function CreatePost ({ user }) {
    return (
        <form onSubmit={e => e.preventDefault()}>
            <div>Author: <b>{user}</b></div>
            <div>
                <label htmlFor="create-title">Title:</label>
                <input type="text" name="create-title" id="create-
title" />
            </div>
            <textarea />
            <input type="submit" value="Create" />
        </form>
    )
}
```

3. As always, we can test our component by editing the `src/App.js` file:

```
import React from 'react'

import CreatePost from './post/CreatePost'

export default function App () {
    return <CreatePost />
}
```

As we can see, the `CreatePost` component renders fine. We can now move on to the `PostList` component.

The PostList component

After implementing the other post-related components, we can now implement the most important part of our blog app: the feed of blog posts. For now, the feed is simply going to show a list of blog posts.

Let's start implementing the `PostList` component now:

1. We start by importing `React` and the `Post` component:

```
import React from 'react'

import Post from './Post'
```

2. Then, we define our `PostList` function component, accepting a `posts` array as a prop. If `posts` is not defined, we set it to an empty array, by default:

```
export default function PostList ({ posts = [] }) {
```

3. Next, we render all `posts` by using the `.map` function and the spread syntax:

```
    return (
        <div>
            {posts.map((p, i) => <Post {...p} key={'post-' + i}
/>)}
        </div>
    )
}
```

If we are rendering a list of elements, we have to give each element a unique `key` prop. React uses this `key` prop to efficiently compute the difference of two lists, when the data has changed.

Here, we use the `map` function, which applies a function to all the elements of an array. This is similar to using a `for` loop, and storing all the results, but it is much more concise, declarative, and easier to read! Alternatively, we could do the following instead of using the `map` function:

```
let renderedPosts = []
let i = 0
for (let p of posts) {
    renderedPosts.push(<Post {...p} key={'post-' + i} />)
    i++
}

return (
    <div>
        {renderedPosts}
    </div>
)
```

We then return the `<Post>` component for each post, and pass all the keys from the post object, `p`, to the component as props. We do this by using the spread syntax, which has the same effect as listing all the keys from the object manually as props, as follows: `<Post title={p.title} content={p.content} author={p.author} />`

4. In the mock-up, we have a horizontal line after each blog post. We can implement this without an additional `<div>` container element, by using `React.Fragment`:

```
{posts.map((p, i) => (
    <React.Fragment key={'post-' + i} >
        <Post {...p} />
        <hr />
    </React.Fragment>
))}
```

 The `key` prop always has to be added to the uppermost parent element that is rendered within the `map` function. In this case, we had to move the `key` prop from the `Post` component to the `React.Fragment` component.

5. Again, we test our component by editing the `src/App.js` file:

```
import React from 'react'

import PostList from './post/PostList'

const posts = [
    { title: 'React Hooks', content: 'The greatest thing since
sliced bread!', author: 'Daniel Bugl' },
    { title: 'Using React Fragments', content: 'Keeping the DOM
tree clean!', author: 'Daniel Bugl' }
]

export default function App () {
    return <PostList posts={posts} />
}
```

Now, we can see that our app lists all the posts that we defined in the `posts` array:

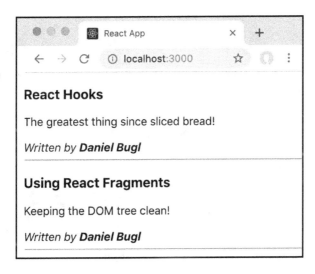

Showing multiple posts using the PostList component

As we can see, listing multiple posts via the `PostList` component works fine. We can now move on to putting the app together.

Putting the app together

After implementing all components, in order to reproduce the mock-up, we now only have to put everything together in the App component. Then, we will have successfully reproduced the mock-up!

Let's start modifying the App component, and putting our app together:

1. Edit src/App.js, and remove all of the current code.
2. First, we import React, PostList, CreatePost, and the UserBar components:

```
import React from 'react'

import PostList from './post/PostList'
import CreatePost from './post/CreatePost'
import UserBar from './user/UserBar'
```

3. Then, we define some mock data for our app:

```
const user = 'Daniel Bugl'
const posts = [
    { title: 'React Hooks', content: 'The greatest thing since
sliced bread!', author: 'Daniel Bugl' },
    { title: 'Using React Fragments', content: 'Keeping the DOM
tree clean!', author: 'Daniel Bugl' }
]
```

4. Next, we define the App component, and return a `<div>` container element, where we set some padding:

```
export default function App () {
    return (
        <div style={{ padding: 8 }}>
```

5. Now, we insert the UserBar and CreatePost components, passing the user prop to the CreatePost component:

```
<UserBar />
<br />
<CreatePost user={user} />
<br />
<hr />
```

Please note that you should always prefer spacing via CSS, rather than using the `<br />` HTML tag. However, at the moment, we are focusing on the UI, rather than its style, so we simply use HTML whenever possible.

6. Finally, we display the `PostList` component, listing all `posts`:

```
        <PostList posts={posts} />
    </div>
  )
}
```

7. After saving the file, `http://localhost:3000` should automatically refresh, and we can now see the full UI:

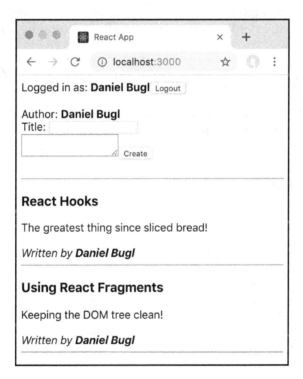

Full implementation of our static blog app, according to the mock-up

As we can see, all of the static components that we defined earlier are rendered together in one `App` component. Our app now looks just like the mock-up. Next, we can move on to making all of the components dynamic.

Example code

The example code for the static implementation of our blog app can be found in the `Chapter03/chapter3_2` folder.

Just run `npm install` to install all dependencies and `npm start` to start the application, then visit `http://localhost:3000` in your browser (if it did not open automatically).

Implementing stateful components with Hooks

Now that we have implemented the static structure of our application, we are going to add `useState` Hooks to it, in order to be able to handle state and dynamic interactions!

Adding Hooks for the users feature

To add Hooks for the users feature, we are going to have to replace the static `user` value with a State Hook. Then, we need to adjust the value when we log in, register and log out.

Adjusting UserBar

Recall that when we created the `UserBar` component, we statically defined the `user` value. We are now going to replace this value with a State Hook!

Let's start modifying the `UserBar` component to make it dynamic:

1. Edit `src/user/UserBar.js`, and import the `useState` Hook by adjusting the `React` import statement, as follows:

   ```
   import React, { useState } from 'react'
   ```

2. Remove the following line of code:

   ```
   const user = 'Daniel Bugl'
   ```

   Replace it with a State Hook, using an empty user `' '` as the default value:

   ```
   const [ user, setUser ] = useState('')
   ```

3. Then, we pass the `setUser` function to the `Login`, `Register`, and `Logout` components:

```
if (user) {
    return <Logout user={user} setUser={setUser} />
} else {
    return (
        <React.Fragment>
            <Login setUser={setUser} />
            <Register setUser={setUser} />
        </React.Fragment>
    )
}
```

Now, the `UserBar` component provides a `setUser` function, which can be used in the `Login`, `Register`, and `Logout` components to set or unset the `user` value.

Adjusting the Login and Register components

In the `Login` and `Register` components, we need to use the `setUser` function to set the value of `user` accordingly, when we log in or register.

Login

In the `Login` component, we just ignore the **Password** field for now, and only process the **Username** field.

Let's start by modifying the `Login` component in order to make it dynamic:

1. Edit `src/user/Login.js`, and import the `useState` Hook:

```
import React, { useState } from 'react'
```

2. Then, adjust the function definition to accept the `setUser` prop:

```
export default function Login ({ setUser }) {
```

3. Now, we define a new State Hook for the value of the **Username** field:

```
const [ username, setUsername ] = useState('')
```

4. Next, we define a handler function:

```
function handleUsername (evt) {
    setUsername(evt.target.value)
}
```

5. Then, we adjust the `input` field, in order to use the `username` value, and call the `handleUsername` function when the input changes:

```
<input type="text" value={username}
onChange={handleUsername} name="login-username" id="login-username"
/>
```

6. Finally, we need to call the `setUser` function when the **Login** button is pressed, and thus the `form` is submitted:

```
<form onSubmit={e => { e.preventDefault();
setUser(username) }} />
```

7. Additionally, we can disable the **Login** button when the `username` value is empty:

```
<input type="submit" value="Login"
disabled={username.length === 0} />
```

And it works—we can now enter a username, press the **Login** button, and then our `UserBar` component will change its state, and show the `Logout` component!

Register

For registration, we are additionally going to check whether the entered passwords are the same, and only then will we set the `user` value.

Let's start by modifying the `Register` component in order to make it dynamic:

1. First, we do the same steps as we did for `Login`, in order to handle the `username` field:

```
import React, { useState } from 'react'

export default function Register ({ setUser }) {
    const [ username, setUsername ] = useState('')

    function handleUsername (evt) {
        setUsername(evt.target.value)
    }
```

```
      return (
          <form onSubmit={e => { e.preventDefault();
setUser(username) }}>
              <label htmlFor="register-username">Username:</label>
              <input type="text" value={username}
onChange={handleUsername} name="register-username" id="register-
username" />
              <label htmlFor="register-password">Password:</label>
              <input type="password" name="register-password"
id="register-password" />
              <label htmlFor="register-password-repeat">Repeat
password:</label>
              <input type="password" name="register-password-repeat"
id="register-password-repeat" />
              <input type="submit" value="Register"
disabled={username.length === 0} />
          </form>
      )
  }
```

2. Now, we define two new State Hooks for the **Password** and **Repeat password** fields:

```
const [ password, setPassword ] = useState('')
const [ passwordRepeat, setPasswordRepeat ] = useState('')
```

3. Then, we define two handler functions for them:

```
function handlePassword (evt) {
    setPassword(evt.target.value)
}

function handlePasswordRepeat (evt) {
    setPasswordRepeat(evt.target.value)
}
```

You might have noticed that we are always writing similar handler functions for `input` fields. Actually, this is the perfect use case for creating a custom Hook! We are going to learn how to do that in a future chapter.

4. Next, we assign the `value` and `onChange` handler functions to the `input` fields:

```
              <label htmlFor="register-password">Password:</label>
              <input type="password" value={password}
onChange={handlePassword} name="register-password" id="register-
password" />
              <label htmlFor="register-password-repeat">Repeat
```

```
password:</label>
            <input type="password" value={passwordRepeat}
onChange={handlePasswordRepeat} name="register-password-repeat"
id="register-password-repeat" />
```

5. Finally, we check if the passwords match, and if they do not, we keep the button `disabled`:

```
            <input type="submit" value="Register"
disabled={username.length === 0 || password.length === 0 ||
password !== passwordRepeat} />
```

And now we have successfully implemented a check on whether the passwords are equal, and we implemented registration!

Adjusting Logout

There is still one thing missing for the users feature—we cannot log out yet.

Let's make the `Logout` component dynamic now:

1. Edit `src/user/Logout.js`, and add the `setUser` prop:

```
export default function Logout ({ user, setUser }) {
```

2. Then, adjust the `onSubmit` handler of `form` and set the user to `''`:

```
            <form onSubmit={e => { e.preventDefault(); setUser('')
}} />
```

 As we are not creating a new Hook here, we do not need to import the `useState` Hook from React. We can simply use the `setUser` function passed to the `Logout` component as a prop.

Now, the `Logout` component sets the `user` value to `''` when we click on the **Logout** button.

Passing the user to CreatePost

As you might have noticed, the `CreatePost` component still uses the hardcoded username. To be able to access the `user` value there, we need to move the Hook from the `UserBar` component, to the `App` component.

Let's refactor the definition of the `user` State Hook now:

1. Edit `src/user/UserBar.js`, and cut/remove the Hook definition that is there:

   ```
   const [ user, setUser ] = useState('')
   ```

2. Then, we edit the function definition, and accept these two values as props:

   ```
   export default function UserBar ({ user, setUser }) {
   ```

3. Now, we edit `src/App.js`, and import the `useState` Hook there:

   ```
   import React, { useState } from 'react'
   ```

4. Next, we remove the static `user` value definition:

   ```
   const user = 'Daniel Bugl'
   ```

5. Then, we insert the `user` State Hook that we cut earlier into the `App` component function:

   ```
   const [ user, setUser ] = useState('')
   ```

6. Now, we can pass `user` and `setUser` as props to the `UserBar` component:

   ```
   <UserBar user={user} setUser={setUser} />
   ```

 The `user` state is a global state, so we are going to need it in many components across the app. At the moment, this means that we need to pass down the `user` value and the `setUser` function to each component that needs it. In a future chapter, we are going to learn about React Context Hooks, which solve the problem of having to pass down props in such a way.

7. Finally, we only show the `CreatePost` component when the user is logged in. To do this, we use a pattern, which allows us to show a component based on a condition:

   ```
   {user && <CreatePost user={user} />}
   ```

Now, the users feature is fully implemented—we can use the `Login` and `Register` components, and the `user` value also gets passed to the `CreatePost` component!

Adding Hooks for the posts feature

After implementing the users feature, we are now going to implement the dynamic creation of posts. We do so by first adjusting the App component and then modifying the CreatePost component, in order to be able to insert new posts.

Let's get started by adjusting the App component.

Adjusting the App component

As we know from the users feature, posts are also going to be global state, so we should define it in the App component.

Let's implement the posts value as global state now:

1. Edit src/App.js, and rename the current posts array to defaultPosts:

```
const defaultPosts = [
    { title: 'React Hooks', content: 'The greatest thing since
sliced bread!', author: 'Daniel Bugl' },
    { title: 'Using React Fragments', content: 'Keeping the DOM
tree clean!', author: 'Daniel Bugl' }
]
```

2. Then, define a new State Hook for the posts state:

```
const [ posts, setPosts ] = useState(defaultPosts)
```

3. Now, we pass the posts value and setPosts function as props to the CreatePost component:

```
{user && <CreatePost user={user} posts={posts}
setPosts={setPosts} />}
```

Now, our App component provides the posts array, and a setPosts function to the CreatePost component. Let's move on to adjusting the CreatePost component.

Adjusting the CreatePost component

Next, we need to use the setPosts function in order to insert a new post, when we press the **Create** button.

Let's start modifying the `CreatePost` component in order to make it dynamic:

1. Edit `src/posts/CreatePost.js`, and import the `useState` Hook:

   ```
   import React, { useState } from 'react'
   ```

2. Then, adjust the function definition to accept the `posts` and `setPosts` props:

   ```
   export default function CreatePost ({ user, posts, setPosts }) {
   ```

3. Next, we define two new State Hooks—one for the `title` value, and one for the `content` value:

   ```
   const [ title, setTitle ] = useState('')
   const [ content, setContent ] = useState('')
   ```

4. Now, we define two handler functions—one for the `input` field, and one for the `textarea`:

   ```
   function handleTitle (evt) {
       setTitle(evt.target.value)
   }

   function handleContent (evt) {
       setContent(evt.target.value)
   }
   ```

5. We also define a handler function for the **Create** button:

   ```
   function handleCreate () {
   ```

6. In this function, we first create a `newPost` object from the `input` field values:

   ```
   const newPost = { title, content, author: user }
   ```

In newer JavaScript versions, we can shorten the following object assignment: `{ title: title }`, to `{ title }`, and it will have the same effect. So, instead of doing `{ title: title, contents: contents }`, we can simply do `{ title, contents }`.

7. Then, we set the new `posts` array by first adding `newPost` to the array, then using the spread syntax to list all of the existing `posts`:

   ```
   setPosts([ newPost, ...posts ])
   }
   ```

8. Next, we add the `value` and handler functions to the `input` field and `textarea` element:

```
<div>
    <label htmlFor="create-title">Title:</label>
    <input type="text" value={title}
onChange={handleTitle} name="create-title"
                id="create-title" />
</div>
<textarea value={content} onChange={handleContent} />
```

 Usually in HTML, we put the value of `textarea` as its children. However, in React, `textarea` can be handled like any other `input` field, by using the `value` and `onChange` props.

9. Finally, we pass the `handleCreate` function to the `onSubmit` handler of the `form` element:

```
<form onSubmit={e => { e.preventDefault(); handleCreate()
}}>
```

10. Now, we can log in and create a new post, and it will be inserted at the beginning of the feed:

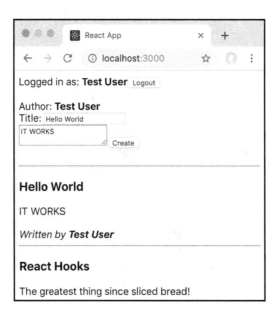

Our first version of the blog app using Hooks, after inserting a new blog post

As we can see, now our application is fully dynamic, and we can use all of its features!

Example code

The example code for the dynamic implementation of our blog app with Hooks can be found in the `Chapter03/chapter3_3` folder.

Just run `npm install` to install all dependencies, and `npm start` to start the application, then visit `http://localhost:3000` in your browser (if it did not open automatically).

Summary

In this chapter, we developed our own blog application from scratch! We started with a mock-up, then created static components to resemble it. Afterward, we implemented Hooks, to allow for dynamic behavior. Throughout the chapter, we learned how to deal with local and global states, using Hooks. Furthermore, we learned how to use multiple Hooks, and in which components to define Hooks and store state. We also learned how to solve common use cases, such as handling input fields with the use of Hooks.

In the next chapter, we are going to learn about the `useReducer` Hook, which allows us to deal with certain state changes more easily. Furthermore, we are going to learn about the `useEffect` Hook, which allows us to run code with side effects.

Questions

To recap what we have learned in this chapter, try to answer the following questions:

1. What is the best practice for folder structures in React?
2. Which principle should we use when splitting up React components?
3. What does the `map` function do?
4. How does destructuring work, and when do we use it?
5. How does the spread operator work, and when do we use it?
6. How do we deal with input fields using React Hooks?
7. Where should local State Hooks be defined?
8. What is global state?
9. Where should global State Hooks be defined?

Further reading

If you are interested in more information about the concepts that we have learned in this chapter, take a look at the following reading material:

- Official docs on *Thinking in React*: `https://reactjs.org/docs/thinking-in-react.html`
- Handling input fields with React: `https://reactjs.org/docs/forms.html`

Section 2: Understanding Hooks in Depth

In this part of the book, we will learn about various React Hooks and how to use them. Additionally, we will learn about the rules of Hooks and how to write our own Hooks.

In this section, we will cover the following chapters:

- Chapter 4, *Using the Reducer and Effect Hooks*
- Chapter 5, *Implementing React Context*
- Chapter 6, *Implementing Requests and React Suspense*
- Chapter 7, *Using Hooks for Routing*
- Chapter 8, *Using Community Hooks*
- Chapter 9, *Rules of Hooks*
- Chapter 10, *Building Your Own Hooks*

Using the Reducer and Effect Hooks

After developing our own blog application using the State Hook, we are now going to learn about two other very important Hooks that are provided by React: the **Reducer** and **Effect** Hooks. We are first going to learn when we should use a Reducer Hook instead of a State Hook. Then, we learn how to turn an existing State Hook into a Reducer Hook in order to get a grasp on the concept in practice. Next, we are going to learn about Effect Hooks and what they are used for. Finally, we are going to implement them in our blog application.

The following topics will be covered in this chapter:

- Learning about the differences between Reducer Hooks and State Hooks
- Implementing Reducer Hooks in our blog app
- Using Effect Hooks in our blog app

Technical requirements

A fairly recent version of Node.js should already be installed (v11.12.0 or higher). The npm package manager for Node.js also needs to be installed.

The code for this chapter can be found on the GitHub repository: `https://github.com/PacktPublishing/Learn-React-Hooks/tree/master/Chapter04`.

Check out the following video to see the code in action:

`http://bit.ly/2Mm9yoC`

Please note that it is highly recommended that you write the code on your own. Do not simply run the code examples that have been provided. It is important that you write the code yourself in order for you to be able to learn and understand properly. However, if you run into any issues, you can always refer to the code example.

Now, let's get started with the chapter.

Reducer Hooks versus State Hooks

In the previous chapter, we learned about dealing with local and global states. We used State Hooks for both cases, which is fine for simple state changes. However, when our state logic becomes more complicated, we are going to need to ensure that we keep the state consistent. In order to do so, we should use a Reducer Hook instead of multiple State Hooks, because it is harder to maintain synchronicity between multiple State Hooks that depend on each other. As an alternative, we could keep all state in one State Hook, but then we have to make sure that we do not accidentally overwrite parts of our state.

Problems with the State Hook

The State Hook already supports passing complex objects and arrays to it, and it can handle their state changes perfectly well. However, we are always going to have to change the state directly, which means that we need to use a lot of spread syntax, in order to make sure that we are not overwriting other parts of the state. For example, imagine that we have a state object like this:

```
const [ config, setConfig ] = useState({ filter: 'all', expandPosts: true })
```

Now, we want to change the filter:

```
setConfig({ filter: { byAuthor: 'Daniel Bugl', fromDate: '2019-04-29' } })
```

If we simply ran the preceding code, we would be removing the `expandPosts` part of our state! So, we need to do the following:

```
setConfig({ ...config, filter: { byAuthor: 'Daniel Bugl', fromDate: '2019-04-29' } })
```

Now, if we wanted to change the `fromDate` filter to a different date, we would need to use spread syntax twice, to avoid removing the `byAuthor` filter:

```
setConfig({ ...config, filter: { ...config.filter, fromDate: '2019-04-30' }
})
```

But, what happens if we do this when the `filter` state is still a string? We are going to get the following result:

```
{ filter: { '0': 'a', '1': 'l', '2': 'l', fromDate: '2019-04-30' },
  expandPosts: true }
```

What? Why are there suddenly three new keys—0, 1, and 2? This is because spread syntax also works on strings, which are spread in such a way that each letter gets a key, based on its index in the string.

As you can imagine, using spread syntax and changing the state object directly can become very tedious for larger state objects. Furthermore, we always need to make sure that we do not introduce any bugs, and we need to check for bugs in multiple places all across our app.

Actions

Instead of changing the state directly, we could make a function that deals with state changes. Such a function would only allow state changes via certain actions, such as a `CHANGE_FILTER` or a `TOGGLE_EXPAND` action.

Actions are simply objects that have a `type` key, telling us which action we are dealing with, and additional keys more closely describing the action.

The `TOGGLE_EXPAND` action is quite simple. It is simply an object with the action `type` defined:

```
{ type: 'TOGGLE_EXPAND' }
```

The `CHANGE_FILTER` action could deal with the complex state changes that we had problems with earlier, as follows:

```
{ type: 'CHANGE_FILTER', all: true }
{ type: 'CHANGE_FILTER', fromDate: '2019-04-29' }
{ type: 'CHANGE_FILTER', byAuthor: 'Daniel Bugl' }
{ type: 'CHANGE_FILTER', fromDate: '2019-04-30' }
```

The second, third, and fourth actions would change the `filter` state from a string to an object, and then set the respective key. If the object already exists, we would simply adjust the keys that were defined in the action. After each action, the state would change as follows:

- `{ expandPosts: true, filter: 'all' }`
- `{ expandPosts: true, filter: { fromDate: '2019-04-29' } }`
- `{ expandPosts: true, filter: { fromDate: '2019-04-29', byAuthor: 'Daniel Bugl' } }`
- `{ expandPosts: true, filter: { fromDate: '2019-04-30', byAuthor: 'Daniel Bugl' } }`

Now, take a look at the following code:

```
{ type: 'CHANGE_FILTER', all: true }
```

If we dispatched another action, as in the preceding code, then the state would go back to being the `all` string, as it was in the initial state.

Reducers

Now, we still need to define the function that handles these state changes. Such a function is known as a reducer function. It takes the current `state` and `action` as arguments, and returns a new state.

 If you are aware of the Redux library, you will already be very familiar with the concept of state, actions, and reducers.

Now, we are going to define our `reducer` function:

1. We start with the function definition of our `reducer`:

   ```
   function reducer (state, action) {
   ```

2. Then, we check for `action.type` using a `switch` statement:

   ```
   switch (action.type) {
   ```

3. Now, we are going to handle the `TOGGLE_EXPAND` action, where we simply toggle the current `expandPosts` state:

```
case 'TOGGLE_EXPAND':
    return { ...state, expandPosts: !state.expandPosts }
```

4. Next, we are going to handle the `CHANGE_FILTER` action. Here, we first need to check if `all` is set to `true`, and, in that case, simply set our `filter` to the `'all'` string:

```
case 'CHANGE_FILTER':
    if (action.all) {
        return { ...state, filter: 'all' }
    }
```

5. Now, we have to handle the other `filter` options. First, we check if the `filter` variable is already an `object`. If not, we create a new one. Otherwise, we use the existing object:

```
    let filter = typeof state.filter === 'object' ?
state.filter : {}
```

6. Then, we define the handlers for the various filters, allowing for multiple filters to be set at once, by not immediately returning the new `state`:

```
    if (action.fromDate) {
        filter = { ...filter, fromDate: action.fromDate }
    }
    if (action.byAuthor) {
        filter = { ...filter, byAuthor: action.byAuthor }
    }
```

7. Finally, we return the new `state`:

```
    return { ...state, filter }
```

8. For the `default` case, we throw an error, because this is an unknown action:

```
    default:
        throw new Error()
    }
}
```

Throwing an error in the default case is different to what is best practice with Redux reducers, where we would simply return the current state in the default case. Because React Reducer Hooks do not store all state in one object, we are only going to handle certain actions for certain state objects, so we can throw an error for unknown actions.

Now, our `reducer` function has been defined, and we can move on to defining the Reducer Hook.

The Reducer Hook

Now that we have defined actions and the `reducer` function, we can create a Reducer Hook from the `reducer`. The signature for the `useReducer` Hook is as follows:

```
const [ state, dispatch ] = useReducer(reducer, initialState)
```

The only thing that we still need to define is the `initialState`; then we can define a Reducer Hook:

```
const initialState = { all: true }
```

Now, we can access the state by using the `state` object that was returned from the Reducer Hook, and dispatch actions via the `dispatch` function, as follows:

```
dispatch({ type: 'TOGGLE_EXPAND' })
```

If we want to add additional options to the action, we simply add them to the action object:

```
dispatch({ type: 'CHANGE_FILTER', fromDate: '2019-04-30' })
```

As we can see, dealing with state changes using actions and reducers is much easier than having to adjust the state object directly.

Implementing Reducer Hooks

After learning about actions, reducers, and the Reducer Hook, we are going to implement them in our blog app. Any existing State Hook can be turned into a Reducer Hook, when the state object or state changes become too complex.

If there are multiple `setState` functions that are always called at the same time, it is a good hint that they should be grouped together in a single Reducer Hook.

Global state is usually a good candidate for using a Reducer Hook, rather than a State Hook, because global-state changes can happen anywhere in the app. Then, it is much easier to deal with actions, and update the state-changing logic only in one place. Having all the state-changing logic in one place makes it easier to maintain and fix bugs, without introducing new ones by forgetting to update the logic everywhere.

We are now going to turn some of the existing State Hooks in our blog app into Reducer Hooks.

Turning a State Hook into a Reducer Hook

In our blog app, we have two global State Hooks, which we are going to replace with Reducer Hooks:

- `user` state
- `posts` state

We start by replacing the `user` State Hook.

Replacing the user State Hook

We are going to start with the `user` State Hook, because it is simpler than the `posts` State Hook. Later on, the `user` state will contain complex state changes, so it makes sense to use a Reducer Hook here.

First, we are going to define our actions, then we are going to define the reducer function. Finally, we are going to replace the State Hook with a Reducer Hook.

Defining actions

We start by defining our actions, as these will be important when defining the reducer function.

Let's define the actions now:

1. First, we are going to need an action to allow a user to log in, by providing a `username` value and a `password` value:

   ```
   { type: 'LOGIN', username: 'Daniel Bugl', password: 'notsosecure' }
   ```

2. Then, we are also going to need a `REGISTER` action, which, in our case, is going to be similar to the `LOGIN` action, because we did not implement any registration logic yet:

   ```
   { type: 'REGISTER', username: 'Daniel Bugl', password:
   'notsosecure', passwordRepeat: 'notsosecure' }
   ```

3. Finally, we are going to need a `LOGOUT` action, which is simply going to log out the currently logged-in user:

   ```
   { type: 'LOGOUT' }
   ```

Now, we have defined all the required user-related actions and we can move on to defining the reducer function.

Defining the reducer

Next, we define a reducer function for the `user` state. For now, we are going to place our reducers in the `src/App.js` file.

> Later on, it might make sense to create a separate `src/reducers.js` file, or even a separate `src/reducers/` directory, with separate files for each reducer function.

Let's start defining the `userReducer` function:

1. In the `src/App.js` file, before the `App` function definition, create a `userReducer` function for the `user` state:

   ```
   function userReducer (state, action) {
   ```

2. Again, we use a `switch` statement for the `action` type:

```
switch (action.type) {
```

3. Then, we handle the `LOGIN` and `REGISTER` actions, where we set the `user` state to the given `username` value. In our case, we simply return the `username` value from the `action` object for now:

```
case 'LOGIN':
case 'REGISTER':
    return action.username
```

4. Next, we handle the `LOGOUT` action, where we set the state to an empty string:

```
case 'LOGOUT':
    return ''
```

5. Finally, we throw an error when we encounter an unhandled action:

```
default:
    throw new Error()
    }
}
```

Now, the `userReducer` function is defined, and we can move on to defining the Reducer Hook.

Defining the Reducer Hook

After defining the actions and the reducer function, we are going to define the Reducer Hook, and pass its state and the dispatch function to the components that need it.

Let's start implementing the Reducer Hook:

1. First, we have to import the `useReducer` Hook, by adjusting the following `import` statement in `src/App.js`:

```
import React, { useState, useReducer } from 'react'
```

2. Edit `src/App.js`, and remove the following State Hook:

```
const [ user, setUser ] = useState('')
```

Replace the preceding State Hook with a Reducer Hook—the initial state is an empty string, as we had it before:

```
const [ user, dispatchUser ] = useReducer(userReducer, '')
```

3. Now, pass the `user` state and the `dispatchUser` function to the `UserBar` component, as a `dispatch` prop:

```
<UserBar user={user} dispatch={dispatchUser} />
```

4. We do not need to modify the `CreatePost` component, as we are only passing the `user` state to it, and that part did not change.

5. Next, we edit the `UserBar` component in `src/user/UserBar.js`, and replace the `setUser` prop with the `dispatch` function:

```
export default function UserBar ({ user, dispatch }) {
    if (user) {
        return <Logout user={user} dispatch={dispatch} />
    } else {
        return (
            <React.Fragment>
                <Login dispatch={dispatch} />
                <Register dispatch={dispatch} />
            </React.Fragment>
        )
    }
}
```

6. Now, we can edit the `Login` component in `src/user/Login.js`, and replace the `setUser` function with the `dispatch` function:

```
export default function Login ({ dispatch }) {
```

7. Then, we replace the call to `setUser` with a call to the `dispatch` function, dispatching a `LOGIN` action:

```
<form onSubmit={e => { e.preventDefault(); dispatch({
type: 'LOGIN', username }) }}>
```

We could also make functions that return actions—so-called action creators. Instead of manually creating the action object every time, we could simply call `loginAction('username')` instead, which returns the corresponding `LOGIN` action object.

---

8. We repeat the same process for the `Register` component in `src/user/Register.js`:

```
export default function Register ({ dispatch }) {
    // ...
                <form onSubmit={e => { e.preventDefault(); dispatch({
    type: 'REGISTER', username }) }}>
```

9. Finally, we also repeat the same process for the `Logout` component in `src/user/Logout.js`:

```
export default function Logout ({ user, dispatch }) {
    // ...
                <form onSubmit={e => { e.preventDefault(); dispatch({
    type: 'LOGOUT' }) }}>
```

Now, our app should work the same way as before, but it uses the Reducer Hook instead of a simple State Hook!

Replacing the posts State Hook

It also makes sense to use a Reducer Hook for the `posts` state, because, later on, we are going to have features that can be used to delete and edit posts, so it makes a lot of sense to keep these complex state changes contained. Let's now get started replacing the posts State Hook with a Reducer Hook.

Defining actions

Again, we start by defining actions. At the moment, we are only going to consider a `CREATE_POST` action:

```
{ type: 'CREATE_POST', title: 'React Hooks', content: 'The greatest thing
since sliced bread!', author: 'Daniel Bugl' }
```

That is the only action we are going to need for posts, at the moment.

Defining the reducer

Next, we are going to define the reducer function in a similar way that we did for the user state:

1. We start by editing src/App.js, and defining the reducer function there. The following code defines the postsReducer function:

   ```
   function postsReducer (state, action) {
       switch (action.type) {
   ```

2. In this function, we are going to handle the CREATE_POST action. We first create a newPost object, and then we insert it at the beginning of the current posts state by using spread syntax, in a similar way to how we did it in the src/post/CreatePost.js component earlier:

   ```
   case 'CREATE_POST':
       const newPost = { title: action.title, content:
   action.content, author: action.author }
           return [ newPost, ...state ]
   ```

3. For now, this will be the only action that we handle in this reducer, so we can now define the default statement:

   ```
           default:
               throw new Error()
       }
   }
   ```

Now, the postsReducer function is defined, and we can move on to creating the Reducer Hook.

Defining the Reducer Hook

Finally, we are going to define and use the Reducer Hook for the posts state:

1. We start by removing the following State Hook in src/App.js:

   ```
   const [ posts, setPosts ] = useState(defaultPosts)
   ```

   We replace it with the following Reducer Hook:

   ```
   const [ posts, dispatchPosts ] = useReducer(postsReducer,
   defaultPosts)
   ```

2. Then, we pass the `dispatchPosts` function to the `CreatePost` component, as a `dispatch` prop:

```
{user && <CreatePost user={user} posts={posts}
dispatch={dispatchPosts} />}
```

3. Next, we edit the `CreatePost` component in `src/post/CreatePost.js`, and replace the `setPosts` function with the `dispatch` function:

```
export default function CreatePost ({ user, posts, dispatch }) {
```

4. Finally, we use the `dispatch` function in the `handleCreate` function:

```
function handleCreate () {
    dispatch({ type: 'CREATE_POST', title, content, author:
user })
    }
```

Now, the `posts` state also uses a Reducer Hook instead of a State Hook, and it works in the same way as before! However, if we want to add more logic for managing posts, such as searching, filtering, deleting, and editing, later on, it will be much easier to do so.

Example code

The example code for using Reducer Hooks in our blog app can be found in the `Chapter04/chapter4_1` folder.

Just run `npm install` in order to install all dependencies and `npm start` to start the application; then visit `http://localhost:3000` in your browser (if it did not open automatically).

Merging Reducer Hooks

Currently, we have two different dispatch functions: one for the `user` state, and one for the `posts` state. In our case, it makes sense to combine the two reducers into one, which then calls further reducers, in order to deal with the sub-state.

 This pattern is similar to the way in which reducers work in Redux, where we only have one object containing the whole state tree of the application, which in the case of the global state, makes sense. However, for complex local state changes, it might make more sense to keep the reducers separate.

Let's start merging our reducer functions into one reducer function. While we are at it, let's refactor all the reducers into a `src/reducers.js` file, in order to keep the `src/App.js` file more readable:

1. Create a new `src/reducers.js` file.

2. Cut the following code from the `src/App.js` file, and paste it into the `src/reducers.js` file:

```
function userReducer (state, action) {
    switch (action.type) {
        case 'LOGIN':
        case 'REGISTER':
            return action.username

        case 'LOGOUT':
            return ''

        default:
            throw new Error()
    }
}

function postsReducer (state, action) {
    switch (action.type) {
        case 'CREATE_POST':
            const newPost = { title: action.title, content:
action.content, author: action.author }
            return [ newPost, ...state ]

        default:
            throw new Error()
    }
}
```

3. Edit `src/reducers.js`, and define a new reducer function below the existing reducer functions, called `appReducer`:

```
export default function appReducer (state, action) {
```

4. In this `appReducer` function, we are going to call the other two reducer functions, and return the full state tree:

```
    return {
        user: userReducer(state.user, action),
        posts: postsReducer(state.posts, action)
    }
}
```

5. Edit `src/App.js`, and import the `appReducer` there:

    ```
    import appReducer from './reducers'
    ```

6. Then, we remove the following two Reducer Hook definitions:

    ```
    const [ user, dispatchUser ] = useReducer(userReducer,
      '')
    const [ posts, dispatchPosts = useReducer(postsReducer,
    defaultPosts)
    ```

    We replace the preceding Reducer Hook definitions with a single Reducer Hook definition for the `appReducer`:

    ```
    const [ state, dispatch ] = useReducer(appReducer, { user: '',
    posts: defaultPosts })
    ```

7. Next, we extract the `user` and `posts` values from our `state` object, using destructuring:

    ```
    const { user, posts } = state
    ```

8. Now, we still need to replace the `dispatchUser` and `dispatchPosts` functions that we passed to the other components with the `dispatch` function:

    ```
    <UserBar user={user} dispatch={dispatch} />
    <br />
    {user && <CreatePost user={user} posts={posts}
    dispatch={dispatch} />}
    ```

As we can see, now there is only one `dispatch` function, and a single state object.

Ignoring unhandled actions

However, if we try logging in now, we are going to see an error from the `postsReducer`. This is because we are still throwing an error on unhandled actions. In order to avoid this, we have to instead ignore unhandled actions, and simply return the current state:

Edit the `userReducer` and `postsReducer` functions in `src/reducers.js`, and remove the following code:

```
default:
    throw new Error()
```

Replace the preceding code with a `return` statement that returns the current `state`:

```
default:
    return state
```

As we can see, now our app still works in exactly the same way as before, but we are using a single reducer for our whole app state!

Example code

The example code for using a single Reducer Hook in our blog app can be found in the `Chapter04/chapter4_2` folder.

Just run `npm install` in order to install all dependencies, and `npm start` to start the application, and then visit `http://localhost:3000` in your browser (if it did not open automatically).

Using Effect Hooks

The last essential Hook that we are going to be using frequently is the Effect Hook. Using the Effect Hook, we can perform side effects from our components, such as fetching data when the component mounts or updates.

In the case of our blog, we are going to implement a feature that updates the title of our web page when we log in, so that it contains the username of the currently logged-in user.

Remember componentDidMount and componentDidUpdate?

If you have worked with React before, you have probably used the `componentDidMount` and `componentDidUpdate` life cycle methods. For example, we can set the document `title` to a given prop as follows, using a React class component. In the following code section, the life cycle method is highlighted in bold:

```
import React from 'react'

class App extends React.Component {
    componentDidMount () {
        const { title } = this.props
```

```
        document.title = title
    }

    render () {
        return (
            <div>Test App</div>
        )
    }
}
```

This works fine. However, when the title prop updates, the change does not get reflected in the title of our web page. To solve this problem, we need to define the componentDidUpdate life cycle method (new code in bold), as follows:

```
import React from 'react'

class App extends React.Component {
    componentDidMount () {
        const { title } = this.props
        document.title = title
    }

    componentDidUpdate (prevProps) {
        const { title } = this.props
        if (title !== prevProps.title) {
            document.title = title
        }
    }

    render () {
        return (
            <div>Test App</div>
        )
    }
}
```

You might have noticed that we are writing almost the same code twice; therefore, we could create a new method to deal with updates to title, and then call it from both life cycle methods. In the following code section, the updated code is highlighted in bold:

```
import React from 'react'

class App extends React.Component {
    updateTitle () {
        const { title } = this.props
        document.title = title
    }
```

```
componentDidMount () {
    this.updateTitle()
}

componentDidUpdate (prevProps) {
    if (this.props.title !== prevProps.title) {
        this.updateTitle()
    }
}

render () {
    return (
        <div>Test App</div>
    )
}
}
```

However, we still need to call this.updateTitle() twice. When we update the code later on, and, for example, pass an argument to this.updateTitle(), we always need to remember to pass it in both calls to the method. If we forget to update one of the life cycle methods, we might introduce bugs. Furthermore, we need to add an if condition to componentDidUpdate, in order to avoid calling this.updateTitle() when the title prop did not change.

Using an Effect Hook

In the world of Hooks, the componentDidMount and componentDidUpdate life cycle methods are combined in the useEffect Hook, which—when not specifying a dependency array—triggers whenever any props in the component change.

So, instead of using a class component, we can now define a function component with an Effect Hook, which does the same thing as before. The function passed to the Effect Hook is called "effect function":

```
import React, { useEffect } from 'react'

function App ({ title }) {
    useEffect(() => {
        document.title = title
    })

    return (
        <div>Test App</div>
    )
}
```

And that's all we need to do! The Hook that we have defined will call our effect function every time any props change.

Trigger effect only when certain props change

If we want to make sure that our effect function only gets called when the `title` prop changes, for example, for performance reasons, we can specify which values should trigger the changes, as a second argument to the `useEffect` Hook:

```
useEffect(() => {
    document.title = title
}, [title])
```

And this is not just restricted to props, we can use any value here, even values from other Hooks, such as a State Hook or a Reducer Hook:

```
const [ title, setTitle ] = useState('')
useEffect(() => {
    document.title = title
}, [title])
```

As we can see, using an Effect Hook is much more straightforward than using life cycle methods when dealing with changing values.

Trigger effect only on mount

If we want to replicate the behavior of only adding a `componentDidMount` life cycle method, without triggering when the props change, we can do this by passing an empty array as the second argument to the `useEffect` Hook:

```
useEffect(() => {
    document.title = title
}, [])
```

Passing an empty array means that our effect function will only trigger once when the component mounts, and it will not trigger when props change. However, instead of thinking about the mounting of components, with Hooks, we should think about the dependencies of effects. In this case, the effect does not have any dependencies, which means it will only trigger once. If an effect has dependencies specified, it will trigger again when any of the dependencies change.

Cleaning up effects

Sometimes effects need to be cleaned up when the component unmounts. To do so, we can return a function from the effect function of the Effect Hook. This returned function works similarly to the `componentWillUnmount` life cycle method:

```
useEffect(() => {
    const updateInterval = setInterval(() => console.log('fetching
update'), updateTime)

    return () => clearInterval(updateInterval)
}, [updateTime])
```

The code marked in bold above is called the cleanup function. The cleanup function will be called when the component unmounts and before running the effect again. This avoids bugs when, for example, the `updateTime` prop changes. In that case, the previous effect will be cleaned up and a new interval with the updated `updateTime` value will be defined.

Implementing an Effect Hook in our blog app

Now that we have learned how the Effect Hook works, we are going to use it in our blog app, to implement the title changing when we log in/log out (when the `user` state changes).

Let's get started implementing an Effect Hook in our blog app:

1. Edit `src/App.js`, and import the `useEffect` Hook:

   ```
   import React, { useReducer, useEffect } from 'react'
   ```

2. After defining our `useReducer` Hook and the state destructuring, define a `useEffect` Hook that adjusts the `document.title` variable, based on the `username` value:

   ```
   useEffect(() => {
   ```

3. If the user is logged in, we set the `document.title` to `<username> - React Hooks Blog`. We use template strings for this, which allow us to include variables, or JavaScript expressions, in a string via the `${ }` syntax. Template strings are defined using `` ` ``:

   ```
   if (user) {
       document.title = `${user} - React Hooks Blog`
   ```

4. Otherwise, if the user is not logged in, we simply set the `document.title` to `React Hooks Blog`:

```
    } else {
        document.title = 'React Hooks Blog'
    }
```

5. Finally, we pass the `user` value as the second argument to the Effect Hook, in order to ensure that whenever the `user` value updates, our effect function triggers again:

```
    }, [user])
```

If we start our app now, we can see that the `document.title` gets set to `React Hooks Blog`, because the Effect Hook triggers when the `App` component mounts, and the `user` value is not defined yet:

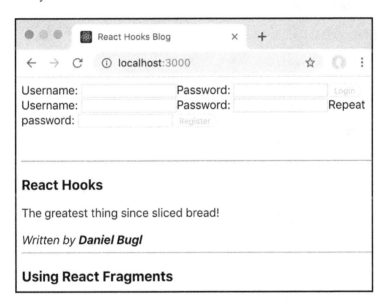

The effect of our Effect Hook: changing the web page title

After logging in with `Test User`, we can see that the `document.title` changes to `Test User - React Hooks Blog`:

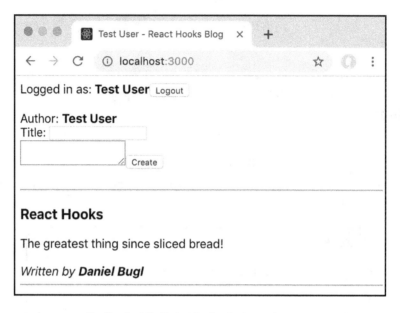

The effect of our Effect Hook re-triggering, after the user value changes

As we can see, our Effect Hook re-triggers successfully after the `user` value changes!

Example code

The example code for implementing Effect Hooks in our blog app can be found in the `Chapter04/chapter4_3` folder.

Just run `npm install` in order to install all dependencies, and `npm start` to start the application, and then visit `http://localhost:3000` in your browser (if it did not open automatically).

Summary

In this chapter, we first learned about actions, reducers, and Reducer Hooks. We also learned when we should use Reducer Hooks instead of State Hooks. Then, we replaced our existing global State Hooks for the `user` and `posts` states, with two Reducer Hooks. Next, we merged the two Reducer Hooks into a single app Reducer Hook. Finally, we learned about Effect Hooks, and how they can be used instead of `componentDidMount` and `componentDidUpdate`.

In the next chapter, we are going to learn about React context, and how to use it with Hooks. Then, we are going to add Context Hooks to our app, in order to avoid having to pass down props over multiple layers of components.

Questions

In order to recap what we have learned in this chapter, try to answer the following questions:

1. What are the common problems with State Hooks?
2. What are actions?
3. What are reducers?
4. When should we use a Reducer Hook instead of a State Hook?
5. Which steps are needed in order to turn a State Hook into a Reducer Hook?
6. How can we create actions more easily?
7. When should we merge Reducer Hooks?
8. What do we need to watch out for when merging Reducer Hooks?
9. What is the equivalent of an Effect Hook in class components?
10. What are the advantages of using an Effect Hook, versus class components?

Further reading

If you are interested in more information about the concepts that we have explored in this chapter, take a look at the following reading material:

- Official docs regarding the Reducer Hook: `https://reactjs.org/docs/hooks-reference.html#usereducer`
- Official docs and tips for using Effect Hooks: `https://reactjs.org/docs/hooks-effect.html`
- *Learning Redux* published by *Packt* for more in-depth information about actions, reducers, and managing the app state: `https://www.packtpub.com/web-development/learning-redux`

Implementing React Context 5

In the previous chapters, we learned about the most fundamental Hooks, such as the State Hook, the Reducer Hook, and the Effect Hook. We developed a small blog application using these Hooks. We have noticed during the development of our blog app, that we have to pass down the user state from the App component to the UserBar component, and from the UserBar component to the Login, Register, and Logout components. To avoid having to pass down the state like this, we are now going to learn about React context and Context Hooks.

We are going to begin by learning what React context is, and what providers and consumers are. Then, we are going to use Context Hooks as a context consumer, and discuss when context should be used. Finally, we are going to implement themes and global state via contexts.

The following topics will be covered in this chapter:

- Introducing React context as an alternative to passing down props
- Implementing themes via context
- Using context for global state

Technical requirements

A fairly recent version of Node.js should already be installed (v11.12.0 or higher). The npm package manager for Node.js also needs to be installed.

The code for this chapter can be found on the GitHub repository: hhttps://github.com/PacktPublishing/Learn-React-Hooks/tree/master/Chapter05

Check out the following video to see the code in action:

http://bit.ly/2Mm9yoC

Please note that it is highly recommended that you write the code on your own. Do not simply run the code examples that have been provided. It is important that you write the code yourself in order for you to be able to learn and understand properly. However, if you run into any issues, you can always refer to the code example.

Now, let's get started with the chapter.

Introducing React context

In the previous chapters, we passed down the `user` state and `dispatch` function from the `App` component, to the `UserBar` component; and then from the `UserBar` component to the `Logout`, `Login`, and `Register` components. React context provides a solution to this cumbersome way of passing down props over multiple levels of components, by allowing us to share values between components, without having to explicitly pass them down via props. As we are going to see, React context is perfect for sharing values across the whole application.

First, we are going to have a closer look at the problem of passing down props. Then, we are going to introduce React context as a solution to the problem.

Passing down props

Before learning about React context in depth, let's recap what we implemented in the earlier chapters, in order to get a feeling for the problem that contexts solve:

1. In `src/App.js`, we defined the `user` state and the `dispatch` function:

```
const [ state, dispatch ] = useReducer(appReducer, { user: '',
posts: defaultPosts })
const { user, posts } = state
```

2. Then, we passed the `user` state and the `dispatch` function to the `UserBar` component (and the `CreatePost` component):

```
return (
    <div style={{ padding: 8 }}>
        <UserBar user={user} dispatch={dispatch} />
        <br />
        {user && <CreatePost user={user} posts={posts}
dispatch={dispatch} />}
        <br />
```

```
            <hr />
            <PostList posts={posts} />
        </div>
    )
```

3. In the `src/user/UserBar.js` component, we took the `user` state as a prop, and then passed it down to the `Logout` component. We also took the `dispatch` function as a prop, and passed it to the `Logout`, `Login`, and `Register` components:

```
export default function UserBar ({ user, dispatch }) {
    if (user) {
        return <Logout user={user} dispatch={dispatch} />
    } else {
        return (
            <React.Fragment>
                <Login dispatch={dispatch} />
                <Register dispatch={dispatch} />
            </React.Fragment>
        )
    }
}
```

4. Finally, we used the `dispatch` and `user` props in the `Logout`, `Login`, and `Register` components.

React context allows us to skip steps 2 and 3, and jump straight from step 1 to step 4. As you can imagine, with larger apps, context becomes even more useful, because we might have to pass down props over many levels.

Introducing React context

React context is used to share values across a tree of React components. Usually, we want to share global values, such as the `user` state and the `dispatch` function, the theme of our app, or the chosen language.

React context consists of two parts:

- The **provider**, which provides (sets) the value
- The **consumer**, which consumes (uses) the value

We are first going to look at how contexts work, using a simple example, and, in the next section, we are going to implement them in our blog app. We create a new project with the `create-react-app` tool. In our simple example, we are going to define a theme context, containing the primary color of an app.

Defining the context

First, we have to define the context. The way this works has not changed since Hooks were introduced.

We simply use the `React.createContext(defaultValue)` function to create a new context object. We set the default value to `{ primaryColor: 'deepskyblue' }`, so our default primary color, when no provider is defined, will be `'deepskyblue'`.

In `src/App.js`, add the following definition before the `App` function:

```
export const ThemeContext = React.createContext({ primaryColor:
'deepskyblue' })
```

 Note how we are exporting `ThemeContext` here, because we are going to need to import it for the consumer.

That is all we need to do to define a context with React. Now we just need to define the consumer.

Defining the consumer

Now, we have to define the consumer in our `Header` component. We are going to do this in the traditional way for now, and in the next steps use Hooks to define the consumer:

1. Create a new `src/Header.js` file
2. First, we have to import `ThemeContext` from the `App.js` file:

```
import React from 'react'
import { ThemeContext } from './App'
```

3. Now, we can define our component, where we use the `ThemeContext.Consumer` component and a `render` function as `children` prop, in order to make use of the context value:

```
const Header = ({ text }) => (
    <ThemeContext.Consumer>
        {theme => (
```

4. Inside the `render` function, we can now make use of the context value to set the `color` style of our `Header` component:

```
            <h1 style={{ color: theme.primaryColor }}>{text}</h1>
        )}
    </ThemeContext.Consumer>
)

export default Header
```

5. Now, we still need to import the `Header` component in `src/App.js`, by adding the following `import` statement:

```
import Header from './Header'
```

6. Then, we replace the current `App` function with the following code:

```
const App = () => (
    <Header text="Hello World" />
)

export default App
```

Using contexts like this works, but, as we have learned in the first chapter, using components with `render` function props in this way clutters our UI tree, and makes our app harder to debug and maintain.

Using Hooks

A better way to use contexts is with the `useContext` Hook! That way, we can use context values like any other value, in a similar way to the `useState` Hook:

1. Edit `src/Header.js`. First, we import the `useContext` Hook from React, and the `ThemeContext` object from `src/App.js`:

```
import React, { useContext } from 'react'
import { ThemeContext } from './App'
```

2. Then, we create our `Header` component, where we now define the `useContext` Hook:

```
const Header = ({ text }) => {
    const theme = useContext(ThemeContext)
```

3. The rest of our component will be the same as before, except that, now, we can simply return our `Header` component, without using an additional component for the consumer:

```
    return <h1 style={{ color: theme.primaryColor }}>{text}</h1>
}

export default Header
```

As we can see, using Hooks makes our context consumer code much more concise. Furthermore, it will be easier to read, maintain, and debug.

We can see that the header now has the color `deepskyblue`:

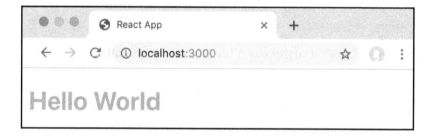

A simple app with a Context Hook!

As we can see, our theme context successfully provides the theme for the header.

Defining the provider

Contexts use the default value that is passed to `React.createContext`, when there is no provider defined. This is useful for debugging the components when they are not embedded in the app. For example, we could debug a single component as a standalone component. In an app, we usually want to use a provider to provide the value for the context, which we are going to define now.

Edit `src/App.js`, and in our `App` function, we simply wrap the `Header` component with a `<ThemeContext.Provider>` component, where we pass `coral` as `primaryColor`:

```
const App = () => (
    <ThemeContext.Provider value={{ primaryColor: 'coral' }}>
        <Header text="Hello World" />
    </ThemeContext.Provider>
)

export default App
```

We can now see that our header color changed from `deepskyblue` to `coral`:

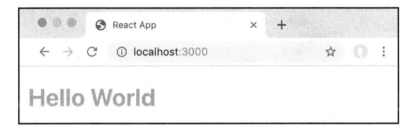

Our provider changed the color of the header

If we want to change the value of our context, we can simply adjust the `value` prop that is passed to the `Provider` component.

 Please note that the default value of a context is not used when we define a provider without passing the `value` prop to it! If we define a provider without a `value` prop, then the value of the context will be `undefined`.

Now that we have defined a single provider for our context, let's move on to defining multiple, nested providers.

Nested providers

With React context, it is also possible to define multiple providers for the same context. Using this technique, we can override the context value in certain parts of our app. Let's consider the earlier example, and add a second header to it:

1. Edit `src/App.js`, and add a second `Header` component:

```
const App = () => (
    <ThemeContext.Provider value={{ primaryColor: 'coral' }}>
```

```
        <Header text="Hello World" />
        <Header text="This is a test" />
      </ThemeContext.Provider>
    )

    export default App
```

2. Now, define a second `Provider` component with a different `primaryColor`:

```
    const App = () => (
      <ThemeContext.Provider value={{ primaryColor: 'coral' }}>
        <Header text="Hello World" />
        <ThemeContext.Provider value={{ primaryColor: 'deepskyblue'
    }}>
          <Header text="This is a test" />
        </ThemeContext.Provider>
      </ThemeContext.Provider>
    )

    export default App
```

If we open the app in our browser, the second header now has a different color from the first one:

Overriding context values with nested providers

As we can see, we can override React context values by defining providers. Providers can also be nested, therefore overriding the values of other providers that are higher up in the component tree.

Example code

The example code for the small theme context example can be found in the `Chapter05/chapter5_1` folder.

Just run `npm install` in order to install all dependencies, and `npm start` to start the application; then visit `http://localhost:3000` in your browser (if it did not open automatically).

Alternative to contexts

However, we should be careful, and not use React context too often, because it makes reusing components more difficult. We should only use contexts when we need to access data in many components, which are at different nesting levels. Furthermore, we need to make sure that we only use contexts for non-frequently changing data. Frequently changing values of contexts can cause our whole component tree to re-render, resulting in performance problems. That is why, for frequently changing values, we should use a state management solution such as Redux or MobX, instead.

If we only want to avoid having to pass down props, we can pass down the rendered component instead of the data. For example, let's say we have a `Page` component, which renders a `Header` component, which renders a `Profile` component, which then renders an `Avatar` component. We get a `headerSize` prop passed to the `Page` component, which we need in the `Header` component, but also in the `Avatar` component. Instead of passing down props through multiple levels, we could do the following:

```
function Page ({ headerSize }) {
    const profile = (
        <Profile>
            <Avatar size={headerSize} />
        </Profile>
    )
    return <Header size={headerSize} profile={profile} />
}
```

Now, only the `Page` component needs to know about the `headerSize` prop, and there is no need to pass it down further in the tree. In this case, contexts are not necessary.

Such a pattern is called **inversion of control**, and it can make your code much cleaner than passing down props or using a context. However, we should not always use this pattern either, because it makes the higher-level component more complicated.

Implementing themes

After learning how to implement themes in a small example, we are now going to implement themes in our blog app, using React context and Hooks.

Defining the context

First, we have to define the context. Instead of defining it in the `src/App.js` file, in our blog app, we are going to create a separate file for the context. Having a separate file for contexts makes it easier to maintain them later on. Furthermore, we always know where to import the contexts from, because it is clear from the filename.

Let's start defining a theme context:

1. Create a new `src/contexts.js` file.
2. Then, we import `React`:

   ```
   import React from 'react'
   ```

3. Next, we define the `ThemeContext`. As before in our small example, we set the default `primaryColor` to `deepskyblue`. Additionally, we set the `secondaryColor` to `coral`:

   ```
   export const ThemeContext = React.createContext({
       primaryColor: 'deepskyblue',
       secondaryColor: 'coral'
   })
   ```

Now that we have defined our context, we can move on to defining the Context Hooks.

Defining the Context Hooks

After defining the context, we are going to define our consumers, using Context Hooks. We start by creating a new component for the header, then define a Context Hook for our existing `Post` component.

Creating the Header component

First, we create a new `Header` component, which is going to display `React Hooks Blog` in the `primaryColor` of our app.

Let's create the `Header` component now:

1. Create a new `src/Header.js` file.
2. In this file, we import `React`, and the `useContext` Hook:

   ```
   import React, { useContext } from 'react'
   ```

3. Next, we import the `ThemeContext` from the previously created `src/contexts.js` file:

   ```
   import { ThemeContext } from './contexts'
   ```

4. Then, we define our `Header` component, and the Context Hook. Instead of storing the context value in a `theme` variable, we use destructuring to directly extract the `primaryColor` value:

   ```
   const Header = ({ text }) => {
       const { primaryColor } = useContext(ThemeContext)
   ```

5. Finally, we return the `h1` element, as we did before in our small example, and `export` the `Header` component:

   ```
       return <h1 style={{ color: primaryColor }}>{text}</h1>
   }

   export default Header
   ```

Now our `Header` component is defined, and we can use it.

Using the Header component

After creating the `Header` component, we are going to use it in the `App` component, as follows:

1. Edit `src/App.js`, and import the `Header` component:

   ```
   import Header from './Header'
   ```

2. Then, render the `Header` component before the `UserBar` component:

   ```
   return (
       <div style={{ padding: 8 }}>
           <Header text="React Hooks Blog" />
           <UserBar user={user} dispatch={dispatch} />
   ```

> You might want to refactor the `React Hooks Blog` value into a prop that is passed to the `App` component (app config), because we are already using it three times in this component.

Now, our `Header` component will be rendered in the app and we can move on to implementing the Context Hook in the Post component.

Implementing the Context Hook for the Post component

Next, we want to display the `Post` headers in the secondary color. To do this, we need to define a Context Hook for the `Post` component, as follows:

1. Edit `src/post/Post.js`, and adjust the `import` statement to import the `useContext` Hook:

   ```
   import React, { useContext } from 'react'
   ```

2. Next, we import the `ThemeContext`:

   ```
   import { ThemeContext } from '../contexts'
   ```

3. Then, we define a Context Hook in the `Post` component, and get the `secondaryColor` value from the theme, via destructuring:

   ```
   export default function Post ({ title, content, author }) {
     const { secondaryColor } = useContext(ThemeContext)
   ```

4. Finally, we use the `secondaryColor` value to style our `h3` element:

   ```
   return (
     <div>
       <h3 style={{ color: secondaryColor }}>{title}</h3>
   ```

If we look at our app now, we can see that both colors are used properly from
the `ThemeContext`:

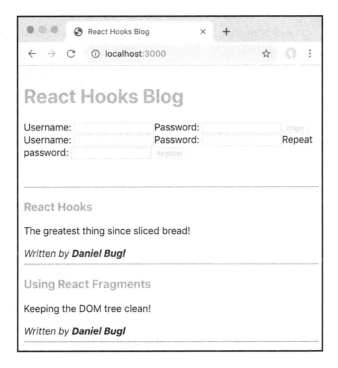

As we can see, our app now uses the primary color for the main header, and the secondary
color for the post titles.

Defining the provider

Right now, our Context Hooks use the default value that is specified by the context, when
no provider is defined. To be able to change the value, we need to define a provider.

Let's start defining the provider:

1. Edit `src/App.js`, and import the `ThemeContext`:

```
import { ThemeContext } from './contexts'
```

2. Wrap the whole app with the `ThemeContext.Provider` component, providing the same theme that we set as the default value earlier:

```
return (
    <ThemeContext.Provider value={{ primaryColor:
'deepskyblue', secondaryColor: 'coral' }}>
        <div style={{ padding: 8 }}>
            <Header text="React Hooks Blog" />
            ...
            <PostList posts={posts} />
        </div>
    </ThemeContext.Provider>
)
```

Our app should look exactly the same way as before, but now we are using the value from the provider!

Dynamically changing the theme

Now that we have defined a provider, we can use it to dynamically change the theme. Instead of passing a static value to the provider, we are going to use a State Hook that defines the current theme. Then, we are going to implement a component that changes the theme.

Using a State Hook with the context provider

First, we are going to define a new State Hook, which we are going to use to set the value for the context provider.

Let's define a State Hook, and use it in the context provider:

1. Edit `src/App.js`, and import the `useState` Hook:

```
import React, { useReducer, useEffect, useState } from 'react'
```

2. Define a new State Hook at the beginning of the `App` component; here we set the default value to our default theme:

```
export default function App () {
    const [ theme, setTheme ] = useState({
        primaryColor: 'deepskyblue',
        secondaryColor: 'coral'
    })
```

3. Then, we pass the `theme` value to the `ThemeContext.Provider` component:

```
return (
    <ThemeContext.Provider value={theme}>
```

Our app is still going to look the same way as before, but we are now ready to dynamically change our theme!

Implementing the ChangeTheme component

The final part of our theme feature is a component that can be used to change the theme dynamically, by making use of the State Hook that we defined earlier. The State Hook is going to re-render the `App` component, which will change the value that is passed to the `ThemeContext.Provider`, which, in turn, is going to re-render all the components that make use of the `ThemeContext` Context Hook.

Let's start implementing the `ChangeTheme` component:

1. Create a new `src/ChangeTheme.js` file.

2. As always, we have to import `React` first, before we can define a component:

```
import React from 'react'
```

3. In order to be able to easily add new themes later on, we are going to create a constant `THEMES` array, instead of manually copying and pasting the code for the different themes. This is going to make our code much more concise, and easier to read:

```
const THEMES = [
    { primaryColor: 'deepskyblue', secondaryColor: 'coral' },
    { primaryColor: 'orchid', secondaryColor: 'mediumseagreen' }
]
```

It is a good idea to give constant values that are hardcoded a special name, such as writing the whole variable name in caps. Later on, it might make sense to put all these configurable hardcoded values in a separate `src/config.js` file.

4. Next, we define a component to render a single `theme`:

```
function ThemeItem ({ theme, active, onClick }) {
```

5. Here, we render a link, and display a small preview of the theme, by showing the **Primary** and **Secondary** colors:

```
return (
    <span onClick={onClick} style={{ cursor: 'pointer',
paddingLeft: 8, fontWeight: active ? 'bold' : 'normal' }}>
        <span style={{ color: theme.primaryColor
}}>Primary</span> / <span style={{ color: theme.secondaryColor
}}>Secondary</span>
    </span>
)
}
```

 Here, we set the cursor to `pointer`, in order to make the element appear clickable. We could also use an `<a>` element; however, this is not recommended if we do not have a valid link target, such as a separate page.

6. Then, we define the `ChangeTheme` component, which accepts the `theme` and `setTheme` props:

```
export default function ChangeTheme ({ theme, setTheme }) {
```

7. Next, we define a function to check if a theme object is the currently active theme:

```
function isActive (t) {
    return t.primaryColor === theme.primaryColor &&
t.secondaryColor === theme.secondaryColor
    }
```

8. Now, we use the `.map` function to render all of the available themes, and call the `setTheme` function when clicking on them:

```
return (
    <div>
        Change theme:
        {THEMES.map((t, i) =>
            <ThemeItem key={'theme-' + i} theme={t}
active={isActive(t)} onClick={() => setTheme(t)} />
        )}
    </div>
)
}
```

9. Finally, we can import and render the `ChangeTheme` component, after the `Header` component in `src/App.js`:

```
import ChangeTheme from './ChangeTheme'
// ...
    return (
        <ThemeContext.Provider value={theme}>
            <div style={{ padding: 8 }}>
                <Header text="React Hooks Blog" />
                <ChangeTheme theme={theme} setTheme={setTheme} />
                <br />
```

As we can see, we now have a way to change the theme in our app:

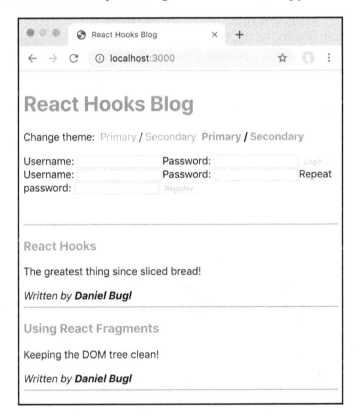

Our app after changing the theme, using Context Hooks in combination with a State Hook

Now, we have a context that is consumed via Hooks, which can also be changed via Hooks!

Example code

The example code for the theme feature in our blog app can be found in the `Chapter05/chapter5_2` folder.

Just run `npm install` in order to install all dependencies, and `npm start` to start the application; then visit `http://localhost:3000` in your browser (if it did not open automatically).

Using context for global state

After learning how to use React context to implement themes in our blog app, we are now going to use a context to avoid having to manually pass down the `state` and `dispatch` props for our global app state.

Defining StateContext

We start by defining the context in our `src/contexts.js` file.

In `src/contexts.js`, we define the `StateContext`, which is going to store the `state` value and the `dispatch` function:

```
export const StateContext = React.createContext({
    state: {},
    dispatch: () => {}
})
```

We initialized the `state` value as an empty object, and the `dispatch` function as an empty function, which will be used when no provider is defined.

Defining the context provider

Now, we are going to define the context provider in our `src/App.js` file, which is going to get the values from the existing Reducer Hook.

Let's define the context provider for global state now:

1. In `src/App.js`, import the `StateContext` by adjusting the existing `import` statement:

```
import { ThemeContext, StateContext } from './contexts'
```

2. Then, we define a new context provider, by returning it from our `App` function:

```
return (
    <StateContext.Provider value={{ state, dispatch }}>
        <ThemeContext.Provider value={theme}>
            . . .
        </ThemeContext.Provider>
    </StateContext.Provider>
)
```

Now, our context provider provides the `state` object and the `dispatch` function to the rest of our app, and we can move on to consuming the context value.

Using StateContext

Now that we have defined our context and provider, we can use the `state` object and the `dispatch` function in various components.

We start by removing the props that we manually passed to our components in `src/App.js`. Delete the following code segments marked in bold:

```
<div style={{ padding: 8 }}>
    <Header text="React Hooks Blog" />
    <ChangeTheme theme={theme} setTheme={setTheme} />
    <br />
    <UserBar user={user} dispatch={dispatch} />
    <br />
    {user && <CreatePost user={user} posts={posts}
dispatch={dispatch} />}
    <br />
    <hr />
    <PostList posts={posts} />
</div>
```

As we are using contexts, there is no need to pass down props manually anymore. We can now move on to refactoring the components.

Refactoring user components

First, we refactor the user components, and then we move on to the post components.

Let's refactor the user-related components now:

1. Edit `src/user/UserBar.js`, and also remove the props there (code marked in bold should be removed), since we do not need to manually pass them down anymore:

```
export default function UserBar ({ user, dispatch }) {
    if (user) {
        return <Logout user={user} dispatch={dispatch} />
    } else {
        return (
            <React.Fragment>
                <Login dispatch={dispatch} />
                <Register dispatch={dispatch} />
            </React.Fragment>
        )
    }
}
```

2. Then, we import the `useContext` Hook and the `StateContext` in `src/user/UserBar.js`, in order to be able to tell whether the user is logged in or not:

```
import React, { useContext } from 'react'
import { StateContext } from '../contexts'
```

3. Now, we can use the Context Hook to get the `user` state from our `state` object:

```
export default function UserBar () {
    const { state } = useContext(StateContext)
    const { user } = state
```

4. Again, we import `useContext` and `StateContext` in `src/user/Login.js`:

```
import React, { useState, useContext } from 'react'
import { StateContext } from '../contexts'
```

5. Then, we remove the `dispatch` prop, and use the Context Hook instead:

```
export default function Login () {
    const { dispatch } = useContext(StateContext)
```

6. We repeat the same process in the `src/user/Register.js` component:

```
import React, { useState, useContext } from 'react'
import { StateContext } from '../contexts'

export default function Register () {
    const { dispatch } = useContext(StateContext)
```

7. In the `src/user/Logout.js` component, we do the same, but also get the `user` state from the `state` object:

```
import React, { useContext } from 'react'
import { StateContext } from '../contexts'

export default function Logout () {
    const { state, dispatch } = useContext(StateContext)
    const { user } = state
```

Our user-related components now use a context instead of props. Let's move on to refactoring the post-related components.

Refactoring post components

Now, all that is left to do is refactoring the post components; then our whole app will be using React context for global state:

1. We start with the `src/post/PostList.js` component, where we import `useContext` and `StateContext`, remove the props, and use the Context Hook instead:

```
import React, { useContext } from 'react'
import { StateContext } from '../contexts'

import Post from './Post'

export default function PostList () {
    const { state } = useContext(StateContext)
    const { posts } = state
```

2. We do the same for the `CreatePost` component, which is the last component that we need to refactor:

```
import React, { useState, useContext } from 'react'
import { StateContext } from '../contexts'

export default function CreatePost () {
    const { state, dispatch } = useContext(StateContext)
    const { user } = state
```

Our app works in the same way as before, but now we use a context for global state, which makes our code much cleaner, and avoids having to pass down props!

Example code

The example code for the global state context in our blog app can be found in the `Chapter05/chapter5_3` folder.

Just run `npm install` in order to install all dependencies, and `npm start` to start the application; then visit `http://localhost:3000` in your browser (if it did not open automatically).

Summary

In this chapter, we first learned about React context as an alternative to passing down props over multiple levels of React components. We then learned about context providers and consumers, and the new way to define consumers, via Hooks. Next, we learned when it does not make sense to use contexts, and when we should use inversion of control instead. Then, we used what we learned in practice, by implementing themes in our blog app. Finally, we used React context for the global state in our blog app.

In the next chapter, we are going to learn how to request data from a server, using React and Hooks. Then, we are going to learn about `React.memo` to prevent unnecessary re-rendering of components, and React Suspense to lazily load components when they are needed.

Questions

In order to recap what we have learned in this chapter, try to answer the following questions:

1. Which problem do contexts avoid?
2. What are the two parts that contexts consist of?
3. Are both parts required to be defined in order to use contexts?
4. What is the advantage of using Hooks, instead of traditional context consumers?
5. What is an alternative to contexts, and when should we use it?
6. How can we implement dynamically changing contexts?
7. When does it make sense to use contexts for state?

Further reading

If you are interested in more information about the concepts that we have explored in this chapter, take a look at the following reading material:

- Official docs on React context: `https://reactjs.org/docs/context.html`
- More information on composition versus inheritance: `https://reactjs.org/docs/composition-vs-inheritance.html`
- List of HTML color codes (if you want to define new themes): `https://www.rapidtables.com/web/color/html-color-codes.html`.

6
Implementing Requests and React Suspense

In the previous chapters, we learned how to use React context as an alternative to manually passing down props. We learned about context providers, consumers, and how to use Hooks as a context consumer. Next, we learned about inversion of control as an alternative to contexts. Finally, we implemented themes and global state, using contexts in our blog app.

In this chapter, we are going to set up a simple backend server, which will be generated from a **JavaScript Object Notation** (**JSON**) file, using the `json-server` tool. Then, we are going to implement requesting resources, by using an Effect Hook in combination with a State Hook. Next, we are going to do the same, using the `axios` and `react-request-hook` libraries. Finally, we are going to take a look at preventing unnecessary re-rendering, using `React.memo`, and lazily loading components through the use of React Suspense.

The following topics will be covered in this chapter:

- Requesting resources using Hooks
- Preventing unnecessary re-rendering with `React.memo`
- Implementing lazy loading using React Suspense

Technical requirements

A fairly recent version of Node.js should already be installed (v11.12.0 or higher). The `npm` package manager for Node.js also needs to be installed.

The code for this chapter can be found on the GitHub repository: `https://github.com/PacktPublishing/Learn-React-Hooks/tree/master/Chapter06`.

Check out the following video to see the code in action:

`http://bit.ly/2Mm9yoC`

 Please note that it is highly recommended that you write the code on your own. Do not simply run the code examples that have been provided. It is important that you write the code yourself in order for you to be able to learn and understand properly. However, if you run into any issues, you can always refer to the code example.

Now, let's get started with the chapter.

Requesting resources with Hooks

In this section, we are going to learn how to request resources from a server, using Hooks. First, we are going to implement requests by only using the JavaScript `fetch` function, and the `useEffect`/`useState` Hooks. Then, we are going to learn how to request resources, using the `axios` library in combination with `react-request-hook`.

Setting up a dummy server

Before we can implement requests, we need to create a backend server. Since we are focusing on the user interface at the moment, we are going to set up a dummy server, which will allow us to test out requests. We are going to use the `json-server` tool to create a full **Representational State Transfer** (**REST**) API from a JSON file.

Creating the db.json file

To be able to use the `json-server` tool, first we need to create a `db.json` file, which is going to contain our full database for the server. The `json-server` tool will allow you to make the following:

- `GET` requests, to fetch data from the file
- `POST` requests, to insert new data into the file

- PUT and PATCH requests, to adjust existing data
- DELETE requests, to remove data

For all modifying actions (POST, PUT, PATCH, and DELETE), the updated file will automatically be saved by the tool.

We can use our existing structure for posts, which we defined as the default state of the posts reducer. However, we need to make sure that we provide an id value, so that we can query the database later:

```
[
    { "id": "react-hooks", "title": "React Hooks", "content": "The greatest
thing since sliced bread!", "author": "Daniel Bugl" },
    { "id": "react-fragments", "title": "Using React Fragments", "content":
"Keeping the DOM tree clean!", "author": "Daniel Bugl" }
]
```

As for the users, we need to come up with a way to store usernames and passwords. For simplicity, we just store the password in plain text (do not do this in a production environment!). Here, we also need to provide an id value:

```
[
    { "id": 1, "username": "Daniel Bugl", "password": "supersecure42" }
]
```

Additionally, we are going to store themes in our database. In order to investigate whether pulling themes from our database works properly, we are now going to define a third theme. As always, each theme needs an id value:

```
[
    { "id": 1, "primaryColor": "deepskyblue", "secondaryColor": "coral" },
    { "id": 2, "primaryColor": "orchid", "secondaryColor": "mediumseagreen"
},
    { "id": 3, "primaryColor": "darkslategray", "secondaryColor":
"slategray" }
]
```

Now, all that is left to do is to combine these three arrays into a single JSON object, by storing the posts array under a posts key, the users array under a users key, and the themes array under a themes key.

Let's start creating the JSON file that is used as a database for our backend server:

1. Create a new `server/` directory in the root of our application folder.
2. Create a `server/db.json` file with the following contents. We can use the existing state from our Reducer Hook. However, since this is a database, we need to give each element an `id` value (marked in bold):

```
{
    "posts": [
        { "id": "react-hooks", "title": "React Hooks", "content":
"The greatest thing since sliced bread!", "author": "Daniel Bugl"
},
        { "id": "react-fragments", "title": "Using React
Fragments", "content": "Keeping the DOM tree clean!", "author":
"Daniel Bugl" }
    ],
    "users": [
        { "id": 1, "username": "Daniel Bugl", "password":
"supersecure42" }
    ],
    "themes": [
        { "id": 1, "primaryColor": "deepskyblue", "secondaryColor":
"coral" },
        { "id": 2, "primaryColor": "orchid", "secondaryColor":
"mediumseagreen" },
        { "id": 3, "primaryColor": "darkslategray",
"secondaryColor": "slategray" }
    ]
}
```

For the `json-server` tool, we simply need a JSON file as the database, and the tool will create a full REST API for us.

Installing the json-server tool

Now, we are going to install and start our backend server by using the `json-server` tool:

1. First, we are going to install the `json-server` tool via npm:

```
> npm install --save json-server
```

2. Now, we can start our backend server, by calling the following command:

```
> npx json-server --watch server/db.json
```

The `npx` command executes commands that were installed locally in a project. We need to use `npx` here, because we did not globally install the `json-server` tool (via `npm install -g json-server`).

We executed the `json-server` tool, and made it watch the `server/db.json` file that we created earlier. The `--watch` flag means that it will listen to changes to the file, and refresh automatically.

Now, we can go to `http://localhost:3000/posts/react-hooks` in order to see our post object:

Our simple JSON server working and serving a post!

As we can see, the tool created a full REST API from the database JSON file for us!

Configuring package.json

Next, we need to adjust our `package.json` file, in order to start the server, in addition to our client (running via `webpack-dev-server`).

Let's start adjusting the `package.json` file:

1. First, we create a new package script called `start:server`, by inserting it in the `scripts` section of the `package.json` file. We also make sure that we change the port, so that it does not run on the same port as our client:

```
"scripts": {
    "start:server": "npx json-server --watch server/db.json --port 4000",
    "start": "react-scripts start",
```

2. Then, we rename the `start` script to `start:client`:

```
"scripts": {
    "start:server": "npx json-server --watch server/db.json",
    "start:client": "react-scripts start",
```

3. Next, we install a tool called `concurrently`, which lets us start the server and the client at the same time:

```
> npm install --save concurrently
```

4. Now, we can define a new `start` script by using the `concurrently` command, and then passing the server and client commands as arguments to it:

```
"scripts": {
    "start": "npx concurrently \"npm run start:server\" \"npm run start:client\"",
```

Now, running `npm start` will run the client, as well as the backend server.

Configuring a proxy

Finally, we have to define a proxy, to make sure that we can request our API from the same **Uniform Resource Locator (URL)** as the client. This is needed because, otherwise, we would have to deal with cross-site requests, which are a bit more complicated to handle. We are going to define a proxy that will forward requests from `http://localhost:3000/api/` to `http://localhost:4000/`.

Now, let's configure the proxy:

1. First, we have to install the `http-proxy-middleware` package:

```
> npm install --save http-proxy-middleware
```

2. Then, we create a new `src/setupProxy.js` file, with the following contents:

```
const proxy = require('http-proxy-middleware')

module.exports = function (app) {
    app.use(proxy('/api', {
```

3. Next, we have to define the target of our proxy, which will be the backend server, running at `http://localhost:4000`:

```
target: 'http://localhost:4000',
```

4. Finally, we have to define a path-rewrite rule, which removes the /api prefix before forwarding the request to our server:

```
        pathRewrite: { '^/api': '' }
    }))
}
```

The preceding proxy configuration will link /api to our backend server; therefore, we can now start both the server and the client via the following command:

> **npm start**

Then, we can access the API by opening
http://localhost:3000/api/posts/react-hooks!

Defining routes

By default, the json-server tool defines the following routes: https://github.com/typicode/json-server#routes.

We can also define our own routes, by creating a routes.json file, where we can rewrite existing routes to other routes: https://github.com/typicode/json-server#add-custom-routes.

For our blog app, we are going to define a single custom route:
/login/:username/:password. We are going to link this to a
/users?username=:username&password=:password query, in order to find a user with the given username and password combination.

We are now going to define the custom login route for our app:

1. Create a new server/routes.json file with the following contents:

```
{
    "/login/:username/:password":
"/users?username=:username&password=:password"
}
```

2. Then, adjust the start:server script in the package.json file, and add the --routes option, as follows:

```
    "start:server": "npx json-server --watch server/db.json --port 4000 --routes server/routes.json",
```

Now, our server will be serving our custom login route, which we are going to use later on in this chapter! We can try logging in by opening the following URL in our browser: `http://localhost:3000/api/login/Daniel%20Bugl/supersecure42`. This returns a user object; therefore, the login was successful!

We can see the user object being returned as text in our browser:

Accessing our custom route directly in the browser

As we can see, accessing our custom route works! We can now use it to log in users.

Example code

The example code can be found in the `Chapter06/chapter6_1` folder.

Just run `npm install` in order to install all dependencies, and `npm start` to start the application; then visit `http://localhost:3000` in your browser (if it did not open automatically).

Implementing requests using Effect and State/Reducer Hooks

Before we use a library to implement requests using Hooks, we are going to implement them manually, using an Effect Hook to trigger the request, and State/Reducer Hooks to store the result.

Requests with Effect and State Hooks

First, we are going to request themes from our server, instead of hardcoding the list of themes.

Let's implement requesting themes using an Effect Hook and a State Hook:

1. In the `src/ChangeTheme.js` file, adjust the React `import` statement in order to import the `useEffect` and `useState` Hooks:

    ```
    import React, { useEffect, useState } from 'react'
    ```

2. Remove the `THEMES` constant, which is all of the following code:

    ```
    const THEMES = [
        { primaryColor: 'deepskyblue', secondaryColor: 'coral' },
        { primaryColor: 'orchid', secondaryColor: 'mediumseagreen' }
    ]
    ```

3. In the `ChangeTheme` component, define a new `useState` Hook in order to store the themes:

    ```
    export default function ChangeTheme ({ theme, setTheme }) {
        const [ themes, setThemes ] = useState([])
    ```

4. Then define a `useEffect` Hook, where we are going to make the request:

    ```
    useEffect(() => {
    ```

5. In this Hook, we use `fetch` to request a resource; in this case, we request `/api/themes`:

    ```
    fetch('/api/themes')
    ```

6. Fetch makes use of the Promise API; therefore, we can use `.then()` in order to work with the result. First, we have to parse the result as JSON:

    ```
    .then(result => result.json())
    ```

7. Finally, we call `setThemes` with the themes array from our request:

    ```
    .then(themes => setThemes(themes))
    ```

 We can also shorten the preceding function to `.then(setThemes)`, as we are only passing down the `themes` argument from `.then()`.

8. For now, this Effect Hook should only trigger when the component mounts, so we pass an empty array as the second argument to `useEffect`. This ensures that the Effect Hook has no dependencies, and thus will only trigger when the component mounts:

```
}, [])
```

9. Now, all that is left to do is to replace the `THEMES` constant with our `themes` value from the Hook:

```
{themes.map(t =>
```

As we can see, there are now three themes available, all loaded from our database through our server:

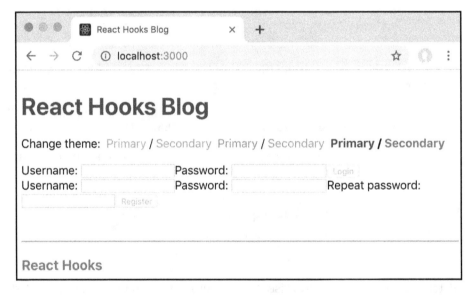

Three themes loaded from our server by using hooks!

Our themes are now loaded from the backend server and we can move on to requesting posts via Hooks.

Requests with Effect and Reducer Hooks

We are now going to use our backend server to request the posts array, instead of hardcoding it as the default value for the `postsReducer`.

Let's implement requesting posts using an Effect Hook and a Reducer Hook:

1. **Remove** the `defaultPosts` constant definition from `src/App.js`, which is all of the following code:

```
const defaultPosts = [
    { title: 'React Hooks', content: 'The greatest thing since
sliced bread!', author: 'Daniel Bugl' },
    { title: 'Using React Fragments', content: 'Keeping the DOM
tree clean!', author: 'Daniel Bugl' }
]
```

2. Replace the `defaultPosts` constant in the `useReducer` function with an empty array:

```
const [ state, dispatch ] = useReducer(appReducer, { user: '',
posts: [] })
```

3. In `src/reducers.js`, define a new action type, called `FETCH_POSTS`, in the `postsReducer` function. This action type will replace the current state with a new posts array:

```
function postsReducer (state, action) {
    switch (action.type) {
        case 'FETCH_POSTS':
            return action.posts
```

4. In `src/App.js`, define a new `useEffect` Hook, which precedes the current one:

```
useEffect(() => {
```

5. In this Hook, we again use `fetch` in order to request a resource; in this case, we request `/api/posts`:

```
fetch('/api/posts')
    .then(result => result.json())
```

6. Finally, we dispatch a `FETCH_POSTS` action with the `posts` array from our request:

```
    .then(posts => dispatch({ type: 'FETCH_POSTS', posts
}))
```

7. For now, this Effect Hook should only trigger when the component mounts, so we pass an empty array as the second argument to `useEffect`:

```
}, [])
```

As we can see, the posts now get requested from the server! We can have a look at the DevTools **Network** tab to see the request:

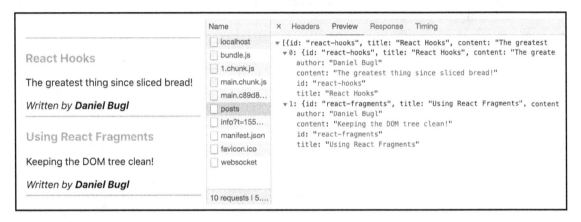

Posts being requested from our server!

The posts are now being requested from the backend server. In the next section, we are going to use `axios` and the `react-request-hook` to request resources from our server.

Example code

The example code can be found in the `Chapter06/chapter6_2` folder.

Just run `npm install` in order to install all dependencies, and `npm start` to start the application; then visit `http://localhost:3000` in your browser (if it did not open automatically).

Using axios and react-request-hook

In the previous section, we used an Effect Hook to trigger the request, and a Reducer/State Hook to update the state, using the result from the request. Instead of manually implementing requests like this, we can use the `axios` and `react-request-hook` libraries to easily implement requests using Hooks.

Setting up the libraries

Before we can start using `axios` and `react-request-hook`, we have to set up an `axios` instance and a `RequestProvider` component.

Let's get started setting up the libraries:

1. First, we install the libraries:

   ```
   > npm install --save react-request-hook axios
   ```

2. Then, we import them in `src/index.js`:

   ```
   import { RequestProvider } from 'react-request-hook'
   import axios from 'axios'
   ```

3. Now, we define an `axios` instance, where we set the `baseURL` to `http://localhost:3000/api/`—our backend server:

   ```
   const axiosInstance = axios.create({
       baseURL: 'http://localhost:3000/api/'
   })
   ```

    In the config for our `axios` instance, we can also define other options, such as a default timeout for requests, or custom headers. For more information, check out the `axios` documentation: `https://github.com/axios/axios#axioscreateconfig`.

4. Finally, we wrap our `<App />` component with the `<RequestProvider>` component. Remove the following line of code:

   ```
   ReactDOM.render(<App />, document.getElementById('root'));
   ```

   Replace it with this code:

   ```
   ReactDOM.render(
       <RequestProvider value={axiosInstance}>
           <App />
       </RequestProvider>,
       document.getElementById('root')
   )
   ```

Now, our app is ready to use Resource Hooks!

Using the useResource Hook

A more powerful way of dealing with requests, is using the `axios` and `react-request-hook` libraries. Using these libraries, we have access to features that can cancel a single request, or even clear all pending requests. Furthermore, using these libraries makes it easier to deal with errors and loading states.

We are now going to implement the `useResource` Hook in order to request themes from our server:

1. In `src/ChangeTheme.js`, import the `useResource` Hook from the `react-request-hook` library:

   ```
   import { useResource } from 'react-request-hook'
   ```

2. Remove the previously defined State and Effect Hooks.

3. Then, we define a `useResource` Hook within the `ChangeTheme` component. The Hook returns a value and a getter function. Calling the getter function will request the resource:

   ```
   export default function ChangeTheme ({ theme, setTheme }) {
       const [ themes, getThemes ] = useResource(() => ({
   ```

 Here, we are using the shorthand syntax for `() => { return { } }`, which is `() => ({ })`. Using this shorthand syntax allows us to concisely write functions that only return an object.

4. In this Hook we pass a function, which returns an object with information about the request:

   ```
           url: '/themes',
           method: 'get'
       }))
   ```

 With `axios`, we only need to pass `/themes` as the `url`, because we already defined the `baseURL`, which contains `/api/`.

5. The Resource Hook returns an object with a `data` value, an `isLoading` boolean, an `error` object, and a `cancel` function to cancel the pending request. Now, we pull out the `data` value and the `isLoading` boolean from the `themes` object:

```
const { data, isLoading } = themes
```

6. Then, we define a `useEffect` Hook to trigger the `getThemes` function. We only want it to trigger once, when the component mounts; therefore, we pass an empty array as the second argument:

```
useEffect(getThemes, [])
```

7. Additionally, we use the `isLoading` flag to display a loading message while waiting for the server to respond:

```
{isLoading && ' Loading themes...'}
```

8. Finally, we rename the `themes` value to the `data` value that is returned from the `useResource` Hook, and add a conditional check to ensure the `data` value is already available:

```
{data && data.map(t =>
```

If we have a look at our app now, we can see that the **Loading themes...** message gets displayed for a very short time, and, then the themes from our database get displayed! We can now move on to requesting posts using the Resource Hook.

Using useResource with a Reducer Hook

The `useResource` Hook already handles the state for the result of our request, so we do not need an additional `useState` Hook to store the state. If we already have an existing Reducer Hook, however, we can use it in combination with the `useResource` Hook.

We are now going to implement the `useResource` Hook in combination with a Reducer Hook in our app:

1. In `src/App.js`, import the `useResource` Hook from the `react-request-hook` library:

```
import { useResource } from 'react-request-hook'
```

2. Remove the previously defined `useEffect` Hook that uses `fetch` to request `/api/posts`.

3. Define a new `useResource` Hook, where we request `/posts`:

```
const [ posts, getPosts ] = useResource(() => ({
    url: '/posts',
    method: 'get'
}))
```

4. Define a new `useEffect` Hook, which simply calls `getPosts`:

```
useEffect(getPosts, [])
```

5. Finally, define a `useEffect` Hook, which dispatches the `FETCH_POSTS` action, after checking if the data already exists:

```
useEffect(() => {
    if (posts && posts.data) {
        dispatch({ type: 'FETCH_POSTS', posts: posts.data })
    }
```

6. We make sure that this Effect Hook triggers every time the `posts` object updates:

```
}, [posts])
```

Now, when we fetch new posts, a `FETCH_POSTS` action will be dispatched. Next, we move on to handling errors during requests.

Handling error state

We have already handled the loading state in the `ChangeTheme` component. Now, we are going to implement the error state for posts.

Let's get started handling the error state for posts:

1. In `src/reducers.js`, define a new `errorReducer` function with a new action type, `POSTS_ERROR`:

```
function errorReducer (state, action) {
    switch (action.type) {
        case 'POSTS_ERROR':
            return 'Failed to fetch posts'

        default:
            return state
```

```
        }
    }
```

2. Add the `errorReducer` function to our `appReducer` function:

```
export default function appReducer (state, action) {
    return {
        user: userReducer(state.user, action),
        posts: postsReducer(state.posts, action),
        error: errorReducer(state.error, action)
    }
}
```

3. In `src/App.js`, adjust the default state of our Reducer Hook:

```
const [ state, dispatch ] = useReducer(appReducer, { user: '',
posts: [], error: '' })
```

4. Pull the `error` value out of the `state` object:

```
const { user, error } = state
```

5. Now, we can adjust the existing Effect Hook that handles new data from the `posts` resource, by dispatching a `POSTS_ERROR` action in the case of an error:

```
useEffect(() => {
    if (posts && posts.error) {
        dispatch({ type: 'POSTS_ERROR' })
    }
    if (posts && posts.data) {
        dispatch({ type: 'FETCH_POSTS', posts: posts.data })
    }
}, [posts])
```

6. Finally, we display the error message before the `PostList` component:

```
{error && <b>{error}</b>}
<PostList />
```

If we only start the client now (via `npm run start:client`), the error will be displayed:

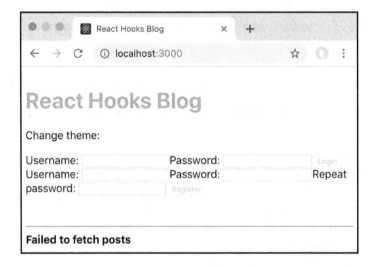

Displaying an error when the request fails!

As we can see, the **Failed to fetch posts** error gets displayed in our app, because the server is not running. We can now move on to implementing post creation via requests.

Implementing post creation

Now that we have a good grasp on how to request data from an API, we are going to use the `useResource` Hook for the creation of new data.

Let's get started implementing post creation using the Resource Hook:

1. Edit `src/post/CreatePost.js`, and import the `useResource` Hook:

   ```
   import { useResource } from 'react-request-hook'
   ```

2. Then, define a new Resource Hook, below the other Hooks, but before our handler function definitions. Here, we set the method to `post` (creates new data) and we pass the data from the `createPost` function, to the request config:

   ```
   const [ , createPost ] = useResource(({ title, content, author
   }) => ({
       url: '/posts',
       method: 'post',
       data: { title, content, author }
   }))
   ```

Here, we are using a shorthand syntax for array destructuring: we are ignoring the first element of the array, by not specifying a value name. Instead of writing const [post, createPost], and then not using post, we just put a comma, as follows: const [, createPost].

3. Now, we can use the `createPost` function in our `handleCreate` handler function. We make sure that we keep the call to the `dispatch` function there, so that we immediately insert the new post client-side, while waiting for the server to respond. The added code is highlighted in bold:

```
function handleCreate () {
    createPost({ title, content, author: user })
    dispatch({ type: 'CREATE_POST', title, content, author:
user })
}
```

 Please note that, in this simple example, we do not expect, or handle the failure of post creations. In this case, we dispatch the action even before the request completes. However, when implementing login, we are going to handle error states from the request, in order to check whether the user was logged in successfully. It is best practice to always handle error states in real-world applications.

4. Note that when we insert a post now, the post will first be at the beginning of the list; however, after refreshing, it will be at the end of the list. Unfortunately, our server inserts new posts at the end of the list. Therefore, we are going to reverse the order, after fetching posts from the server. Edit `src/App.js`, and adjust the following code:

```
if (posts && posts.data) {
    dispatch({ type: 'FETCH_POSTS', posts:
posts.data.reverse() })
}
```

Now, inserting a new post via the server works fine and we can move on to implementing registration!

Implementing registration

Next, we are going to implement registration, which is going to work in very similar way to creating posts.

Let's get started implementing registration:

1. First, import the `useEffect` and `useResource` Hooks in `src/user/Register.js`:

    ```
    import React, { useState, useContext, useEffect } from 'react'
    import { useResource } from 'react-request-hook'
    ```

2. Then, define a new `useResource` Hook, below the other Hooks, and before the handler functions. Unlike we did in the post creation, we now want to also store the resulting `user` object:

    ```
    const [ user, register ] = useResource((username, password) =>
    ({
        url: '/users',
        method: 'post',
        data: { username, password }
    }))
    ```

3. Next, define a new `useEffect` Hook below the `useResource` Hook, which will dispatch a `REGISTER` action when the request completes:

    ```
    useEffect(() => {
        if (user && user.data) {
            dispatch({ type: 'REGISTER', username:
    user.data.username })
        }
    }, [user])
    ```

    Please note that, in this simple example, we do not expect, or handle the failure of registrations. In this case, we dispatch the action only after the successful creation of the user. However, when implementing login, we are going to handle error states from the request, in order to check whether the user was logged in successfully. It is best practice to always handle error states in real-world applications.

4. Finally, we adjust the form submit handler in order to call the `register` function, instead of directly dispatching the action:

    ```
    <form onSubmit={e => { e.preventDefault();
    register(username, password) }}>
    ```

Now, if we enter a **Username** and **Password**, and press **Register**, a new user will be inserted into our `db.json` file and, just like before, we will be logged in. We now move on to implementing login via Resource Hooks.

Implementing login

Finally, we are going to implement login, via requests using our custom route. After doing so, our blog app will be fully connected to the server.

Let's get started implementing login:

1. First, edit `src/user/Login.js` and import the `useEffect` and `useResource` Hooks:

    ```
    import React, { useState, useContext, useEffect } from 'react'
    import { useResource } from 'react-request-hook'
    ```

2. We define a new State Hook that will store a boolean to check if the login failed:

    ```
    const [ loginFailed, setLoginFailed ] = useState(false)
    ```

3. Then, we define a new State Hook for the **Password** field, because we did not handle it before:

    ```
    const [ password, setPassword ] = useState('')
    ```

4. Now, we define a handler function for the **Password** field, below the `handleUsername` function:

    ```
    function handlePassword (evt) {
        setPassword(evt.target.value)
    }
    ```

5. Next, we handle the value change in the `input` field:

    ```
    <input type="password" value={password}
    onChange={handlePassword} name="login-username" id="login-username"
    />
    ```

6. Now, we can define our Resource Hook below the State Hooks, where we are going to pass `username` and `password` to the `/login` route. Since we are passing them as part of the URL, we need to make sure that we encode them properly first:

    ```
    const [ user, login ] = useResource((username, password) => ({
        url:
    `/login/${encodeURI(username)}/${encodeURI(password)}`,
        method: 'get'
    }))
    ```

Please note that it is not secure to send the password in cleartext via a GET request. We only do this for the sake of simplicity when configuring our dummy server. In a real world application, use a POST request for login instead and send the password as part of the POST data. Also make sure to use **Hypertext Transfer Protocol Secure (HTTPS)** so that the POST data will be encrypted.

7. Next, we define an Effect Hook, which will dispatch the LOGIN action if the request completes successfully:

```
useEffect(() => {
    if (user && user.data) {
```

8. Because the login route returns either an empty array (login failed), or an array with a single user, we need to check whether the array contains at least one element:

```
if (user.data.length > 0) {
    setLoginFailed(false)
    dispatch({ type: 'LOGIN', username:
user.data[0].username })
        } else {
```

9. If the array was empty, we set loginFailed to true:

```
setLoginFailed(true)
    }
}
```

10. If we get an error response from the server, we also set the login state to failed:

```
if (user && user.error) {
    setLoginFailed(true)
}
```

11. We make sure that the Effect Hook triggers whenever the user object from the Resource Hook updates:

```
}, [user])
```

12. Then, we adjust the `onSubmit` function of `form`, in order to call the `login` function:

```
<form onSubmit={e => { e.preventDefault();
login(username, password) }}>
```

13. Finally, below the **Submit** button, we display the **Invalid username or password** message, in case `loginFailed` was set to `true`:

```
{loginFailed && <span style={{ color: 'red' }}>Invalid
username or password</span>}
```

As we can see, entering a wrong **Username** or **Password** (or no **Password**) will result in an error, while entering the correct **Username/Password** combination will log us in:

Displaying an error message when the login failed

Now, our app is fully connected to the backend server!

Example code

The example code can be found in the `Chapter06/chapter6_3` folder.

Just run `npm install` in order to install all dependencies, and `npm start` to start the application; then visit `http://localhost:3000` in your browser (if it did not open automatically).

Preventing unnecessary re-rendering with React.memo

With class components we had `shouldComponentUpdate`, which would prevent components from re-rendering if the props did not change.

With function components, we can do the same using `React.memo`, which is a higher-order component. `React.memo` memoizes the result, which means that it will remember the last rendered result, and, in cases where the props did not change, it will skip re-rendering the component:

```
const SomeComponent = () => ...

export default React.memo(SomeComponent)
```

By default, `React.memo` will act like the default definition of `shouldComponentUpdate`, and it will only shallowly compare the props object. If we want to do a special comparison, we can pass a function as a second argument to `React.memo`:

```
export default React.memo(SomeComponent, (prevProps, nextProps) => {
    // compare props and return true if the props are equal and we should
not update
})
```

Unlike `shouldComponentUpdate`, the function that is passed to `React.memo` returns `true` when the props are equal, and thus it should not update, which is the opposite of how `shouldComponentUpdate` works! After learning about `React.memo`, let's try it out in practice by implementing `React.memo` for the Post component.

Implementing React.memo for the Post component

First, let's find out when the `Post` component re-renders. To do this, we are going to add a `console.log` statement to our `Post` component, as follows:

1. Edit `src/post/Post.js`, and add the following debug output when the component renders:

   ```
   export default function Post ({ title, content, author }) {
       console.log('rendering Post')
   ```

2. Now, open the app at `http://localhost:3000`, and open the DevTools (on most browsers: right-click | **Inspect** on the page). Go to the **Console** tab, and you should see the output twice, because we are rendering two posts:

The debug output when rendering two posts

3. So far, so good. Now, let's try logging in, and see what happens:

Posts re-rendering after logging in

As we can see, the Post components unnecessarily re-render after logging in, although their props did not change. We can use `React.memo` to prevent this, as follows:

1. Edit `src/post/Post.js`, and remove the export default part of the function definition (marked in bold):

   export default function Post ({ title, content, author }) {

2. Then, at the bottom of the file, export the Post component, after wrapping it with `React.memo()`:

   ```
   export default React.memo(Post)
   ```

3. Now, refresh the page and log in again. We can see that the two posts get rendered, which produces the initial debug output. However, logging in now does not cause the Post components to re-render anymore!

If we wanted to do a custom check on whether the posts are equal, we could, for example, compare `title`, `content`, and `author`, as follows:

```
export default React.memo(Post,
    (prev, next) => prev.title === next.title && prev.content ===
next.content && prev.author === next.author
)
```

In our case, doing this will have the same effect, because React already does a shallow comparison of all props, by default. This function only becomes useful when we have deep objects to compare, or when we want to ignore changes in certain props. Please note that we should not prematurely optimize our code. Re-renders can be fine, since React is intelligent, and does not paint to the browser if nothing changed. Therefore, it might be overkill to optimize all re-renders, unless a certain case has already been identified as a performance bottleneck.

Example code

The example code can be found in the `Chapter06/chapter6_4` folder.

Just run `npm install` in order to install all dependencies, and `npm start` to start the application; then visit `http://localhost:3000` in your browser (if it did not open automatically).

Implementing lazy loading with React Suspense

React Suspense allows us to let components wait before rendering. At the moment, React Suspense only allows us to dynamically load components with `React.lazy`. In the future, Suspense will support other use cases, such as data fetching.

`React.lazy` is another form of performance optimization. It lets us load a component dynamically in order to reduce the bundle size. Sometimes we want to avoid loading all of the components during the initial render, and only request certain components when they are needed.

For example, if our blog has a member area, we only need to load it after the user has logged in. Doing this will reduce the bundle size for guests who only visit our blog to read blog posts. To learn about React Suspense, we are going to lazily load the `Logout` component in our blog app.

Implementing React.Suspense

First, we have to specify a loading indicator, which will be shown when our lazily-loaded component is loading. In our example, we are going to wrap the `UserBar` component with React Suspense.

Edit `src/App.js`, and replace the `<UserBar />` component with the following code:

```
<React.Suspense fallback={"Loading..."}>
    <UserBar />
</React.Suspense>
```

Now, our app is ready for implementing lazy loading.

Implementing React.lazy

Next, we are going to implement lazy loading for the `Logout` component by wrapping it with `React.lazy()`, as follows:

1. Edit `src/user/UserBar.js`, and remove the import statement for the `Logout` component:

   ```
   import Logout from './Logout'
   ```

2. Then, define the `Logout` component via lazy loading:

   ```
   const Logout = React.lazy(() => import('./Logout'))
   ```

 The `import()` function dynamically loads the `Logout` component from the `Logout.js` file. In contrast to the static `import` statement, this function only gets called when `React.lazy` triggers it, which means it will only be imported when the component is needed.

If we want to see lazy loading in action, we can set **Network Throttling** to **Slow 3G** in Google Chrome:

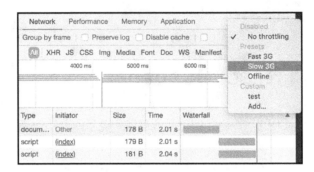

Setting Network Throttling to Slow 3G in Google Chrome

In Firefox, we can do the same by setting **Network Throttling** to **GPRS**. Safari unfortunately does not offer such a feature right now, but we can use the **Network Link Conditioner** tool from Apple's "Hardware IO tools": `https://developer.apple.com/download/more/`

If we refresh the page now, and then log in, we can first see the **Loading...** message, and then the `Logout` component will be shown. If we take a look at the **Network** logs, we can see that the `Logout` component was requested via the network:

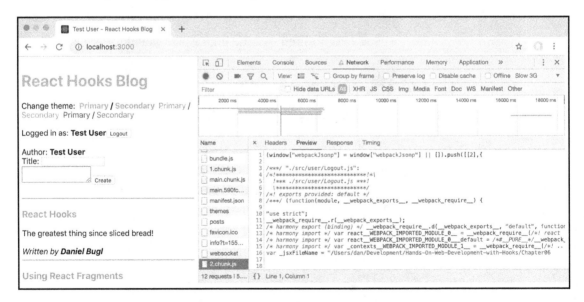

The Logout component being loaded via the network

As we can see, the `Logout` component is now lazily loaded, which means that it will only be requested when needed.

Example code

The example code can be found in the `Chapter06/chapter6_5` folder.

Just run `npm install` in order to install all dependencies, and `npm start` to start the application; then visit `http://localhost:3000` in your browser (if it did not open automatically).

Summary

In this chapter, we first learned how to set up an API server from a JSON file. Then, we learned how to request resources using Effect and State/Reducer Hooks. Next, we learned how to request resources using the `axios` and `react-request-hook` libraries. Finally, we learned how to prevent unnecessary re-rendering using `React.memo`, and how to lazily-load components with React Suspense.

In the next chapter, we are going to add routes to our application, and learn how to use Hooks for routing.

Questions

In order to recap what we have learned in this chapter, try to answer the following questions:

1. How can we easily create a full REST API from a simple JSON file?
2. What are the advantages of using a proxy to access our backend server during development?
3. Which combinations of Hooks can we use to implement requests?
4. Which libraries can we use to implement requests?
5. How can we deal with loading states using `react-request-hook`?
6. How can we deal with errors using `react-request-hook`?
7. How can we prevent the unnecessary re-rendering of components?
8. How can we reduce the bundle size of our app?

Further reading

If you are interested in more information about the concepts that we have explored in this chapter, take a look at the following reading material:

- Official documentation of `json-server`: `https://github.com/typicode/json-server`.
- Official documentation of `concurrently`: `https://github.com/kimmobrunfeldt/concurrently`.
- Official documentation of `axios`: `https://github.com/axios/axios`.
- Official documentation of `react-request-hook`: `https://github.com/schettino/react-request-hook`.
- Create React App documentation on configuring proxies: `https://facebook.github.io/create-react-app/docs/proxying-api-requests-in-development#configuring-the-proxy-manually`.
- Fetching data with React Hooks: `https://www.robinwieruch.de/react-hooks-fetch-data`
- When to use `useMemo`: `https://kentcdodds.com/blog/usememo-and-usecallback`

Using Hooks for Routing

In the previous chapter, we learned how to request resources with Hooks. We first implemented requesting resources using State/Reducer and Effect Hooks. Then, we learned about the `axios` and `react-request-hook` libraries.

In this chapter, we are going to create multiple pages and implement routing in our app. Routing is important in almost every application. To implement routing, we are going to learn how to use use the Navi library, a Hook-based navigation system. Finally, we are also going to learn about dynamic links, and how to access routing information using Hooks.

The following topics will be covered in this chapter:

- Creating multiple pages
- Implementing routing
- Using routing Hooks

Technical requirements

A fairly recent version of Node.js should already be installed (v11.12.0 or higher). The `npm` package manager for Node.js also needs to be installed.

The code for this chapter can be found on the GitHub repository: `https://github.com/PacktPublishing/Learn-React-Hooks/tree/master/Chapter07`.

Check out the following video to see the code in action:

`http://bit.ly/2Mm9yoC`

Please note that it is highly recommended that you write the code on your own. Do not simply run the code examples that have been provided. It is important that you write the code yourself in order to be able to learn and understand properly. However, if you run into any issues, you can always refer to the code example.

Now, let's get started with the chapter.

Creating multiple pages

At the moment, our blog application is a so-called single-page application. However, most larger apps consist of multiple pages. In a blog app, we at least want to have a separate page for each blog post.

Before we can set up routing, we need to create the various pages that we want to render. In our blog app, we are going to define the following pages:

- A home page, which will display a list of all posts
- A post page, which will display a single post

All pages will show a `HeaderBar`, which renders the `Header`, `UserBar`, `ChangeTheme`, and `CreatePost` components. We are now going to start by creating a component for the `HeaderBar`. Afterward, we are going to implement the page components.

Creating the HeaderBar component

First of all, we are going to refactor some contents of our `App` component into a `HeaderBar` component. The `HeaderBar` component will contain everything that we want to display on every page: the `Header`, `UserBar`, `ChangeTheme`, and `CreatePost` components.

Let's start creating the `HeaderBar` component:

1. Create a new folder: `src/pages/`.
2. Create a new file, `src/pages/HeaderBar.js`, import `React` (with the `useContext` Hook), and define the component there. It will accept the `setTheme` function as prop:

```
import React, { useContext } from 'react'

export default function HeaderBar ({ setTheme }) {
    return (
```

```
            <div>
            </div>
        )
    }
```

3. Now, cut the following code from the `src/App.js` component, and insert it between the `<div>` tags of the `HeaderBar` component:

```
<Header text="React Hooks Blog" />
<ChangeTheme theme={theme} setTheme={setTheme} />
<br />
<React.Suspense fallback={"Loading..."}>
    <UserBar />
</React.Suspense>
<br />
{user && <CreatePost />}
```

4. Also, cut the following import statements (and adjust the paths) from `src/App.js` and insert them at the beginning of the `src/pages/HeaderBar.js` file, after the `import React from 'react'` statement:

```
import CreatePost from '../post/CreatePost'
import UserBar from '../user/UserBar'
import Header from '../Header'
import ChangeTheme from '../ChangeTheme'
```

5. Additionally, import the `ThemeContext` and the `StateContext`:

```
import { ThemeContext, StateContext } from '../contexts'
```

6. Then, define two Context Hooks for the `theme` and `state`, and pull the `user` variable out of the `state` object in `src/pages/HeaderBar.js`, as we need it for a conditional check to determine whether we should render the `CreatePost` component:

```
export default function HeaderBar ({ setTheme }) {
    const theme = useContext(ThemeContext)

    const { state } = useContext(StateContext)
    const { user } = state

    return (
```

7. Now, we import the `HeaderBar` component in `src/App.js`:

```
import HeaderBar from './pages/HeaderBar'
```

8. Finally, we render the `HeaderBar` component in `src/App.js`:

```
<div style={{ padding: 8 }}>
    <HeaderBar setTheme={setTheme} />
    <hr />
```

Now, we have a separate component for the `HeaderBar`, which will be shown on all pages. Next, we move on to creating the `HomePage` component.

Creating the HomePage component

Now, we are going to create the `HomePage` component from the `PostList` component and the Resource Hook that is concerned with the posts. Again, we are going to refactor `src/App.js`, in order to create a new component.

Let's start creating the `HomePage` component:

1. Create a new file, `src/pages/HomePage.js`, import `React` with the `useEffect` and `useContext` Hooks, and define the component there. We also define a Context Hook and pull out the `state` object and `dispatch` function:

```
import React, { useEffect, useContext } from 'react'
import { StateContext } from '../contexts'

export default function HomePage () {
    const { state, dispatch } = useContext(StateContext)
    const { error } = state

    return (
        <div>
        </div>
    )
}
```

2. Then, cut the following import statements (and adjust the paths) from `src/App.js`, and add them after the `import React from 'react'` statement in `src/pages/HomePage.js`:

```
import { useResource } from 'react-request-hook'
import PostList from '../post/PostList'
```

3. Next, cut the following Hook definitions from `src/App.js`, and insert them before the `return` statement of the `HomePage` function:

```
const [ posts, getPosts ] = useResource(() => ({
    url: '/posts',
    method: 'get'
}))
useEffect(getPosts, [])
useEffect(() => {
    if (posts && posts.error) {
        dispatch({ type: 'POSTS_ERROR' })
    }
    if (posts && posts.data) {
        dispatch({ type: 'FETCH_POSTS', posts:
posts.data.reverse() })
    }
}, [posts])
```

4. Now, cut the following rendered code from `src/App.js`, and insert it in between the `<div>` tags of `src/pages/HomePage.js`:

```
{error && <b>{error}</b>}
<PostList />
```

5. Then, import the `HomePage` component in `src/App.js`:

```
import HomePage from './pages/HomePage'
```

6. Finally, render the `HomePage` component below the `<hr />` tag:

```
<hr />
<HomePage />
```

Now, we have successfully refactored our current code into a `HomePage` component. Next, we move on to creating the `PostPage` component.

Creating the PostPage component

We are now going to define a new page component, where we will only fetch a single post from our API and display it.

Let's start creating the `PostPage` component now:

1. Create a new `src/pages/PostPage.js` file.

2. Import `React`, the `useEffect` and `useResource` Hooks and the `Post` component:

```
import React, { useEffect } from 'react'
import { useResource } from 'react-request-hook'

import Post from '../post/Post'
```

3. Now, define the `PostPage` component, which is going to accept the post `id` as prop:

```
export default function PostPage ({ id }) {
```

4. Here, we define a Resource Hook that will fetch the corresponding `post` object. We pass the `id` as dependency to the Effect Hook so that our resource re-fetches when the `id` changes:

```
const [ post, getPost ] = useResource(() => ({
    url: `/posts/${id}`,
    method: 'get'
}))
useEffect(getPost, [id])
```

5. Finally, we render the `Post` component:

```
return (
    <div>
        {(post && post.data)
            ? <Post {...post.data} />
            : 'Loading...'
        }
        <hr />
    </div>
)
}
```

We now also have a separate page for single posts.

Testing out the PostPage

To test out the new page, we are going to replace the HomePage component in src/App.js with the PostPage component, as follows:

1. Import the PostPage component in src/App.js:

   ```
   import PostPage from './pages/PostPage'
   ```

2. Now, replace the HomePage component with the PostPage component:

   ```
   <PostPage id={'react-hooks'} />
   ```

As we can see, now only one post, the **React Hooks** post, gets rendered.

Example code

The example code can be found in the Chapter07/chapter7_1 folder.

Just run npm install in order to install all dependencies and npm start to start the application, and then visit http://localhost:3000 in your browser (if it did not open automatically).

Implementing routing

We are going to use the Navi library for routing. Navi supports React Suspense, Hooks, and error boundary APIs of React natively, which makes it the perfect fit to implement routing through the use of Hooks. To implement routing, we are first going to define routes from the pages that we defined in the previous section. Finally, we are going to define links from the main page to the corresponding post pages, and from these pages back to the main page.

Toward the end of this chapter, we are going to extend our routing functionality by implementing routing Hooks.

Defining routes

The first step when implementing routing is to install the `navi` and `react-navi` libraries. Then, we define the routes. Follow the given steps to do so:

1. First, we have to install the libraries using npm:

   ```
   > npm install --save navi react-navi
   ```

2. Then, in `src/App.js`, we import the `Router` and `View` components and the `mount` and `route` functions from the Navi library:

   ```
   import { Router, View } from 'react-navi'
   import { mount, route } from 'navi'
   ```

3. Make sure that the `HomePage` component is imported:

   ```
   import HomePage from './pages/HomePage'
   ```

4. Now, we can define the `routes` object using the `mount` function:

   ```
   const routes = mount({
   ```

5. In this function, we define our routes, starting with the main route:

   ```
   '/': route({ view: <HomePage /> }),
   ```

6. Next, we define the route for a single post, here we use URL parameters (`:id`), and a function to dynamically create the `view`:

   ```
   '/view/:id': route(req => {
       return { view: <PostPage id={req.params.id} /> }
   }),
   })
   ```

7. Finally, we wrap our rendered code with the `<Router>` component, and replace the `<PostPage>` component with the `<View>` component in order to dynamically render the current page:

   ```
   <Router routes={routes}>
       <div style={{ padding: 8 }}>
           <HeaderBar setTheme={setTheme} />
           <hr />
           <View />
       </div>
   </Router>
   ```

Now, if we go to `http://localhost:3000`, we can see a list of all posts, and when we go to `http://localhost:3000/view/react-hooks`, we can see a single post: the **React Hooks** post.

Defining links

Now, we are going to define links from each post to the page of the corresponding single post, and then back to the main page from the post page. The links will be used to access the various routes that have been defined in our app. First, we are going to define links from the home page to the single post pages. Next, we are going to define links from the single post pages back to the main page.

Defining links to the posts

We start by shortening the post `content` in the list, and defining links from the `PostList` to the corresponding post pages. To do so, we have to define static links from the `PostList` on the home page to the specific post pages.

Let's define those links now:

1. Edit `src/post/Post.js`, and import the `Link` component from `react-navi`:

   ```
   import { Link } from 'react-navi'
   ```

2. Then, we are going to add two new props to the `Post` component: `id` and `short`, which will be set to `true` when we want to display the shortened version of the post. Later, we are going to set `short` to `true` in the `PostList` component:

   ```
   function Post ({ id, title, content, author, short = false }) {
   ```

3. Next, we are going to add some logic to trim the post `content` to 30 characters when listing it:

   ```
   let processedContent = content
   if (short) {
       if (content.length > 30) {
           processedContent = content.substring(0, 30) + '...'
       }
   }
   ```

4. Now, we can display the `processedContent` value instead of the `content` value, and a `Link` to view the full post:

```
<div>{processedContent}</div>
{short &&
    <div>
        <br />
        <Link href={`/view/${id}`}>View full
post</Link>
    </div>
}
```

5. Finally, we set the `short` prop to `true` within the `PostList` component. Edit `src/post/PostList.js`, and adjust the following code:

```
<Post {...p} short={true} />
```

Now we can see that each post on the main page is trimmed to 30 characters, and has a link to the corresponding single post page:

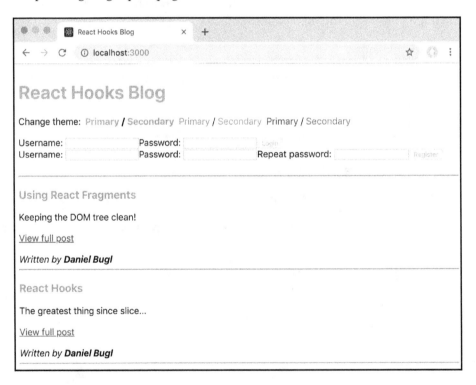

Displaying a link in the PostList

As we can see, routing is quite simple. Now, each post has a link to its corresponding full post page.

Defining the links to the main page

Now, we just need a way to get back to the main page from a single post page. We are going to repeat a similar process to what we have done previously. Let's define the links back to the main page now:

1. Edit `src/pages/PostPage.js`, and import the `Link` component there:

   ```
   import { Link } from 'react-navi'
   ```

2. Then, insert a new link back to the main page, before displaying the post:

   ```
   return (
       <div>
           <div><Link href="/">Go back</Link></div>
   ```

3. After going to a page, we can now use the **Go back** link in order to return to the main page:

Displaying a link on the single post page

Now, our app also provides a way back to the home page.

Adjusting the CREATE_POST action

Previously, we dispatched a CREATE_POST action when a new post gets created. However, this action does not contain the post id, which means that links to newly created posts will not work.

We are now going to adjust the code to pass the post id to the CREATE_POST action:

1. Edit src/post/CreatePost.js, and import the useEffect Hook:

   ```
   import React, { useState, useContext, useEffect } from 'react'
   ```

2. Next, adjust the existing Resource Hook to pull out the post object after the creation of the post finishes:

   ```
   const [ post, createPost ] = useResource(({ title, content,
   author }) => ({
   ```

3. Now, we can create a new Effect Hook after the Resource Hook, and dispatch the CREATE_POST action once the result of the create post request becomes available:

   ```
   useEffect(() => {
       if (post && post.data) {
           dispatch({ type: 'CREATE_POST', ...post.data })
       }
   }, [post])
   ```

4. Next, we remove the call to the dispatch function in the handleCreate handler function:

   ```
   function handleCreate () {
       createPost({ title, content, author: user })
       dispatch({ type: 'CREATE_POST', title, content, author:
   user })
       }
   ```

5. Finally, we edit src/reducers.js, and adjust the postsReducer as follows:

   ```
   function postsReducer (state, action) {
       switch (action.type) {
           case 'FETCH_POSTS':
               return action.posts

           case 'CREATE_POST':
               const newPost = { title: action.title, content:
   action.content, author: action.author, id: action.id }
               return [ newPost, ...state ]
   ```

Now, links to the newly created posts work fine, because the `id` value is added to the inserted `post` object.

Example code

The example code can be found in the `Chapter07/chapter7_2` folder.

Just run `npm install` in order to install all dependencies and `npm start` to start the application, and then visit `http://localhost:3000` in your browser (if it did not open automatically).

Using routing Hooks

After implementing basic routing using `navi` and `react-navi`, we are now going to implement more advanced use cases using routing Hooks, which are provided by `react-navi`. Routing Hooks can be used to make routing more dynamic. For example, by allowing navigation to different routes from other Hooks. Furthermore, we can use Hooks to access all route-related information within a component.

Overview of Navi's Hooks

First, we will have a look at three of the Hooks that are provided by the Navi library:

- The `useNavigation` Hook
- The `useCurrentRoute` Hook
- The `useLoadingRoute` Hook

The useNavigation Hook

The `useNavigation` Hook has the following signature:

```
const navigation = useNavigation()
```

It returns the `navigation` object of Navi, which contains the following functions to manage the navigation state of the app:

- `extractState()`: Returns the current value of `window.history.state`; this is useful when dealing with server-side rendering.
- `getCurrentValue()` : Returns the `Route` object that corresponds to the current URL.
- `getRoute()`: Returns a promise to the fully loaded `Route` object that corresponds to the current URL. The promise will only resolve once the `Route` object is fully loaded.
- `goBack()`: Goes back one page; this is similar to how pressing the back button of the browser works.
- `navigate(url, options)`: Navigates to the provided URL using the provided options (`body`, `headers`, `method`, `replace`, and `state`). More information about the options can be found on the official Navi documentation: `https://frontarm.com/navi/en/reference/navigation/#navigationnavigate`.

The useCurrentRoute Hook

The `useCurrentRoute` Hook has the following signature:

```
const route = useCurrentRoute()
```

It returns the latest non-busy route, which contains all information that Navi knows about the current page:

- `data`: Contains merged values from all `data` chunks.
- `title`: Contains the `title` value that should be set on `document.title`.
- `url`: Contains information about the current route, such as the `href`, `query`, and `hash`.
- `views`: Contains an array of components or elements that will be rendered in the route's view.

The useLoadingRoute Hook

The `useLoadingRoute` Hook has the following signature:

```
const loadingRoute = useLoadingRoute()
```

It returns the `Route` object for the page that is currently being fetched. If no page is currently being fetched, it outputs `undefined`. The object looks the same as the `Route` object of the `useCurrentRoute` Hook.

Programmatic navigation

First, we are going to use the `useNavigation` Hook to implement programmatic navigation. We want to automatically redirect to the corresponding post page after creating a new post.

Let's implement programmatic navigation in the `CreatePost` component using Hooks:

1. Edit `src/post/CreatePost.js`, and import the `useNavigation` Hook there:

       import { useNavigation } from 'react-navi'

2. Now, define a Navigation Hook after the existing Resource Hook:

       const navigation = useNavigation()

3. Finally, we adjust the Effect Hook to call `navigation.navigate()`, once the result of the create post request becomes available:

       useEffect(() => {
           if (post && post.data) {
               dispatch({ type: 'CREATE_POST', ...post.data })
               navigation.navigate(`/view/${post.data.id}`)
           }
       }, [post])

If we create a new `post` object now, we can see that after pressing the **Create** button, we automatically get redirected to the page of the corresponding post. We can now move on to accessing route information using Hooks.

Accessing route information

Next, we are going to use the `useCurrentRoute` Hook to access information about the current route/URL. We are going to use this Hook to implement a footer, which will display the `href` value of the current route.

Let's get started implementing the footer now:

1. First, we create a new component for the footer. Create a new `src/pages/FooterBar.js` file, and import React, as well as the `useCurrentRoute` Hook from `react-navi`:

   ```
   import React from 'react'
   import { useCurrentRoute } from 'react-navi'
   ```

2. Then, we define a new `FooterBar` component:

   ```
   export default function FooterBar () {
   ```

3. We use the `useCurrentRoute` Hook, and pull out the `url` object to be able to show the current `href` value in the footer:

   ```
   const { url } = useCurrentRoute()
   ```

4. Finally, we render a link to the current `href` value in the footer:

   ```
   return (
       <div>
           <a href={url.href}>{url.href}</a>
       </div>
   )
   }
   ```

Now, when we, for example, open a post page, we can see the `href` value of the current post in the footer:

Displaying a footer with the current href value

As we can see, our footer works properly—it always shows the `href` value of the current page.

Example code

The example code can be found in the `Chapter07/chapter7_3` folder.

Just run `npm install` in order to install all dependencies and `npm start` to start the application, and then visit `http://localhost:3000` in your browser (if it did not open automatically).

Summary

In this chapter, we first defined two pages for our blog: the home page and a page for single posts. We also created a component for the `HeaderBar`. Afterward, we implemented routing by defining routes, links to the single posts, and links back to the main page. Finally, we used routing Hooks to implement dynamic navigation when creating a new post, and implemented a footer that shows the current URL.

Routing is very important, and is used in almost every application. We now know how to define separate pages and how to link between them. Furthermore, we learned how to dynamically navigate between pages using Hooks. We also learned how to access routing information with Hooks for more advanced use cases.

There are many more things that the Navi library can do. However, this book focuses on Hooks, so most features of Navi are out of scope. For example, we can fetch data using Navi, implement error pages (for example, a 404 page), lazy loading and compose routes. Feel free to read up on those features in the official documentation of Navi.

In the next chapter, we are going to learn about the various Hooks that are provided by the React community: for input handling, for responsive design, to implement undo/redo, and to implement various data structures and React life cycle methods using Hooks. We are also going to learn where to find more Hooks provided by the community.

Questions

In order to recap what we have learned in this chapter, try answering the following questions:

1. Why do we need to define separate pages?
2. How do we define routes using the Navi library?
3. How do we define routes with URL parameters?
4. How are static links defined with Navi?
5. How can we implement dynamic navigation?
6. Which Hook is used to access the route information of the current route?
7. Which Hook is used to access the route information of the currently loading route?

Further reading

If you are interested in more information about the concepts that we have learned in this chapter, take a look at the official documentation of the Navi library: `https://frontarm.com/navi/en/`.

Using Community Hooks

8

In the previous chapter, we implemented routing using the Navi library. We started by implementing pages, then defining routes and static links. Finally, we implemented dynamic links and accessed route information using Hooks.

In this chapter, we are going to learn about various Hooks that are provided by the React community. These Hooks can be used to simplify input handling, and implement React life cycles in order to simplify migration from React class components. Furthermore, there are Hooks that implement various behaviors such as timers, checking if the client is online, hover and focus events, and data manipulation. Finally, we are going to learn about responsive design and implementing undo/redo functionality using Hooks.

The following topics will be covered in this chapter:

- Simplifying input handling using the Input Hook
- Implementing React life cycles with Hooks
- Learning about various useful Hooks (`usePrevious`, timer, online, focus, hover, and data manipulation Hooks)
- Implementing responsive design with Hooks
- Implementing undo/redo functionality and debouncing with Hooks
- Learning where to find other Hooks

Technical requirements

A fairly recent version of Node.js should already be installed (v11.12.0 or higher). The npm package manager for Node.js also needs to be installed.

The code for this chapter can be found on the GitHub repository: https://github.com/PacktPublishing/Learn-React-Hooks/tree/master/Chapter08.

Check out the following video to see the code in action:

```
http://bit.ly/2Mm9yoC
```

 Please note that it is highly recommended that you write the code on your own. Do not simply run the code examples that have been provided. It is important that you write the code yourself in order to be able to learn and understand properly. However, if you run into any issues, you can always refer to the code example.

Now, let's get started with the chapter.

Exploring the input handling Hook

A very common use case when dealing with Hooks, is to store the current value of an input field using State and Effect Hooks. We have already done this many times throughout this book.

The useInput Hook greatly simplifies this use case, by providing a single Hook that deals with the value variable of an input field. It works as follows:

```
import React from 'react'
import { useInput } from 'react-hookedup'

export default function App () {
    const { value, onChange } = useInput('')

    return <input value={value} onChange={onChange} />
}
```

This code will bind an onChange handler function and value to the input field. This means that whenever we enter text into the input field, the value will automatically be updated.

Additionally, there is a function that will clear the input field. This clear function is also returned from the Hook:

```
const { clear } = useInput('')
```

Calling the clear function will set the value to an empty value, and clear all text from the input field.

Furthermore, the Hook provides two ways to bind an `input` field:

- `bindToInput`: Binds the `value` and `onChange` props to an `input` field using `e.target.value` as the `value` argument for the `onChange` function. This is useful when dealing with HTML `input` fields.
- `bind`: Binds the `value` and `onChange` props to an `input` field using only `e` as the value for the `onChange` function. This is useful for React components that directly pass the value to the `onChange` function.

The `bind` and `bindToInput` objects can be used with the spread operator, as follows:

```
import React from 'react'
import { useInput } from 'react-hookedup'

const ToggleButton = ({ value, onChange }) => { ... } // custom component
that renders a toggle button

export default function App () {
    const { bind, bindToInput } = useInput('')

    return (
        <div>
            <input {...bindToInput} />
            <ToggleButton {...bind} />
        </div>
    )
}
```

As we can see, for the `input` field we can use the `{...bindToInput}` props to assign the `value` and `onChange` functions. For `ToggleButton`, we need to use the `{...bind}` props instead, because we are not dealing with input events here, and the value is directly passed to the change handler (not via `e.target.value`).

Now that we have learned about the Input Hook, we can move on to implementing it in our blog app.

Implementing Input Hooks in our blog app

Now that we have learned about the Input Hook, and how it simplifies dealing with the `input` field state, we are going to implement Input Hooks in our blog app.

First, we have to install the `react-hookedup` library in our blog app project:

```
> npm install --save react-hookedup
```

We are now going to implement Input Hooks in the following components:

- The `Login` component
- The `Register` component
- The `CreatePost` component

Let's get started implementing Input Hooks.

The Login component

We have two `input` fields in the `Login` component: the **Username** and **Password** fields. We are now going to replace the State Hooks with Input Hooks.

Let's start implementing Input Hooks in the `Login` component now:

1. Import the `useInput` Hook at the beginning of the `src/user/Login.js` file:

   ```
   import { useInput } from 'react-hookedup'
   ```

2. Then, we remove the following `username` State Hook:

   ```
   const [ username, setUsername ] = useState('')
   ```

   It is replaced with an Input Hook, as follows:

   ```
   const { value: username, bindToInput: bindUsername } =
   useInput('')
   ```

    Since we are using two Input Hooks, in order to avoid name collisions, we are using the rename syntax (`{ from: to }`) in object destructuring to rename the `value` key to `username`, and `bindToInput` key to `bindUsername`.

3. We also remove the following `password` State Hook:

   ```
   const [ password, setPassword ] = useState('')
   ```

   It is replaced with an Input Hook, as follows:

   ```
   const { value: password, bindToInput: bindPassword } =
   useInput('')
   ```

4. We can now remove the following handler functions:

```
function handleUsername (evt) {
    setUsername(evt.target.value)
}

function handlePassword (evt) {
    setPassword(evt.target.value)
}
```

5. Finally, instead of passing the `onChange` handlers manually, we use the bind objects from the Input Hooks:

```
<input type="text" value={username} {...bindUsername}
name="login-username" id="login-username" />
<input type="password" value={password}
{...bindPassword} name="login-password" id="login-password" />
```

The login functionality will still work in exactly the same way as before, but we are now using the much more concise Input Hook, instead of the generic State Hook. We also do not have to define the same kind of handler function for each `input` field anymore. As we can see, using community Hooks can greatly simplify the implementation of common use-cases, such as input handling. We are now going to repeat the same process for the `Register` component.

The Register component

The `Register` component works similarly to the `Login` component. However, it has three `input` fields: **Username**, **Password**, and **Repeat Password**.

Let's implement Input Hooks in the `Register` component now:

1. Import the `useInput` Hook at the beginning of the `src/user/Register.js` file:

```
import { useInput } from 'react-hookedup'
```

2. Then, we remove the following State Hooks:

```
const [ username, setUsername ] = useState('')
const [ password, setPassword ] = useState('')
const [ passwordRepeat, setPasswordRepeat ] = useState('')
```

They are replaced with the corresponding Input Hooks:

```
const { value: username, bindToInput: bindUsername } =
useInput('')
const { value: password, bindToInput: bindPassword } =
useInput('')
const { value: passwordRepeat, bindToInput: bindPasswordRepeat
} = useInput('')
```

3. Again, we can remove all of the handler functions:

```
function handleUsername (evt) {
    setUsername(evt.target.value)
}

function handlePassword (evt) {
    setPassword(evt.target.value)
}

function handlePasswordRepeat (evt) {
    setPasswordRepeat(evt.target.value)
}
```

4. Finally, we replace all of the onChange handlers with the corresponding bind objects:

```
<input type="text" value={username} {...bindUsername}
name="register-username" id="register-username" />
<input type="password" value={password}
{...bindPassword} name="register-password" id="register-password"
/>
<input type="password" value={passwordRepeat}
{...bindPasswordRepeat} name="register-password-repeat"
id="register-password-repeat/>
```

The register functionality will also still work in the same way, but now using Input Hooks. Next up is the CreatePost component, where we are going to implement Input Hooks as well.

The CreatePost component

The CreatePost component uses two input fields: one for the title, and one for the content. We are going to replace both of them with Input Hooks.

Let's implement Input Hooks in the `CreatePost` component now:

1. Import the `useInput` Hook at the beginning of
   the `src/user/CreatePost.js` file:

   ```
   import { useInput } from 'react-hookedup'
   ```

2. Then, we remove the following State Hooks:

   ```
   const [ title, setTitle ] = useState('')
   const [ content, setContent ] = useState('')
   ```

   We replace them with the corresponding Input Hooks:

   ```
   const { value: title, bindToInput: bindTitle } = useInput('')
   const { value: content, bindToInput: bindContent } =
   useInput('')
   ```

3. Again, we can remove the following input handler functions:

   ```
   function handleTitle (evt) {
       setTitle(evt.target.value)
   }

   function handleContent (evt) {
       setContent(evt.target.value)
   }
   ```

4. Finally, we replace all of the `onChange` handlers with the corresponding bind
   objects:

   ```
   <input type="text" value={title} {...bindTitle}
   name="create-title" id="create-title" />
       </div>
       <textarea value={content} {...bindContent} />
   ```

The create post functionality will also work in the same way with Input Hooks.

Example code

The example code can be found in the `Chapter08/chapter8_1` folder.

Just run `npm install` in order to install all dependencies and `npm start` to start the
application, and then visit `http://localhost:3000` in your browser (if it does not open
automatically).

React life cycles with Hooks

As we have learned in the previous chapters, we can use the `useEffect` Hook to model most of React's life cycle methods. However, if you prefer dealing with React life cycle directly, instead of using Effect Hooks, there is a library called `react-hookedup`, which provides various Hooks, including Hooks for the various React life cycles. Additionally, the library provides a merging State Hook, which works similarly to `this.setState()` in React's class components.

The useOnMount Hook

The `useOnMount` Hook has a similar effect to the `componentDidMount` life cycle. It is used as follows:

```
import React from 'react'
import { useOnMount } from 'react-hookedup'

export default function UseOnMount () {
    useOnMount(() => console.log('mounted'))

    return <div>look at the console :)</div>
}
```

The preceding code will output **mounted** to the console when the component gets mounted (when the React component is rendered for the first time). It will not be called again when the component re-renders due to, for example, a prop change.

Alternatively, we could just use a `useEffect` Hook with an empty array as the second argument, which will have the same effect:

```
import React, { useEffect } from 'react'

export default function OnMountWithEffect () {
    useEffect(() => console.log('mounted with effect'), [])

    return <div>look at the console :)</div>
}
```

As we can see, using an Effect Hook with an empty array as the second argument results in the same behavior as the `useOnMount` Hook or the `componentDidMount` life cycle method.

The useOnUnmount Hook

The useOnUnmount Hook has a similar effect to the componentWillUnmount life cycle. It is used as follows:

```
import React from 'react'
import { useOnUnmount } from 'react-hookedup'

export default function UseOnUnmount () {
    useOnUnmount(() => console.log('unmounting'))

    return <div>click the "unmount" button above and look at the
console</div>
}
```

The preceding code will output **unmounting** to the console when the component gets unmounted (before the React component is removed from the DOM).

If you remember from Chapter 4, *Using the Reducer and Effect Hooks,* we can return a cleanup function from the useEffect Hook, which will be called when the component unmounts. This means that we could alternatively implement the useOnMount Hook using useEffect, as follows:

```
import React, { useEffect } from 'react'

export default function OnUnmountWithEffect () {
    useEffect(() => {
        return () => console.log('unmounting with effect')
    }, [])

    return <div>click the "unmount" button above and look at the
console</div>
}
```

As we can see, using the cleanup function that is returned from an Effect Hook, with an empty array as the second argument, has the same effect as the useOnUnmount Hook, or the componentWillUnmount life cycle method.

The useLifecycleHooks Hook

The `useLifecycleHooks` Hook combines the previous two Hooks into one. We can combine the `useOnMount` and `useOnUnmount` Hooks as follows:

```
import React from 'react'
import { useLifecycleHooks } from 'react-hookedup'

export default function UseLifecycleHooks () {
    useLifecycleHooks({
        onMount: () => console.log('lifecycle mounted'),
        onUnmount: () => console.log('lifecycle unmounting')
    })

    return <div>look at the console and click the button</div>
}
```

Alternatively, we could use the two Hooks separately:

```
import React from 'react'
import { useOnMount, useOnUnmount } from 'react-hookedup'

export default function UseLifecycleHooksSeparate () {
    useOnMount(() => console.log('separate lifecycle mounted'))
    useOnUnmount(() => console.log('separate lifecycle unmounting'))

    return <div>look at the console and click the button</div>
}
```

However, if you have this kind of pattern, I would recommend simply using the `useEffect` Hook, as follows:

```
import React, { useEffect } from 'react'

export default function LifecycleHooksWithEffect () {
    useEffect(() => {
        console.log('lifecycle mounted with effect')
        return () => console.log('lifecycle unmounting with effect')
    }, [])

    return <div>look at the console and click the button</div>
}
```

Using `useEffect`, we can put our whole effect into a single function, and then simply return a function for cleanup. This pattern is especially useful when we learn about making our own Hooks in the next chapters.

Effects make us think differently about React components. We do not have to think about the life cycle of a component at all. Instead, we think about effects, dependencies, and the cleanup of effects.

The useMergeState Hook

The `useMergeState` Hook works similarly to the `useState` Hook. However, it does not replace the current state, but instead merges the current state with the new state, just like `this.setState()` works in React class components.

The Merge State Hook returns the following objects:

- `state`: The current state
- `setState`: A function to merge the current state with the given state object

For example, let's consider the following component:

1. First, we import the `useState` Hook:

   ```
   import React, { useState } from 'react'
   ```

2. Then, we define our app component and a State Hook with an object containing a `loaded` value and a `counter` value:

   ```
   export default function MergeState () {
       const [ state, setState ] = useState({ loaded: true, counter: 0
   })
   ```

3. Next, we define a `handleClick` function, where we set the new `state`, increasing the current `counter` value by 1:

   ```
   function handleClick () {
       setState({ counter: state.counter + 1 })
   }
   ```

4. Finally, we render the current `counter` value and a **+1** button in order to increase the `counter` value by 1. The button will be disabled if `state.loaded` is `false` or `undefined`:

   ```
   return (
       <div>
           Count: {state.counter}
           <button onClick={handleClick}
   disabled={!state.loaded}>+1</button>
   ```

```
            </div>
        )
    }
```

As we can see, we have a simple counter app, showing the current count and a **+1** button. The **+1** button will only be enabled when the `loaded` value is set to `true`.

If we now click on the **+1** button, `counter` will increase from 0 to 1, but the button will get disabled, because we have overwritten the current `state` object with a new `state` object.

To solve this problem, we would have to adjust the `handleClick` function as follows:

```
function handleClick () {
    setState({ ...state, counter: state.counter + 1 })
}
```

Alternatively, we could use the `useMergeState` Hook in order to avoid this problem altogether, and get the same behavior that we had with `this.setState()` in class components:

```
import React from 'react'
import { useMergeState } from 'react-hookedup'

export default function UseMergeState () {
    const { state, setState } = useMergeState({ loaded: true, counter: 0 })
```

As we can see, by using the `useMergeState` Hook, we can reproduce the same behavior that we had with `this.setState()` in class components. So, we do not need to use spread syntax anymore. However, often, it is better to simply use multiple State Hooks or a Reducer Hook instead.

Example code

The example code can be found in the `Chapter08/chapter8_2` folder.

Just run `npm install` in order to install all dependencies and `npm start` to start the application, and then visit `http://localhost:3000` in your browser (if it does not open automatically).

Various useful Hooks

In addition to life cycle Hooks, `react-hookedup` also provides Hooks for timers, checking the network status, and various other useful Hooks for dealing with, for example, arrays and input fields. We are now going to cover the rest of the Hooks that `react-hookedup` provides.

These Hooks are as follows:

- The `usePrevious` Hook, to get the previous value of a Hook or prop
- Timer Hooks, to implement intervals and timeouts
- The `useOnline` Hook, to check whether the client has an active internet connection
- Various data manipulation Hooks for dealing with booleans, arrays, and counters
- Hooks to deal with focus and hover events

The usePrevious Hook

The `usePrevious` Hook is a simple Hook that lets us get the previous value of a prop or Hook value. It will always store and return the previous value of any given variable, and it works as follows:

1. First, we import the `useState` and `usePrevious` Hooks:

```
import React, { useState } from 'react'
import { usePrevious } from 'react-hookedup'
```

2. Then, we define our `App` component, and a Hook in which we store the current `count` state:

```
export default function UsePrevious () {
    const [ count, setCount ] = useState(0)
```

3. Now, we define the `usePrevious` Hook, passing the `count` value from the State Hook to it:

```
const prevCount = usePrevious(count)
```

The usePrevious Hook works with any variable, including component props and values from other Hooks.

4. Next, we define a handler function, which will increase count by 1:

```
function handleClick () {
    setCount(count + 1)
}
```

5. Finally, we render the previous value of count, the current value of count, and a button to increase count:

```
return (
    <div>
        Count was {prevCount} and is {count} now.
        <button onClick={handleClick}>+1</button>
    </div>
)
}
```

The previously defined component will first show **Count was and is 0 now.**, because the default value for the Previous Hook is null. When clicking the button once, it will show the following: **Count was 0 and is 1 now.**.

Timer Hooks

The react-hookedup library also provides Hooks for dealing with timers. If we simply create a timer using setTimeout or setInterval in our component, it will get instantiated again every time the component is re-rendered. This not only causes bugs and unpredictability, but can also cause a memory leak if the old timers are not freed properly. Using timer Hooks, we can avoid these problems completely, and easily use intervals and timeouts.

The following timer Hooks are provided by the library:

- The useInterval Hook, which is used to define setInterval timers (timers that trigger multiple times) in React components
- The useTimeout Hook, which is used to define setTimeout timers (timers that trigger only once after a certain amount of time)

The useInterval Hook

The `useInterval` Hook can be used just like `setInterval`. We are now going to implement a small counter that counts the number of seconds since mounting the component:

1. First, import the `useState` and `useInterval` Hooks:

    ```
    import React, { useState } from 'react'
    import { useInterval } from 'react-hookedup'
    ```

2. Then, we define our component and a State Hook:

    ```
    export default function UseInterval () {
        const [ count, setCount ] = useState(0)
    ```

3. Next, we define the `useInterval` Hook, which is going to increase the `count` by 1 every `1000` ms, which is equal to 1 second:

    ```
    useInterval(() => setCount(count + 1), 1000)
    ```

4. Finally, we display the current `count` value:

    ```
    return <div>{count} seconds passed</div>
    }
    ```

Alternatively, we could use an Effect Hook in combination with `setInterval`, instead of the `useInterval` Hook, as follows:

```
import React, { useState, useEffect } from 'react'

export default function IntervalWithEffect () {
    const [ count, setCount ] = useState(0)
    useEffect(() => {
        const interval = setInterval(() => setCount(count + 1), 1000)
        return () => clearInterval(interval)
    })

    return <div>{count} seconds passed</div>
}
```

As we can see, the `useInterval` Hook makes our code much more concise and easily readable.

useTimeout Hook

The useTimeout Hook can be used just like setTimeout. We are now going to implement a component that triggers after 10 seconds have passed:

1. First, import the useState and useTimeout Hooks:

   ```
   import React, { useState } from 'react'
   import { useTimeout } from 'react-hookedup'
   ```

2. Then, we define our component and a State Hook:

   ```
   export default function UseTimeout () {
       const [ ready, setReady ] = useState(false)
   ```

3. Next, we define the useTimeout Hook, which is going to set ready to true, after 10000 ms (10 seconds):

   ```
   useTimeout(() => setReady(true), 10000)
   ```

4. Finally, we display whether we are ready or not:

   ```
   return <div>{ready ? 'ready' : 'waiting...'}</div>
   }
   ```

Alternatively, we could use an Effect Hook in combination with setTimeout, instead of the useTimeout Hook, as follows:

```
import React, { useState, useEffect } from 'react'

export default function TimeoutWithEffect () {
    const [ ready, setReady ] = useState(false)
    useEffect(() => {
        const timeout = setTimeout(() => setReady(true), 10000)
        return () => clearTimeout(timeout)
    })

    return <div>{ready ? 'ready' : 'waiting...'}</div>
}
```

As we can see, the useTimeout Hook makes our code much more concise and easily readable.

The Online Status Hook

In some web apps, it makes sense to implement an offline mode; for example, if we want to be able to edit and save drafts for posts locally, and sync them to the server whenever we are online again. To be able to implement this use case, we can use the `useOnlineStatus` Hook.

The Online Status Hook returns an object with an `online` value, which contains `true` if the client is online; otherwise, it contains `false`. It works as follows:

```
import React from 'react'
import { useOnlineStatus } from 'react-hookedup'

export default function App () {
    const { online } = useOnlineStatus()

    return <div>You are {online ? 'online' : 'offline'}!</div>
}
```

The previous component will display **You are online!**, when an internet connection is available, or **You are offline!**, otherwise.

We could then use a Previous Hook, in combination with an Effect Hook, in order to sync data to the server when we are online again:

```
import React, { useEffect } from 'react'
import { useOnlineStatus, usePrevious } from 'react-hookedup'

export default function App () {
    const { online } = useOnlineStatus()
    const prevOnline = usePrevious(online)

    useEffect(() => {
        if (prevOnline === false && online === true) {
            alert('syncing data')
        }
    }, [prevOnline, online])

    return <div>You are {online ? 'online' : 'offline'}!</div>
}
```

Now, we have an Effect Hook that triggers whenever the value of `online` changes. It then checks whether the previous value of `online` was `false`, and the current one is `true`. If that is the case, it means we were offline, and are now online again, so we need to sync our updated data to the server.

As a result, our app will show an alert displaying **syncing data** when we go offline and then online again.

Data manipulation Hooks

The `react-hookedup` library provides various utility Hooks for dealing with data. These Hooks simplify dealing with common data structures and provide an abstraction over the State Hook.

The following data manipulation Hooks are provided:

- The `useBoolean` Hook: To deal with toggling boolean values
- The `useArray` Hook: To deal with handling arrays
- The `useCounter` Hook: To deal with counters

The useBoolean Hook

The `useBoolean` Hook is used to deal with toggling boolean values (`true`/`false`), and provides functions to set the value to `true`/`false`, and a `toggle` function to toggle the value.

The Hook returns an object with the following:

- `value`: The current value of the boolean
- `toggle`: A function to toggle the current value (sets `true` if currently `false`, and `false` if currently `true`)
- `setTrue`: Sets the current value to `true`
- `setFalse`: Sets the current value to `false`

The Boolean Hook works as follows:

1. First, we import the `useBoolean` Hook from `react-hookedup`:

   ```
   import React from 'react'
   import { useBoolean } from 'react-hookedup'
   ```

2. Then, we define our component and the Boolean Hook, which returns an object with the `toggle` function and `value`. We pass `false` as the default value:

   ```
   export default function UseBoolean () {
       const { toggle, value } = useBoolean(false)
   ```

3. Finally, we render a button, which can be turned **on/off**:

```
return (
    <div>
        <button onClick={toggle}>{value ? 'on' :
'off'}</button>
    </div>
    )
}
```

The button will initially be rendered with the text **off**. When clicking the button, it will show the text **on**. When clicking again, it will be **off** again.

The useArray Hook

The useArray Hook is used to easily deal with arrays, without having to use the rest/spread syntax.

The Array Hook returns an object with the following:

- value: The current array
- setValue: Sets a new array as the value
- add: Adds a given element to the array
- clear: Removes all elements from the array
- removeIndex: Removes an element from the array by its index
- removeById: Removes an element from the array by its id (assuming that the elements in the array are objects with an id key)

It works as follows:

1. First, we import the useArray Hook from react-hookedup:

```
import React from 'react'
import { useArray } from 'react-hookedup'
```

2. Then, we define the component and the Array Hook, with the default value of ['one', 'two', 'three']:

```
export default function UseArray () {
    const { value, add, clear, removeIndex } = useArray(['one',
'two', 'three'])
```

3. Now, we display the current array as JSON:

```
return (
    <div>
        <p>current array: {JSON.stringify(value)}</p>
```

4. Then, we display a button to `add` an element:

```
        <button onClick={() => add('test')}>add
element</button>
```

5. Next, we display a button to remove the first element by index:

```
        <button onClick={() => removeIndex(0)}>remove first
element</button>
```

6. Finally, we add a button to `clear` all elements:

```
        <button onClick={() => clear()}>clear elements</button>
    </div>
)
}
```

As we can see, using the `useArray` Hook makes dealing with arrays much simpler.

The useCounter Hook

The `useCounter` Hook can be used to define various kinds of counters. We can define a lower/upper limit, specify whether the counter should loop or not, and specify the step amount by which we increase/decrease the counter. Furthermore, the Counter Hook provides functions in order to increase/decrease the counter.

It accepts the following configuration options:

- `upperLimit`: Defines the upper limit (maximum value) of our counter
- `lowerLimit`: Defines the lower limit (minimum value) of our counter
- `loop`: Specifies whether the counter should loop (for example, when the maximum value is reached, we go back to the minimum value)
- `step`: Sets the default step amount for the increase and decrease functions

It returns the following object:

- `value`: The current value of our counter.
- `setValue`: Sets the current value of our counter.
- `increase`: Increases the value by a given step amount. If no amount is specified, then the default step amount is used.
- `decrease`: Decreases the value by a given step amount. If no amount is specified, then the default step amount is used.

The Counter Hook can be used as follows:

1. First, we import the `useCounter` Hook from `react-hookedup`:

   ```
   import React from 'react'
   import { useCounter } from 'react-hookedup'
   ```

2. Then, we define our component and the Hook, specifying 0 as the default value. We also specify `upperLimit`, `lowerLimit`, and `loop`:

   ```
   export default function UseCounter () {
       const { value, increase, decrease } = useCounter(0, {
       upperLimit: 3, lowerLimit: 0, loop: true })
   ```

3. Finally, we render the current value and two buttons to `increase`/`decrease` the value:

   ```
   return (
       <div>
           <b>{value}</b>
           <button onClick={increase}>+</button>
           <button onClick={decrease}>-</button>
       </div>
   )
   }
   ```

As we can see, the Counter Hook makes implementing counters much simpler.

Focus and Hover Hooks

Sometimes, we want to check whether the user has hovered over an element or focused on an `input` field. To do so, we can use the Focus and Hover Hooks that are provided by the `react-hookedup` library.

The library provides two Hooks for these features:

- The `useFocus` Hook: To handle focus events (for example, a selected `input` field)
- The `useHover` Hook: To deal with hover events (for example, when hovering the mouse pointer over an area)

The useFocus Hook

In order to know whether an element is currently focused, we can use the `useFocus` Hook as follows:

1. First, we import the `useFocus` Hook:

   ```
   import React from 'react'
   import { useFocus } from 'react-hookedup'
   ```

2. Then, we define our component and the Focus Hook, which returns the `focused` value and a `bind` function, to bind the Hook to an element:

   ```
   export default function UseFocus () {
       const { focused, bind } = useFocus()
   ```

3. Finally, we render an `input` field, and bind the Focus Hook to it:

   ```
   return (
       <div>
           <input {...bind} value={focused ? 'focused' : 'not
   focused'} />
       </div>
   )
   }
   ```

As we can see, the Focus Hook makes it much easier to handle focus events. There is no need to define our own handler functions anymore.

The useHover Hook

In order to know whether the user is currently hovering over an element, we can use the useHover Hook, as follows:

1. First, we import the useHover Hook:

```
import React from 'react'
import { useHover } from 'react-hookedup'
```

2. Then, we define our component and the Hover Hook, which returns the hovered value and a bind function, to bind the Hook to an element:

```
export default function UseHover () {
    const { hovered, bind } = useHover()
```

3. Finally, we render an element, and bind the Hover Hook to it:

```
return (
    <div {...bind}>Hover me {hovered && 'THANKS!!!'}</div>
)
}
```

As we can see, the Hover Hook makes it much easier to handle hover events. There is no need to define our own handler functions anymore.

Example code

The example code can be found in the Chapter08/chapter8_3 folder.

Just run npm install in order to install all dependencies and npm start to start the application, and then visit http://localhost:3000 in your browser (if it does not open automatically).

Responsive design with Hooks

In web apps, it is often important to have a responsive design. Responsive design makes your web app render well on various devices and window/screen sizes. Our blog app might be viewed on a desktop, a mobile phone, a tablet, or maybe even a very large screen, such as a TV.

Often, it makes the most sense to simply use CSS media queries for responsive design. However, sometimes that is not possible, for example, when we render elements within a canvas or **Web Graphics Library** (**WebGL**). Sometimes, we also want to use the window size in order to decide whether to load a component or not, instead of simply rendering it and then hiding it via CSS later.

The `@rehooks/window-size` library provides the `useWindowSize` Hook, which returns the following values:

- `innerWidth`: Equal to the `window.innerWidth` value
- `innerHeight`: Equal to the `window.innerHeight` value
- `outerWidth`: Equal to the `window.outerWidth` value
- `outerHeight`: Equal to the `window.outerHeight` value

To show the difference between `outerWidth`/`outerHeight`, and `innerWidth`/`innerHeight`, take a look at the following diagram:

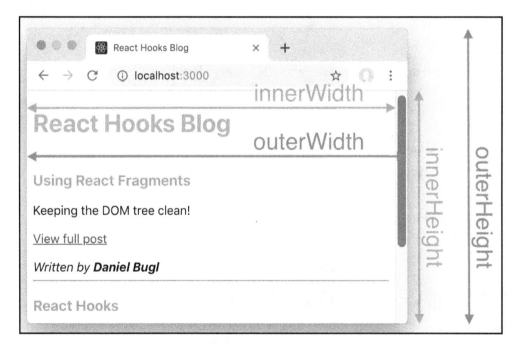

Visualization of the window width/height properties

As we can see, `innerHeight` and `innerWidth` specify the innermost part of the browser window, while `outerHeight` and `outerWidth` specify the full dimensions of the browser window, including the URL bar, scroll bars, and so on.

We are now going to hide components based on the window size in our blog app.

Responsively hiding components

In our blog app, we are going to hide the `UserBar` and `ChangeTheme` components completely when the screen size is very small so that, when reading a post on a mobile phone, we can focus on the content.

Let's get started implementing the Window Size Hook:

1. First, we have to install the `@rehooks/window-size` library:

    ```
    > npm install --save @rehooks/window-size
    ```

2. Then, we import the `useWindowSize` Hook at the start of the `src/pages/HeaderBar.js` file:

    ```
    import useWindowSize from '@rehooks/window-size'
    ```

3. Next, we define the following Window Size Hook after the existing Context Hooks:

    ```
    const { innerWidth } = useWindowSize()
    ```

4. If the window width is smaller than `640` pixels, we assume that the device is a mobile phone:

    ```
    const mobilePhone = innerWidth < 640
    ```

5. Finally, we only show the `ChangeTheme` and `UserBar` components when we are not on a mobile phone:

    ```
    {!mobilePhone && <ChangeTheme theme={theme}
    setTheme={setTheme} />}
    {!mobilePhone && <br />}
    {!mobilePhone && <React.Suspense
    fallback={"Loading..."}>
        <UserBar />
    </React.Suspense>}
    {!mobilePhone && <br />}
    ```

If we now resize our browser window to a width smaller than 640 pixels, we can see that the ChangeTheme and UserBar components will not be rendered anymore:

Hiding the ChangeTheme and UserBar components on smaller screen sizes

Using the Window Size Hook, we can avoid rendering elements on smaller screen sizes.

Example code

The example code can be found in the Chapter08/chapter8_4 folder.

Just run npm install in order to install all dependencies and npm start to start the application, and then visit http://localhost:3000 in your browser (if it does not open automatically).

Undo/Redo with Hooks

In some apps, we want to implement undo/redo functionality, which means that we can go back and forth in the state of our app. For example, if we have a text editor in our blog app, we want to provide a feature to undo/redo changes. If you learned about Redux, you might already be familiar with this kind of functionality. Since React now provides a Reducer Hook, we can reimplement the same functionality using only React. The use-undo library provides exactly this functionality.

The useUndo Hook takes the default state object as an argument, and returns an array with the following contents: [state, functions].

The state object looks as follows:

- present: The current state
- past: Array of past states (when we undo, we go here)
- future: Array of future states (after undoing, we can redo to go here)

The functions object returns various functions to interact with the Undo Hook:

- set: Sets the current state, and assigns a new value to present.
- reset: Resets the current state, clears the past and future arrays (undo/redo history), and assigns a new value to present.
- undo: Undoes to the previous state (goes through the elements of the past array).
- redo: Redoes to the next state (goes through the elements of the future array).
- canUndo: Equals true if it is possible to do an undo action (past array not empty).
- canRedo: Equals true if it is possible to do a redo action (future array not empty).

We are now going to implement undo/redo functionality in our post editor.

Implementing Undo/Redo in our post editor

In the simple post editor of our blog app, we have a textarea where we can write the contents of a blog post. We are now going to implement the useUndo Hook there, so that we can undo/redo any changes that we made to the text:

1. First, we have to install the use-undo library via npm:

   > **npm install --save use-undo**

2. Then, we import the useUndo Hook from the library in src/post/CreatePost.js:

   ```
   import useUndo from 'use-undo'
   ```

3. Next, we define the Undo Hook by replacing the current `useInput` Hook. Remove the following line of code:

```
const { value: content, bindToInput: bindContent } =
useInput('')
```

Replace it with the `useUndo` Hook, as follows. We set the default state to `''`. We also save the state to `undoContent`, and get the `setContent`, `undo`, and `redo` functions, as well as the `canUndo` and `canRedo` values:

```
const [ undoContent, {
    set: setContent,
    undo,
    redo,
    canUndo,
    canRedo
} ] = useUndo('')
```

4. Now, we assign the `undoContent.present` state to the `content` variable:

```
const content = undoContent.present
```

5. Next, we define a new handler function in order to update the `content` value using the `setContent` function:

```
function handleContent (e) {
    setContent(e.target.value)
}
```

6. Then, we have to replace the `bindContent` object with the `handleContent` function, as follows:

```
<textarea value={content} onChange={handleContent} />
```

7. Finally, we define buttons to **Undo/Redo** our changes, after the `textarea` element:

```
<button type="button" onClick={undo}
disabled={!canUndo}>Undo</button>
        <button type="button" onClick={redo}
disabled={!canRedo}>Redo</button>
```

It is important that `<button>` elements in a `<form>` element have a `type` attribute defined. If the `type` attribute is not defined, buttons are assumed to be `type="submit"`, which means that they will trigger the `onSubmit` handler function when clicked.

Now, after entering text we can press **Undo** to remove one character at a time, and **Redo** to add the characters again. Next, we are going to implement debouncing, which means that our changes will only be added to the undo history after a certain amount of time, not after every character that we entered.

Debouncing with Hooks

As we have seen in the previous section, when we press **Undo**, it undoes a single character at a time. Sometimes, we do not want to store every change in our undo history. To avoid storing every change, we need to implement debouncing, which means that the function that stores our content to the undo history is only called after a certain amount of time.

The use-debounce library provides the useDebounce Hook, which can be used, as follows, for simple values:

```
const [ text, setText ] = useState('')
const [ value ] = useDebounce(text, 1000)
```

Now, if we change the text via setText, the text value will be updated instantly, but the value variable will only be updated after 1000 ms (1 second).

However, for our use case, this is not enough. We are going to need debounced callbacks in order to implement debouncing in combination with use-undo. The use-debounce library also provides the useDebouncedCallback Hook, which can be used as follows:

```
const [ text, setText ] = useState('')
const [ debouncedSet, cancelDebounce ] = useDebouncedCallback(
    (value) => setText(value),
    1000
)
```

Now, if we call debouncedSet('text'), the text value will be updated after 1000 ms (1 second). If debouncedSet is called multiple times, the timeout will get reset every time, so that only after 1000 ms of no further calls to the debouncedSet function, the setText function will be called. Next, we are going to move on to implementing debouncing in our post editor.

Debouncing changes in our post editor

Now that we have learned about debouncing, we are going to implement it in combination with the Undo Hook in our post editor, as follows:

1. First, we have to install the `use-debounce` library via npm:

   ```
   > npm install --save use-debounce
   ```

2. In `src/post/CreatePost.js`, first make sure that you import the `useState` Hook, if it is not imported already:

   ```
   import React, { useState, useContext, useEffect } from 'react'
   ```

3. Next, import the `useDebouncedCallback` Hook from the `use-debounce` library:

   ```
   import { useDebouncedCallback } from 'use-debounce'
   ```

4. Now, before the Undo Hook, define a new State Hook, which we are going to use for the non-debounced value, to update the `input` field:

   ```
   const [ content, setInput ] = useState('')
   ```

5. After the Undo Hook, we remove the assignment of the `content` value. Remove the following code:

   ```
   const content = undoContent.present
   ```

6. Now, after the Undo Hook, define the Debounced Callback Hook:

   ```
   const [ setDebounce, cancelDebounce ] = useDebouncedCallback(
   ```

7. Within the Debounced Callback Hook, we define a function in order to set the content of the Undo Hook:

   ```
   (value) => {
       setContent(value)
   },
   ```

8. We trigger the `setContent` function after `200` ms:

```
        200
    )
```

9. Next, we have to define an Effect Hook, which will trigger whenever the undo state changes. In this Effect Hook, we cancel the current debouncing, and set the `content` value to the current `present` value:

```
useEffect(() => {
    cancelDebounce()
    setInput(undoContent.present)
}, [undoContent])
```

10. Finally, we adjust the `handleContent` function in order to trigger the `setInput` function, as well as the `setDebounce` function:

```
function handleContent (e)
    const { value } = e.target
    setInput(value)
    setDebounce(value)
}
```

As a result, we instantly set the input `value`, but we do not store anything to the undo history yet. After the debouncing callback triggers (after `200` ms), we store the current value to the undo history. Whenever the undo state updates, for example, when we press the **Undo/Redo** buttons, we cancel the current debouncing to avoid overwriting the value after undoing/redoing. Then, we set the `content` value to the new `present` value of the Undo Hook.

If we now type some text into our editor, we can see that the **Undo** button only activates after a while. It then looks like this:

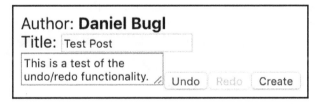

Undo button activated after typing some text

If we now press the **Undo** button, we can see that we will not undo character by character, but more text at once. For example, if we press **Undo** three times, we get the following result:

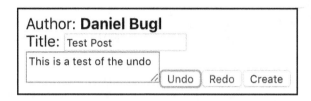

Going back in time using the Undo button

As we can see, **Undo/Redo** and debouncing now work perfectly fine!

Example code

The example code can be found in the `Chapter08/chapter8_5` folder.

Just run `npm install` in order to install all dependencies and `npm start` to start the application, and then visit `http://localhost:3000` in your browser (if it does not open automatically).

Finding other Hooks

There are many other Hooks that are provided by the community. You can find a searchable list of various Hooks on the following page: `https://nikgraf.github.io/react-hooks/`.

To give you an idea of which other Hooks are out there, the following features are provided by community Hooks. We now list a couple more interesting Hooks provided by the community. Of course, there are many more Hooks to be found:

- `use-events` (`https://github.com/sandiiarov/use-events`): Various JavaScript events that have been turned into Hooks, such as mouse position, touch events, clicking outside, and so on.
- `react-apollo-hooks` (`https://github.com/trojanowski/react-apollo-hooks`): Use Apollo Client (a caching **GraphQL** client) with React Hooks.

- `react-use` (https://github.com/streamich/react-use): Various Hooks to deal with sensors (`useBattery`, `useIdle`, `useGeolocation`, and so on), UI (`useAudio`, `useCss`, `useFullscreen`, and so on), animations (`useSpring`, `useTween`, `useRaf`, and so on), and side effects (`useAsync`, `useDebounce`, `useFavicon`, and so on).
- `react-use-clipboard` (https://github.com/danoc/react-use-clipboard): Clipboard functionality to copy text.

Summary

In this chapter, we first learned about the `react-hookedup` library. We used this library to simplify input handling with Hooks in our blog app. Then, we had a look at implementing various React life cycles with Hooks. Next, we covered various useful Hooks, such as the `usePrevious` Hook, Interval/Timeout Hooks, the Online Status Hook, data manipulation Hooks, and the Focus and Hover Hooks. Afterward, we covered responsive design using Hooks, by not rendering certain components on mobile phones. Finally, we learned about implementing undo/redo functionality and debouncing using Hooks.

Using community Hooks is a very important skill, as React only provides a handful of Hooks out of the box. In real applications, you will probably be using many Hooks that are provided by the community, from various libraries and frameworks. We also learned about various community Hooks that will make our life so much easier when writing React applications.

In the next chapter, we will gain an in-depth knowledge about the rules of Hooks, which are important to know before we can start writing our own Hooks.

Questions

In order to recap what we have learned in this chapter, try answering the following questions:

1. Which Hook can we use to simplify input field handling?
2. How are the `componentDidMount` and `componentWillUnmount` life cycles implemented using Effect Hooks?
3. How can we use Hooks to get the behavior of `this.setState()`?

4. Why should we use timer Hooks instead of calling `setTimeout` and `setInterval` directly?
5. Which Hooks can we use to simplify dealing with common data structures?
6. When should we use responsive design with Hooks, versus simply using CSS media queries?
7. Which Hook can we use to implement undo/redo functionality?
8. What is debouncing? Why do we need to do it?
9. Which Hooks can we use for debouncing?

Further reading

If you are interested in more information about the concepts that we have learned in this chapter, take a look at the following reading material:

- `react-hookedup` library documentation: `https://github.com/zakariaharti/react-hookedup`
- `window-size` library documentation: `https://github.com/rehooks/window-size`
- `use-undo` library documentation: `https://github.com/xxhomey19/use-undo`
- `use-debounce` library documentation: `https://github.com/xnimorz/use-debounce.`
- Collection of React Hooks: `https://nikgraf.github.io/react-hooks/`
- *Learning Redux* book published by *Packt* for more in-depth information about undo/redo functionality: `https://www.packtpub.com/web-development/learning-redux`

Rules of Hooks

In the previous chapter, we learned about using various Hooks that have been developed by the React community, as well as where to find more of them. We learned about replacing React life cycle methods with Hooks, utility and data management Hooks, responsive design with Hooks, and implementing undo/redo functionality with Hooks. Finally, we learned where to find other Hooks.

In this chapter, we are going to learn about everything that there is to know about using Hooks, and what to watch out for when using and developing our own Hooks. Hooks have certain limitations regarding the order that they are called. Violating the rules of Hooks can cause bugs or unexpected behavior, so we need to make sure that we learn and enforce the rules.

The following topics will be covered in this chapter:

- Calling Hooks
- Order of Hooks
- Names of Hooks
- Enforcing the rules of Hooks
- Dealing with `useEffect` dependencies

Technical requirements

A fairly recent version of Node.js should already be installed (v11.12.0 or higher). The `npm` package manager for Node.js also needs to be installed.

The code for this chapter can be found on the GitHub repository: `https://github.com/PacktPublishing/Learn-React-Hooks/tree/master/Chapter09`.

Check out the following video to see the code in action:

`http://bit.ly/2Mm9yoC`

 Please note that it is highly recommended that you write the code on your own. Do not simply run the code examples that have been provided. It is important to write the code yourself in order to learn and understand properly. However, if you run into any issues, you can always refer to the code example.

Now, let's get started with the chapter.

Calling Hooks

Hooks should only be called in *React function components* or *custom Hooks*. They cannot be used in class components or regular JavaScript functions.

Hooks can be called at the top level of the following:

- React function components
- Custom Hooks (we are going to learn about creating custom Hooks in the next chapter)

As we can see, Hooks are mostly normal JavaScript functions, except that they rely on being defined in a React function component. Of course, custom Hooks that use other Hooks can be *defined* outside of React function components, but when *using* Hooks, we always need to make sure that we call them inside a React function component. Next, we are going to learn about the rules regarding the order of Hooks.

Order of Hooks

Only call Hooks **at the top level/beginning** of function components or custom Hooks.

Do not call Hooks inside conditions, loops, or nested functions—doing so changes the order of Hooks, which causes bugs. We have already learned that changing the order of Hooks causes the state to get mixed up between multiple Hooks.

In `Chapter 2`, *Using the State Hook,* we learned that we cannot do the following:

```
const [ enableFirstName, setEnableFirstName ] = useState(false)
const [ name, setName ] = enableFirstName
    ? useState('')
    : [ '', () => {} ]
const [ lastName, setLastName ] = useState('')
```

We rendered a checkbox and two input fields for the `firstName` and `lastName`, and then we entered some text in the `lastName` field:

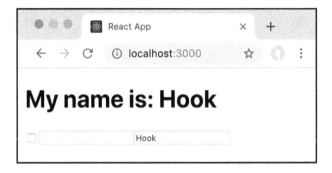

Revisiting our example from Chapter 2, Using the State Hook

At the moment, the order of Hooks is as follows:

1. `enableFirstName`
2. `lastName`

Next, we clicked on the checkbox to enable the `firstName` field. Doing so changed the order of Hooks, because now our Hook definitions look like this:

1. `enableFirstName`
2. `firstName`
3. `lastName`

Since React solely relies on the order of Hooks to manage their state, the `firstName` field is now the second Hook, so it gets the state from the `lastName` field:

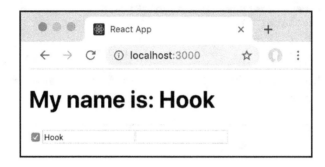

Problem of changing the order of Hooks from Chapter 2, Using the State Hook

If we use the real `useState` Hook from React in example 2 *Can we define conditional Hooks?* from `Chapter 2`, *Using the State Hook*, we can see that React automatically detects when the order of Hooks has changed, and it will show a warning:

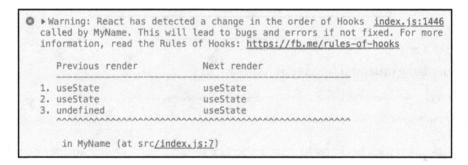

React printing a warning when detecting that the order of Hooks has changed

When running React in development mode, it will additionally crash with an **Uncaught Invariant Violation** error message when rendering more Hooks than in the previous render:

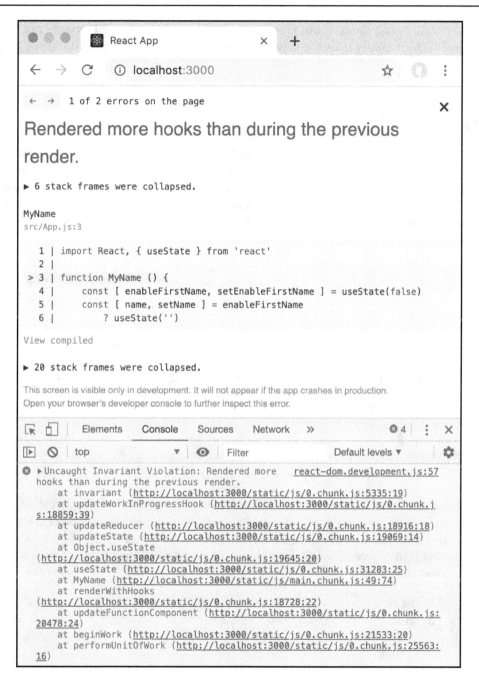

React crashing in development mode when the number of Hooks changed

As we can see, changing the order of Hooks or conditionally enabling Hooks is not possible, as React internally uses the order of Hooks to keep track of which data belongs to which Hook.

Names of Hooks

There is a convention that Hook functions should always be prefixed with use, followed by the Hook name starting with a capital letter; for example: useState, useEffect, and useResource. This is important, because otherwise we would not know which JavaScript functions are Hooks, and which are not. Especially when enforcing the rules of Hooks, we need to know which functions are Hooks so that we can make sure they are not being called conditionally or in loops.

As we can see, naming conventions are not technically required, but they make life a lot easier for developers. Knowing the difference between normal functions and Hooks makes it very easy to automatically enforce the rules of Hooks. In the next section, we are going to learn how to automatically enforce the rules using the eslint tool.

Enforcing the rules of Hooks

If we stick to the convention of prefixing Hook functions with use, we can automatically enforce the other two rules:

- Only call Hooks from React function components or custom Hooks
- Only call Hooks at the top level (not inside loops, conditions, or nested functions)

In order to enforce the rules automatically, React provides an eslint plugin called eslint-plugin-react-hooks, which will automatically detect when Hooks are used, and will ensure that the rules are not broken. ESLint is a linter, which is a tool that analyzes source code and finds problems such as stylistic mistakes, potential bugs, and programming errors.

 In the future, create-react-app is going to include this plugin by default.

Setting up eslint-plugin-react-hooks

We are now going to set up the React Hooks `eslint` plugin to automatically enforce the rules of Hooks.

Let's start installing and enabling the `eslint` plugin:

1. First, we have to install the plugin via `npm`:

    > **npm install --save-dev eslint-plugin-react-hooks**

    We use the `--save-dev` flag here, because `eslint` and its plugins are not required to be installed when deploying the app. We only need them during the development of our app.

2. Then, we create a new `.eslintrc.json` file in the root of our project folder, with the following contents. We start by extending from the `react-app` ESLint configuration:

    ```
    {
        "extends": "react-app",
    ```

3. Next, we include the `react-hooks` plugin that we installed earlier:

    ```
    "plugins": [
        "react-hooks"
    ],
    ```

4. Now we enable two rules. First, we tell `eslint` to show an error when we violate the `rules-of-hooks` rule. Additionally, we enable the `exhaustive-deps` rule as a warning:

    ```
    "rules": {
        "react-hooks/rules-of-hooks": "error",
        "react-hooks/exhaustive-deps": "warn"
    }
    }
    ```

5. Finally, we adjust `package.json` to define a new `lint` script, which is going to call `eslint`:

    ```
    "scripts": {
        "lint": "npx eslint src/",
    ```

Now, we can execute `npm run lint`, and we are going to see that there are **5 warnings** and **0 errors**:

```
● ● ● 1. fish /Users/dan/Development/Hands-On-Web-Development-with-Hooks/Chapter09/chapter...
dan@galaxy ~/D/H/C/chapter9_1 (master)> npm run lint

> chapter8_5@1.0.0 lint /Users/dan/Development/Hands-On-Web-Development-with-Hoo
ks/Chapter09/chapter9_1
> npx eslint src/


/Users/dan/Development/Hands-On-Web-Development-with-Hooks/Chapter09/chapter9_1/
src/pages/HomePage.js
  22:8  warning  React Hook useEffect has a missing dependency: 'dispatch'. Eith
er include it or remove the dependency array  react-hooks/exhaustive-deps

/Users/dan/Development/Hands-On-Web-Development-with-Hooks/Chapter09/chapter9_1/
src/post/CreatePost.js
  32:6  warning  React Hook useEffect has a missing dependency: 'cancelDebounce'
. Either include it or remove the dependency array  react-hooks/exhaustive-deps
  46:6  warning  React Hook useEffect has a missing dependency: 'navigation'. Ei
ther include it or remove the dependency array       react-hooks/exhaustive-deps

/Users/dan/Development/Hands-On-Web-Development-with-Hooks/Chapter09/chapter9_1/
src/user/Login.js
  30:6  warning  React Hook useEffect has a missing dependency: 'dispatch'. Eith
er include it or remove the dependency array  react-hooks/exhaustive-deps

/Users/dan/Development/Hands-On-Web-Development-with-Hooks/Chapter09/chapter9_1/
src/user/Register.js
  23:8  warning  React Hook useEffect has a missing dependency: 'dispatch'. Eith
er include it or remove the dependency array  react-hooks/exhaustive-deps

✖ 5 problems (0 errors, 5 warnings)
  0 errors and 5 warnings potentially fixable with the `--fix` option.
```

Executing ESLint with the react-hooks plugin

We will now try to break the rules of Hooks; for example, by editing
`src/user/Login.js` and making the second Input Hook conditional:

```
const { value: password, bindToInput: bindPassword } = loginFailed ?
useInput('') : [ '', () => {} ]
```

When we execute `npm run lint` again, we can see that there is now an error:

```
● ● ●    1. fish  /Users/dan/Development/Hands-On-Web-Development-with-Hooks/Chapter09/chapter9_1 (fish)
/Users/dan/Development/Hands-On-Web-Development-with-Hooks/Chapter09/chapter9_1/src/u
ser/Login.js
  11:72   error     React Hook "useInput" is called conditionally. React Hooks must be
called in the exact same order in every component render   react-hooks/rules-of-hooks
  30:6    warning   React Hook useEffect has a missing dependency: 'dispatch'. Either i
nclude it or remove the dependency array                    react-hooks/exhaustive-deps

/Users/dan/Development/Hands-On-Web-Development-with-Hooks/Chapter09/chapter9_1/src/u
ser/Register.js
  23:8    warning   React Hook useEffect has a missing dependency: 'dispatch'. Either in
clude it or remove the dependency array   react-hooks/exhaustive-deps

✖ 6 problems (1 error, 5 warnings)
  0 errors and 5 warnings potentially fixable with the `--fix` option.

npm ERR! code ELIFECYCLE
npm ERR! errno 1
npm ERR! chapter8_5@1.0.0 lint: `npx eslint src/`
npm ERR! Exit status 1
npm ERR!
npm ERR! Failed at the chapter8_5@1.0.0 lint script.
npm ERR! This is probably not a problem with npm. There is likely additional logging
output above.

npm ERR! A complete log of this run can be found in:
npm ERR!     /Users/dan/.npm/_logs/2019-06-23T12_51_52_877Z-debug.log
dan@galaxy ~/D/H/C/chapter9_1 (master) [1]>
```

Executing ESLint after breaking the rules of Hooks

As we can see, `eslint` helps us by forcing us to stick to the rules of Hooks. The linter will throw an error when we violate any rules, and show warnings when Effect Hooks have missing dependencies. Listening to `eslint` will help us to avoid bugs and unexpected behavior, so we should never ignore its errors or warnings.

Example code

The example code can be found in the `Chapter09/chapter9_1` folder.

Just run `npm install` in order to install all dependencies and execute `npm run lint` to run the linter.

Dealing with useEffect dependencies

In addition to enforcing the rules of Hooks, we are also checking whether all the variables that are used in an Effect Hook are passed to its dependency array. This *exhaustive dependencies* rule ensures that whenever something that is used inside the Effect Hook changes (a function, value, and so on), the Hook will trigger again.

As we have seen in the previous section, there are a couple warnings related to the exhaustive dependencies rule when running the linter with `npm run lint`. Often, it has to do with the `dispatch` function or other functions not being part of the dependency array. Usually, these functions should not change, but we can never be sure, so it is better to just add them to the dependencies.

Automatically fixing warnings with eslint

As the exhaustive dependencies rule is quite simple and straightforward to fix, we can automatically let `eslint` fix it.

To do so, we need to pass the `--fix` flag to `eslint`. Using `npm run`, we can pass flags by using an additional `--` as a separator, as follows:

```
> npm run lint -- --fix
```

After running the preceding command, we can run `npm run lint` again, and we are going to see that all warnings have automatically been fixed:

No warnings after letting eslint fix them

As we can see, `eslint` not only warns us about problems, it can even fix some of them automatically for us!

Example code

The example code can be found in the `Chapter09/chapter9_2` folder.

Just run `npm install` in order to install all dependencies and execute `npm run lint` to run the linter.

Summary

In this chapter, we first learned about two rules of Hooks: that we should only call Hooks from React function components, and that we need to ensure that the order of Hooks stays the same. Furthermore, we learned about the naming convention of Hooks, and that they should always start with the `use` prefix. Then, we learned how to enforce the rules of Hooks using `eslint`. Finally, we learned about `useEffect` dependencies, and how to fix missing dependencies automatically using `eslint`.

Knowing about the rules of Hooks, and enforcing them, is very important in order to avoid bugs and unexpected behavior. These rules will be especially important when creating our own Hooks. Now that we have a good grasp on how Hooks work, including their rules and conventions, in the next chapter, we are going to learn how to create our own Hooks!

Questions

In order to recap what we have learned in this chapter, try answering the following questions:

1. Where can Hooks be called?
2. Can we use Hooks in React class components?
3. What do we need to watch out for regarding the order of Hooks?
4. Can Hooks be called inside conditions, loops, or nested functions?
5. What is the naming convention for Hooks?
6. How can we automatically enforce the rules of Hooks?
7. What is the exhaustive dependencies rule?
8. How can we automatically fix linter warnings?

Further reading

If you are interested in more information about the concepts that we have learned in this chapter, take a look at the following reading material:

- Rules of Hooks in the official React documentation: `https://reactjs.org/docs/hooks-rules.html`.
- Official website of ESLint: `https://eslint.org/`.

10
Building Your Own Hooks

In the previous chapter, we learned about the limitations and rules of Hooks. We learned where to call Hooks, why the order of Hooks matters, and the naming conventions for Hooks. Finally, we learned about enforcing the rules of Hooks and dealing with `useEffect` dependencies.

In this chapter, we are going to learn how to create custom Hooks by extracting existing code from our components. We are also going to learn how to use custom Hooks and how Hooks can interact with each other. Then, we are going to learn how to write tests for our custom Hooks. Finally, we are going to learn about the full React Hooks API.

The following topics will be covered in this chapter:

- Extracting custom Hooks
- Using custom Hooks
- Interactions between Hooks
- Testing Hooks
- Exploring the React Hooks API

Technical requirements

A fairly recent version of Node.js should already be installed (v11.12.0 or higher). The npm package manager for Node.js also needs to be installed.

The code for this chapter can be found on GitHub: `https://github.com/PacktPublishing/Learn-React-Hooks/tree/master/Chapter10`.

Check out the following video to see the code in action:

`http://bit.ly/2Mm9yoC`

 Please note that it is highly recommended that you write the code on your own. Do not simply run the code examples provided previously. It is important to write the code yourself in order to learn and understand properly. However, if you run into any issues, you can always refer to the code example.

Now let's get started with the chapter.

Extracting custom Hooks

After getting a good grasp on the concept of Hooks by learning about the State and Effect Hooks, community Hooks, and the rules of Hooks, we are now going to build our own Hooks. We start by extracting custom Hooks from existing functionalities of our blog application. Usually, it makes the most sense to first write the component, and then later extract a custom Hook from it if we notice that we use similar code across multiple components. Doing so avoids prematurely defining custom Hooks and making our project unnecessarily complex.

We are going to extract the following Hooks in this section:

- A useTheme Hook
- The useUserState and usePostsState Hooks
- A useDispatch Hook
- API Hooks
- A useDebouncedUndo Hook

Creating a useTheme Hook

In many components, we use the `ThemeContext` to style our blog app. Functionality that is used across multiple components is usually a good opportunity for creating a custom Hook. As you might have noticed, we often do the following:

```
import { ThemeContext } from '../contexts'

export default function SomeComponent () {
    const theme = useContext(ThemeContext)

    // ...
```

We could abstract this functionality into a `useTheme` Hook, which will get the `theme` object from the `ThemeContext`.

Let's start creating a custom `useTheme` Hook:

1. Create a new `src/hooks/` directory, which is where we are going to put our custom Hooks.
2. Create a new `src/hooks/useTheme.js` file.
3. In this newly created file, we first import the `useContext` Hook and the `ThemeContext` as follows:

   ```
   import { useContext } from 'react'
   import { ThemeContext } from '../contexts'
   ```

4. Next, we export a new function called `useTheme`; this will be our custom Hook. Remember, Hooks are just functions prefixed with the `use` keyword:

   ```
   export default function useTheme () {
   ```

5. In our custom Hook, we can now use the essential Hooks provided by React to build our own Hook. In our case, we simply return the `useContext` Hook:

   ```
       return useContext(ThemeContext)
   }
   ```

As we can see, custom Hooks can be quite simple. In this case, the custom Hook only returns a Context Hook with the `ThemeContext` passed to it. Nevertheless, this makes our code more concise and easier to change later. Furthermore, by using a `useTheme` Hook, it is clear that we want to access the theme, which means our code will be easier to read and reason about.

Creating global state Hooks

Another thing that we often do is access the global state. For example, some components need the `user` state and some need the `posts` state. To abstract this functionality, which will also make it easier to adjust the state structure later on, we can create custom Hooks to get certain parts of the state:

- `useUserState`: Gets the `user` part of the `state` object
- `usePostsState`: Gets the `posts` part of the `state` object

Defining the useUserState Hook

Repeating a similar process to what we did for the `useTheme` Hook, we import the `useContext` Hook from React and the `StateContext`. However, instead of returning the result of the Context Hook, we now pull out the `state` object via destructuring and then return `state.user`.

Create a new `src/hooks/useUserState.js` file with the following contents:

```
import { useContext } from 'react'
import { StateContext } from '../contexts'

export default function useUserState () {
    const { state } = useContext(StateContext)
    return state.user
}
```

Similarly to the `useTheme` Hook, the `useUserState` Hook makes our code more concise, easier to change later, and improves readability.

Defining the usePostsState Hook

We repeat the same process for the `posts` state. Create a new `src/hooks/usePostsState.js` file with the following contents:

```
import { useContext } from 'react'
import { StateContext } from '../contexts'

export default function usePostsState () {
    const { state } = useContext(StateContext)
    return state.posts
}
```

Similarly to the `useTheme` and `useUserState` Hooks, the `usePostsState` Hook makes our code more concise, easier to change later, and improves readability.

Creating a useDispatch Hook

In many components, we need the `dispatch` function to do certain actions, so we often have to do the following:

```
import { StateContext } from '../contexts'

export default function SomeComponent () {
    const { dispatch } = useContext(StateContext)

    // ...
```

We can abstract this functionality into a `useDispatch` Hook, which will get the `dispatch` function from our global state context. Doing this will also make it easier to replace the state management implementation later on. For example, later on, we could replace our simple Reducer Hook with a state management library such as Redux or MobX.

Let's define the `useDispatch` Hook now using the following steps:

1. Create a new `src/hooks/useDispatch.js` file.
2. Import the `useContext` Hook from React and the `StateContext` as follows:

   ```
   import { useContext } from 'react'
   import { StateContext } from '../contexts'
   ```

3. Next, we define and export the `useDispatch` function; here, we allow passing a different `context` as an argument for making the Hook more generic (in case we want to use the `dispatch` function from a local state context later on). However, we set the default value of the `context` argument to the `StateContext` like so:

   ```
   export default function useDispatch (context = StateContext) {
   ```

4. Finally, we pull out the `dispatch` function from the Context Hook via destructuring and return it with the following code:

   ```
   const { dispatch } = useContext(context)
   return dispatch
   }
   ```

As we can see, creating a custom Dispatch Hook makes our code easier to change later on, as we only need to adjust the `dispatch` function in one place.

Creating API Hooks

We can also create Hooks for the various API calls. Putting these Hooks in a single file allows us to adjust the API calls easily later on. We are going to prefix our custom API Hooks with `useAPI` so it is easy to tell which functions are API Hooks.

Let's create custom Hooks for our API now using the following steps:

1. Create a new `src/hooks/api.js` file.
2. Import the `useResource` Hook from the `react-request-hook` library as follows:

    ```
    import { useResource } from 'react-request-hook'
    ```

3. First, we define a `useAPILogin` Hook to log in a user; we simply cut and paste the existing code from the `src/user/Login.js` file like so:

    ```
    export function useAPILogin () {
        return useResource((username, password) => ({
            url:
    `/login/${encodeURI(username)}/${encodeURI(password)}`,
            method: 'get'
        }))
    }
    ```

4. Next, we define a `useAPIRegister` Hook; we simply cut and paste the existing code from the `src/user/Register.js` file as follows:

    ```
    export function useAPIRegister () {
        return useResource((username, password) => ({
            url: '/users',
            method: 'post',
            data: { username, password }
        }))
    }
    ```

5. Now we define a `useAPICreatePost` Hook, cutting and pasting the existing code from the `src/post/CreatePost.js` file, as follows:

```
export function useAPICreatePost () {
    return useResource(({ title, content, author }) => ({
        url: '/posts',
        method: 'post',
        data: { title, content, author }
    }))
}
```

6. Finally, we define a `useAPIThemes` Hook, cutting and pasting the existing code from the `src/ChangeTheme.js` file as follows:

```
export function useAPIThemes () {
    return useResource(() => ({
        url: '/themes',
        method: 'get'
    }))
}
```

As we can see, having all API-related functionality in one place makes it easier to adjust our API code later on.

Creating a useDebouncedUndo Hook

We are now going to create a slightly more advanced Hook for debounced undo functionality. We already implemented this functionality in the `CreatePost` component. Now, we are going to extract this functionality into a custom `useDebouncedUndo` Hook.

Let's create the `useDebouncedUndo` Hook with the following steps:

1. Create a new `src/hooks/useDebouncedUndo.js` file.
2. Import the `useState`, `useEffect`, and `useCallback` Hooks from React, as well as the `useUndo` Hook and the `useDebouncedCallback` Hook:

```
import { useState, useEffect, useCallback } from 'react'
import useUndo from 'use-undo'
import { useDebouncedCallback } from 'use-debounce'
```

3. Now we are going to define the `useDebouncedUndo` function, which accepts a `timeout` argument for the debounced callback:

```
export default function useDebouncedUndo (timeout = 200) {
```

4. In this function, we copy over the `useState` Hook from the previous implementation, as shown here:

```
const [ content, setInput ] = useState('')
```

5. Next, we copy over the `useUndo` Hook; however, this time, we store all other undo-related functions in an `undoRest` object:

```
const [ undoContent, { set: setContent, ...undoRest } ] =
useUndo('')
```

6. Then we copy over the `useDebouncedCallback` Hook, replacing the fixed `200` value with our `timeout` argument:

```
const [ setDebounce, cancelDebounce ] = useDebouncedCallback(
    (value) => {
        setContent(value)
    },
    timeout
)
```

7. Now we copy over the Effect Hook, as shown in the following code:

```
useEffect(() => {
    cancelDebounce()
    setInput(undoContent.present)
}, [cancelDebounce, undoContent])
```

8. Then, we define a `setter` function, which is going to set a new input `value` and call `setDebounce`. We can wrap the `setter` function with a `useCallback` Hook here to return a memoized version of the function and avoid recreating the function every time the component that uses the Hook re-renders. Similar to the `useEffect` and `useMemo` Hooks, we also pass a dependency array as the second argument of the `useCallback` Hook:

```
const setter = useCallback(function setterFn (value) {
    setInput(value)
    setDebounce(value)
}, [ setInput, setDebounce ])
```

9. Finally, we return the `content` variable (containing the current input `value`), the `setter` function, and the `undoRest` object (which contains the undo/redo functions and the `canUndo`/`canRedo` booleans):

```
return [ content, setter, undoRest ]
}
```

Creating a custom Hook for debounced undo means that we can reuse that functionality across multiple components. We could even provide this Hook as a public library, allowing others to easily implement debounced undo/redo functionality.

Exporting our custom Hooks

After creating all our custom Hooks, we are going to create an `index.js` file in our Hooks directory and re-export our Hooks there, so that we can import our custom Hooks as follows: `import { useTheme } from './hooks'`

Let's export all our custom Hooks now using the following steps:

1. Create a new `src/hooks/index.js` file.
2. In this file, we first import our custom Hooks as follows:

```
import useTheme from './useTheme'
import useDispatch from './useDispatch'
import usePostsState from './usePostsState'
import useUserState from './useUserState'
import useDebouncedUndo from './useDebouncedUndo'
```

3. Then, we re-export these imported Hooks with the following code:

```
export { useTheme, useDispatch, usePostsState, useUserState,
useDebouncedUndo }
```

4. Finally, we re-export all Hooks from the `api.js` file as follows:

```
export * from './api'
```

Now that we have exported all our custom Hooks, we can simply import Hooks directly from the `hooks` folder, making it easier to import multiple custom Hooks at once.

Example code

The example code can be found in the `Chapter10/chapter10_1` folder.

Just run `npm install` to install all dependencies and `npm start` to start the application, and then visit `http://localhost:3000` in your browser (if it does not open automatically).

Using our custom Hooks

After creating our custom Hooks, we can now start using them throughout our blog application. Using custom Hooks is quite straightforward as they are similar to community Hooks. Just like all other Hooks, custom Hooks are simply JavaScript functions.

We created the following Hooks:

- `useTheme`
- `useDispatch`
- `usePostsState`
- `useUserState`
- `useDebouncedUndo`
- `useAPILogin`
- `useAPIRegister`
- `useAPICreatePost`
- `useAPIThemes`

In this section, we are going to refactor our app to use all of our custom Hooks.

Using the useTheme Hook

Instead of using the `useContext` Hook with the `ThemeContext`, we can now use the `useTheme` Hook directly! If we end up changing the theming system later on, we can simply modify the `useTheme` Hook and our new system will be implemented throughout our application.

Let's refactor our app to use the `useTheme` Hook:

1. Edit `src/Header.js` and replace the existing imports with an import of the `useTheme` Hook. The `ThemeContext` and `useContext` imports can be removed:

   ```
   import { useTheme } from './hooks'
   ```

2. Then, replace the current Context Hook definition with the `useTheme` Hook, as shown here:

   ```
   const { primaryColor } = useTheme()
   ```

3. Now edit `src/post/Post.js` and adjust the imports similarly there:

```
import { useTheme } from './hooks'
```

4. Then, replace the `useContext` Hook with the `useTheme` Hook as follows:

```
const { secondaryColor } = useTheme()
```

As we can see, using a custom Hook makes our code much more concise and easier to read. We now move on to using the global state Hooks.

Using the global state Hooks

Similarly to what we did with the `ThemeContext`, we can also replace our state Context Hooks with the `usePostsState`, `useUserState`, and `useDispatch` Hooks. This is optimal if we want to change the state logic later. For example, if our state grows and we want to use a more sophisticated system such as Redux or MobX, then we can simply adjust the existing Hooks and everything will work the same way as before.

In this section, we are going to adjust the following components:

- `UserBar`
- `Login`
- `Register`
- `Logout`
- `CreatePost`
- `PostList`

Adjusting the UserBar component

First, we are going to adjust the `UserBar` component. Here, we can use the `useUserState` Hook by following these steps:

1. Edit `src/user/UserBar.js` and import the `useUserState` Hook:

```
import { useUserState } from '../hooks'
```

2. Then, we remove the following Hook definition:

```
const { state } = useContext(StateContext)
const { user } = state
```

3. We replace it with our custom `useUserState` Hook:

```
const user = useUserState()
```

Now the `UserBar` component makes use of our custom Hook instead of directly accessing the `user` state.

Adjusting the Login component

Next, we are going to adjust the `Login` component, where we can use the `useDispatch` Hook. This process is outlined in the following steps:

1. Edit `src/user/Login.js` and import the `useDispatch` Hook, as follows:

```
import { useDispatch } from '../hooks'
```

2. Then remove the following Context Hook:

```
const { dispatch } = useContext(StateContext)
```

3. Replace it with our custom `useDispatch` Hook:

```
const dispatch = useDispatch()
```

Now the `Login` component makes use of our custom Hook instead of directly accessing the `dispatch` function. Next, we are going to adjust the `Register` component.

Adjusting the Register component

Similarly to the `Login` component, we can also use the `useDispatch` Hook in the `Register` component, as shown in the following steps:

1. Edit `src/user/Register.js` and import the `useDispatch` Hook:

```
import { useDispatch } from '../hooks'
```

2. Then, replace the current Context Hook with our custom Dispatch Hook, as shown here:

```
const dispatch = useDispatch()
```

Now the `Register` component also makes use of our custom Hook instead of directly accessing the `dispatch` function.

Adjusting the Logout component

Then, we are going to adjust the `Logout` component to use both the `useUserState` and the `useDispatch` Hooks with the following steps:

1. Edit `src/user/Logout.js` and import the `useUserState` and `useDispatch` Hooks:

   ```
   import { useDispatch, useUserState } from '../hooks'
   ```

2. Then, replace the current Hook definitions with the following:

   ```
   const dispatch = useDispatch()
   const user = useUserState()
   ```

Now the `Logout` component makes use of our custom Hooks instead of directly accessing the `user` state and the `dispatch` function.

Adjusting the CreatePost component

Next we are going to adjust the `CreatePost` component, which is similar to what we did with the `Logout` component. This process is outlined in the following steps:

1. Edit `src/post/CreatePost.js` and import the `useUserState` and `useDispatch` Hooks:

   ```
   import { useUserState, useDispatch } from '../hooks'
   ```

2. Then, replace the current Context Hook definition with the following:

   ```
   const user = useUserState()
   const dispatch = useDispatch()
   ```

Now the `CreatePost` component makes use of our custom Hooks instead of directly accessing the `user` state and the `dispatch` function.

Adjusting the PostList component

Finally, we are going to use the `usePostsState` Hook to render the `PostList` component, as follows:

1. Edit `src/post/PostList.js` and import the `usePostsState` Hook:

   ```
   import { usePostsState } from '../hooks'
   ```

2. Then replace the current Hook definition with the following:

```
const posts = usePostsState()
```

Now the `PostList` component makes use of our custom Hook instead of directly accessing the `posts` state.

Using the API Hooks

Next, we are going to replace all the `useResource` Hooks with our custom API Hooks. Doing so allows us to have all the API calls in one file so that we can easily adjust them later on, in case the API changes.

In this section, we are going to adjust the following components:

- `ChangeTheme`
- `Register`
- `Login`
- `CreatePost`

Let's get started.

Adjusting the ChangeTheme component

First, we are going to adjust the `ChangeTheme` component and replace the Resource Hook, accessing `/themes` with our custom `useAPIThemes` Hook in the following steps:

1. In `src/ChangeTheme.js`, remove the following `useResource` Hook import statement:

```
import { useResource } from 'react-request-hook'
```

Replace it with our custom `useAPIThemes` Hook:

```
import { useAPIThemes } from './hooks'
```

2. Then, replace the `useResource` Hook definition with the following custom Hook:

```
const [ themes, getThemes ] = useAPIThemes()
```

Now the `ChangeTheme` component uses our custom API Hook to pull themes from the API.

Adjusting the Register component

Next, we are going to adjust the `Register` component with the following steps:

1. Edit `src/user/Register.js` and adjust the import statement to also import the `useAPIRegister` Hook:

   ```
   import { useDispatch, useAPIRegister } from '../hooks'
   ```

2. Then, replace the current Resource Hook with the following:

   ```
   const [ user, register ] = useAPIRegister()
   ```

Now the `Register` component uses our custom API Hook to `register` users via the API.

Adjusting the Login component

Similar to the `Register` component, we are also going to adjust the `Login` component:

1. Edit `src/user/Login.js` and adjust the import statement to also import the `useAPILogin` Hook:

   ```
   import { useDispatch, useAPILogin } from '../hooks'
   ```

2. Then, replace the current Resource Hook with the following:

   ```
   const [ user, login ] = useAPILogin()
   ```

Now the `Login` component uses our custom API Hook to log in users via the API.

Adjusting the CreatePost component

Finally, we are going to adjust the `CreatePost` component by following these steps:

1. Edit `src/post/CreatePost.js` and adjust the import statement to also import the `useAPICreatePost` Hook:

   ```
   import { useUserState, useDispatch, useAPICreatePost } from
   '../hooks'
   ```

2. Then, replace the current Resource Hook with the following:

   ```
   const [ post, createPost ] = useAPICreatePost()
   ```

Now the `CreatePost` component uses our custom API Hook to create new posts via the API.

Using the useDebouncedUndo Hook

Finally, we are going to replace all debounced undo logic in the `src/post/CreatePost.js` file with our custom `useDebouncedUndo` Hook. Doing so will make our component code much cleaner and easier to read. Furthermore, we can reuse the same debounced undo functionality in other components later.

Let's get started using the Debounced Undo Hook in the `CreatePost` component by following these steps:

1. Edit `src/post/CreatePost.js` and import the `useDebouncedUndo` Hook:

   ```
   import { useUserState, useDispatch, useDebouncedUndo,
   useAPICreatePost } from '../hooks'
   ```

2. Then, remove the following code related to debounced undo handling:

   ```
   const [ content, setInput ] = useState('')
   const [ undoContent, {
       set: setContent,
       undo,
       redo,
       canUndo,
       canRedo
   } ] = useUndo('')

   const [ setDebounce, cancelDebounce ] = useDebouncedCallback(
       (value) => {
           setContent(value)
       },
       200
   )
   useEffect(() => {
       cancelDebounce()
       setInput(undoContent.present)
   }, [cancelDebounce, undoContent])
   ```

   Replace it with our custom `useDebouncedUndo` Hook, as follows:

   ```
   const [ content, setContent, { undo, redo, canUndo, canRedo } ]
   = useDebouncedUndo()
   ```

3. Finally, remove the following setter functions in our `handleContent` function (marked in bold):

```
function handleContent (e) {
    const { value } = e.target
    setInput(value)
    setDebounce(value)
}
```

We can now use the `setContent` function provided by our custom Hook instead:

```
function handleContent (e) {
    const { value } = e.target
    setContent(value)
}
```

As you can see, our code is much cleaner, more concise, and easier to read now. Furthermore, we can reuse the Debounced Undo Hook in other components later on.

Example code

The example code can be found in the `Chapter10/chapter10_2` folder.

Just run `npm install` to install all dependencies and `npm start` to start the application, and then visit `http://localhost:3000` in your browser (if it does not open automatically).

Interactions between Hooks

Our whole blog app now works in the same way as before, but it uses our custom Hooks! Until now, we have always had Hooks that encapsulated the whole logic, with only constant values being passed as arguments to our custom Hooks. However, we can also pass values of other Hooks into custom Hooks!

 Since Hooks are simply JavaScript functions, all Hooks can accept any value as arguments and work with them: constant values, component props, or even values from other Hooks.

We are now going to create local Hooks, which means that they will be placed in the same file as the component, because they are not needed anywhere else. However, they will still make our code easier to read and maintain. These local Hooks will accept values from other Hooks as arguments.

The following local Hooks will be created:

- A local Register Effect Hook
- A local Login Effect Hook

Let's see how to create them in the following subsections.

Creating a local Register Effect Hook

First of all, we are going to extract the Effect Hook from our `Login` component to a separate `useRegisterEffect` Hook function. This function will accept the following values from other Hooks as arguments: `user` and `dispatch`.

Let's create a local Effect Hook for the `Register` component now using the following steps:

1. Edit `src/user/Register.js` and define a new function outside of the component function, right after the import statements:

    ```
    function useRegisterEffect (user, dispatch) {
    ```

2. For the contents of the function, cut the existing Effect Hook from the `Register` component and paste it here:

    ```
    useEffect(() => {
        if (user && user.data) {
            dispatch({ type: 'REGISTER', username:
    user.data.username })
        }
    }, [dispatch, user])
    }
    ```

3. Finally, define our custom `useLoginEffect` Hook where we cut out the previous Effect Hook, and pass the values from the other Hooks to it:

    ```
    useRegisterEffect(user, dispatch)
    ```

As we can see, extracting an effect into a separate function makes our code easier to read and maintain.

Creating a local Login Effect Hook

Repeating a similar process to the local Register Effect Hook, we are also going to extract the Effect Hook from our `Login` component to a separate `useLoginEffect` Hook function. This function will accept the following values from other Hooks as arguments: `user`, `dispatch`, and `setLoginFailed`.

Let's create a local Hook for the `Login` component now using the following steps:

1. Edit `src/user/Login.js` and define a new function outside of the component function, right after the import statements:

   ```
   function useLoginEffect (user, dispatch, setLoginFailed) {
   ```

2. For the contents of the function, cut the existing Effect Hook from the `Login` component and paste it here:

   ```
   useEffect(() => {
       if (user && user.data) {
           if (user.data.length > 0) {
               setLoginFailed(false)
               dispatch({ type: 'LOGIN', username:
   user.data[0].username })
           } else {
               setLoginFailed(true)
           }
       }
       if (user && user.error) {
           setLoginFailed(true)
       }
   }, [dispatch, user, setLoginFailed])
   }
   ```

   Here, we also added `setLoginFailed` to the Effect Hook dependencies. This is to make sure that whenever the `setter` function changes (which could happen eventually when using the Hook) the Hook triggers again. Always passing all dependencies of an Effect Hook, including functions, prevents bugs and unexpected behavior later on.

3. Finally, define our custom `useLoginEffect` Hook, where we cut out the previous Effect Hook, and pass the values from the other Hooks to it:

   ```
   useLoginEffect(user, dispatch, setLoginFailed)
   ```

As we can see, extracting an effect into a separate function makes our code easier to read and maintain.

Example code

The example code can be found in the `Chapter10/chapter10_3` folder.

Just run `npm install` to install all dependencies and `npm start` to start the application, and then visit `http://localhost:3000` in your browser (if it does not open automatically).

Testing Hooks

Now our blog application makes full use of Hooks! We even defined custom Hooks for various functions to make our code more reusable, concise, and easy to read.

When defining custom Hooks, it makes sense to write tests for them to ensure they work properly, even when we change them later on or add more options.

To test our Hooks, we are going to use the Jest test runner, which is included in our `create-react-app` project. However, as a result of the rules of Hooks, we cannot call Hooks from the test functions because they can only be called inside the body of a function component.

Because we do not want to create a component specifically for each test, we are going to use the React Hooks Testing Library to test Hooks directly. This library actually creates a test component and provides various utility functions to interact with the Hook.

Using the React Hooks Testing Library

In addition to the React Hooks Testing Library, we also need a special renderer for React. To render React components to the DOM, we used `react-dom`; for tests, we can use the `react-test-renderer`. We are now going to install the React Hooks Testing Library and the `react-test-renderer` via npm:

```
> npm install --save-dev @testing-library/react-hooks react-test-renderer
```

The React Hooks Testing Library should be used in the following circumstances:

- When writing libraries that define Hooks
- When you have Hooks that are used throughout multiple components (global Hooks)

However, the library should not be used when a Hook is only defined and used in a single component (local Hooks).

In that case, we should test the component directly using the React Testing Library. However, testing React components is beyond the scope of this book. More information about testing components can be found on the library website: `https://testing-library.com/docs/react-testing-library/intro`.

Testing simple Hooks

First of all, we are going to test a very simple Hook that does not make use of contexts or asynchronous code such as timeouts. To do this, we are going to create a new Hook called `useCounter`. Then, we are going to test various parts of the Hook.

The following tasks will be covered in this section:

- Creating the `useCounter` Hook
- Testing the result
- Testing Hook actions
- Testing the initial value
- Testing reset and forcing re-rendering

Let's get started now.

Creating the useCounter Hook

The `useCounter` Hook is going to provide a current `count` and functions to `increment` and `reset` the counter.

Let's create the `useCounter` Hook now using the following steps:

1. Create a new `src/hooks/useCounter.js` file.
2. Import the `useState` and `useCallback` Hooks from React as follows:

   ```
   import { useState, useCallback } from 'react'
   ```

3. We define a new `useCounter` Hook function with an argument for the `initialCount`:

   ```
   export default function useCounter (initialCount = 0) {
   ```

4. Then, we define a new State Hook for the `count` value with the following code:

```
const [ count, setCount ] = useState(initialCount)
```

5. Next, we define functions for incrementing and resetting the `count`, as shown here:

```
const increment = useCallback(() => setCount(count + 1), [])
const reset = useCallback(() => setCount(initialCount),
[initialCount])
```

6. Finally, we return the current `count` and the two functions:

```
    return { count, increment, reset }
}
```

Now that we have defined a simple Hook, we can start testing it.

Testing the useCounter Hook result

Let's now write tests for the `useCounter` Hook we created, by following these steps:

1. Create a new `src/hooks/useCounter.test.js` file.
2. Import the `renderHook` and `act` functions from the React Hooks Testing Library, as we are going to use these later:

```
import { renderHook, act } from '@testing-library/react-hooks'
```

3. Also, import the to-be-tested `useCounter` Hook, as shown here:

```
import useCounter from './useCounter'
```

4. Now we can write our first test. To define a test, we use the `test` function from Jest. The first argument is the name of the test and the second argument is a function to be run as the test:

```
test('should use counter', () => {
```

5. In this test, we use the `renderHook` function to define our Hook. This function returns an object with a `result` key, which is going to contain the result of our Hook:

```
const { result } = renderHook(() => useCounter())
```

6. Now we can check the values of the `result` object using `expect` from Jest. The `result` object contains a `current` key, which will contain the current result from the Hook:

```
    expect(result.current.count).toBe(0)
    expect(typeof result.current.increment).toBe('function')
})
```

As we can see, writing tests for Hook results is quite simple! When creating custom Hooks, especially when they are going to be used publicly, we should always write tests to ensure they work correctly.

Testing useCounter Hook actions

Using the `act` function from the React Hooks Testing Library, we can execute functions from the Hook and then check the new result.

Let's now test actions of our Counter Hook:

1. Write a new `test` function, as shown in the following code:

```
test('should increment counter', () => {
    const { result } = renderHook(() => useCounter())
```

2. Call the `increment` function of the Hook within the `act` function:

```
    act(() => result.current.increment())
```

3. Finally, we check whether the new `count` is now 1:

```
    expect(result.current.count).toBe(1)
})
```

As we can see, we can simply use the `act` function to trigger actions in our Hook and then test the value just like we did before.

Testing the useCounter initial value

We can also check the result before and after calling `act` and pass an initial value to our Hook.

Let's now test the initial value of our Hook:

1. Define a new `test` function, passing the initial value `123` to the Hook:

    ```
    test('should use initial value', () => {
        const { result } = renderHook(() => useCounter(123))
    ```

2. Now we can check if the `current` value equals the initial value, call `increment`, and ensure the `count` was increased from the initial value:

    ```
        expect(result.current.count).toBe(123)
        act(() => result.current.increment())
        expect(result.current.count).toBe(124)
    })
    ```

As we can see, we can simply pass the initial value to the Hook and check whether the value is the same.

Testing reset and forcing re-rendering

We are now going to simulate the props of a component changing. Imagine the initial value for our Hook is a prop and it is initially `0`, which then changes to `123` later on. If we reset our counter now, it should reset to `123` and not `0`. However, to do so, we need to force the re-rendering of our test component after changing the value.

Let's now test resetting and forcing the component to re-render:

1. Define the `test` function and a variable for the `initial` value:

    ```
    test('should reset to initial value', () => {
        let initial = 0
    ```

2. Next, we are going to render our Hook, but this time, we also pull out the `rerender` function via destructuring:

    ```
        const { result, rerender } = renderHook(() =>
    useCounter(initial))
    ```

3. Now we set a new `initial` value and call the `rerender` function:

```
initial = 123
rerender()
```

4. Our `initial` value should now have changed, so when we call `reset`, the `count` will be set to `123`:

```
act(() => result.current.reset())
expect(result.current.count).toBe(123)
})
```

As we can see, the testing library creates a dummy component, which is used for testing the Hook. We can force this dummy component to re-render in order to simulate what would happen when props change in a real component.

Testing Context Hooks

Using the React Hooks Testing Library, we can also test more complex Hooks, such as Hooks making use of React context. Most of the custom Hooks we created for our blog app make use of contexts, so we are now going to test those. To test Hooks that use context, we first have to create a context wrapper, and then we can test the Hook.

In this section, we are going to perform the following:

- Create a `ThemeContextWrapper` component
- Test the `useTheme` Hook
- Create a `StateContextWrapper` component
- Test the `useDispatch` Hook
- Test the `useUserState` Hook
- Test the `usePostsState` Hook

Let's get started.

Creating the ThemeContextWrapper

To be able to test the Theme Hook, we first have to set up the context and provide a wrapper component for the Hook's test component.

Let's now create the `ThemeContextWrapper` component:

1. Create a new `src/hooks/testUtils.js` file.

2. Import `React` and the `ThemeContext`, as follows:

```
import React from 'react'
import { ThemeContext } from '../contexts'
```

3. Define a new function component called `ThemeContextWrapper`; it will accept `children` as props:

```
export function ThemeContextWrapper ({ children }) {
```

 `children` is a special prop of React components. It will contain all other components passed to it as `children`; for example, `<ThemeContextWrapper>{children}</ThemeContextWrapper>`.

4. We return a `ThemeContext.Provider` with our default theme, and then pass `children` to it:

```
return (
    <ThemeContext.Provider value={{ primaryColor:
'deepskyblue', secondaryColor: 'coral' }}>
        {children}
    </ThemeContext.Provider>
)
}
```

As we can see, a context wrapper simply returns a context provider component.

Testing the useTheme Hook

Now that we have defined the `ThemeContextWrapper` component, we can make use of it while testing the `useTheme` Hook.

Let's now test the `useTheme` Hook as outlined in the following steps:

1. Create a new `src/hooks/useTheme.test.js` file.

2. Import the `renderHook` function as well as the `ThemeContextWrapper` and the `useTheme` Hook:

```
import { renderHook } from '@testing-library/react-hooks'
import { ThemeContextWrapper } from './testUtils'
import useTheme from './useTheme'
```

3. Next, define the `test` using the `renderHook` function and pass the `wrapper` as a second argument to it. Doing this will wrap the test component with the defined `wrapper` component, which means that we will be able to use the provided context in the Hook:

```
test('should use theme', () => {
    const { result } = renderHook(
        () => useTheme(),
        { wrapper: ThemeContextWrapper }
    )
```

4. Now we can check the result of our Hook, which should contain the colors defined in the `ThemeContextWrapper`:

```
expect(result.current.primaryColor).toBe('deepskyblue')
expect(result.current.secondaryColor).toBe('coral')
```

As we can see, after providing the context wrapper, we can test Hooks that use context just like we tested our simple Counter Hook.

Creating the StateContextWrapper

For the other Hooks, which make use of the `StateContext`, we have to define another wrapper to provide the `StateContext` to the Hooks.

Let's now define the `StateContextWrapper` component with the following steps:

1. Edit `src/hooks/testUtils.js` and adjust the import statements to import the `useReducer` Hook, the `StateContext`, and the `appReducer` function:

```
import React, { useReducer } from 'react'
import { StateContext, ThemeContext } from '../contexts'
import appReducer from '../reducers'
```

2. Define a new function component called `StateContextWrapper`. Here we are going to use the `useReducer` Hook to define the app state, which is similar to what we did in the `src/App.js` file:

```
export function StateContextWrapper ({ children }) {
    const [ state, dispatch ] = useReducer(appReducer, { user: '',
posts: [], error: '' })
```

3. Next, define and return the `StateContext.Provider`, which is similar to what we did for the `ThemeContextWrapper`:

```
return (
    <StateContext.Provider value={{ state, dispatch }}>
        {children}
    </StateContext.Provider>
)
}
```

As we can see, creating a context wrapper always works similarly. However, this time, we are also defining a Reducer Hook in our wrapper component.

Testing the useDispatch Hook

Now that we have defined the `StateContextWrapper`, we can use it to test the `useDispatch` Hook.

Let's test the `useDispatch` Hook with the following steps:

1. Create a new `src/hooks/useDispatch.test.js` file.

2. Import the `renderHook` function, the `StateContextWrapper` component, and the `useDispatch` Hook:

```
import { renderHook } from '@testing-library/react-hooks'
import { StateContextWrapper } from './testUtils'
import useDispatch from './useDispatch'
```

3. Then, define the `test` function, passing the `StateContextWrapper` component to it:

```
test('should use dispatch', () => {
    const { result } = renderHook(
        () => useDispatch(),
        { wrapper: StateContextWrapper }
    )
```

4. Finally, check whether the result of the Dispatch Hook is a function (the `dispatch` function):

```
        expect(typeof result.current).toBe('function')
    })
```

As we can see, using a `wrapper` component always works the same way, even if we use other Hooks within the `wrapper` component.

Testing the useUserState Hook

Using the `StateContextWrapper` and the Dispatch Hook, we can now test the `useUserState` Hook by dispatching `LOGIN` and `REGISTER` actions and checking the result. To dispatch these actions, we use the `act` function from the testing library.

Let's test the `useUserState` Hook:

1. Create a new `src/hooks/useUserState.test.js` file.
2. Import the necessary functions, the `useDispatch` and `useUserState` Hooks, and the `StateContextWrapper`:

```
    import { renderHook, act } from '@testing-library/react-hooks'
    import { StateContextWrapper } from './testUtils'
    import useDispatch from './useDispatch'
    import useUserState from './useUserState'
```

3. Next, we write a `test` that checks the initial `user` state:

```
    test('should use user state', () => {
        const { result } = renderHook(
            () => useUserState(),
            { wrapper: StateContextWrapper }
        )

        expect(result.current).toBe('')
    })
```

4. Then, we write a `test` that dispatches a `LOGIN` action and then checks the new state. Instead of returning a single Hook, we now return an object with the results of both Hooks:

```
    test('should update user state on login', () => {
        const { result } = renderHook(
            () => ({ state: useUserState(), dispatch: useDispatch() }),
            { wrapper: StateContextWrapper }
```

```
    )

        act(() => result.current.dispatch({ type: 'LOGIN', username:
    'Test User' }))
        expect(result.current.state).toBe('Test User')
    })
```

5. Finally, we write a test that dispatches a REGISTER action and then checks the new state:

```
test('should update user state on register', () => {
    const { result } = renderHook(
        () => ({ state: useUserState(), dispatch: useDispatch() }),
        { wrapper: StateContextWrapper }
    )

    act(() => result.current.dispatch({ type: 'REGISTER', username:
    'Test User' }))
        expect(result.current.state).toBe('Test User')
    })
```

As we can see, we can access both the state object and the dispatch function from our tests.

Testing the usePostsState Hook

Similarly to how we tested the useUserState Hook, we can also test the usePostsState Hook.

Let's test the usePostsState Hook now:

1. Create a new src/hooks/usePostsState.test.js file.

2. Import the necessary functions, the useDispatch and usePostsState Hooks, and the StateContextWrapper:

```
import { renderHook, act } from '@testing-library/react-hooks'
import { StateContextWrapper } from './testUtils'
import useDispatch from './useDispatch'
import usePostsState from './usePostsState'
```

3. Then, we test the initial state of the posts array:

```
test('should use posts state', () => {
    const { result } = renderHook(
        () => usePostsState(),
```

```
            { wrapper: StateContextWrapper }
        )

        expect(result.current).toEqual([])
    })
```

4. Next, we `test` whether a `FETCH_POSTS` action replaces the current `posts` array:

```
test('should update posts state on fetch action', () => {
    const { result } = renderHook(
        () => ({ state: usePostsState(), dispatch: useDispatch()
}),
        { wrapper: StateContextWrapper }
    )

    const samplePosts = [{ id: 'test' }, { id: 'test2' }]
    act(() => result.current.dispatch({ type: 'FETCH_POSTS', posts:
samplePosts }))
    expect(result.current.state).toEqual(samplePosts)
})
```

5. Finally, we `test` whether a new post gets inserted on a `CREATE_POST` action:

```
test('should update posts state on insert action', () => {
    const { result } = renderHook(
        () => ({ state: usePostsState(), dispatch: useDispatch()
}),
        { wrapper: StateContextWrapper }
    )

    const post = { title: 'Hello World', content: 'This is a test',
author: 'Test User' }
    act(() => result.current.dispatch({ type: 'CREATE_POST',
...post }))
    expect(result.current.state[0]).toEqual(post)
})
```

As we can see, the tests for the `posts` state are similar to the `user` state, but with different actions being dispatched.

Testing async Hooks

Sometimes, we need to test Hooks that do asynchronous actions. This means that we need to wait a certain period of time until we check the result. To implement tests for these kind of Hooks, we can use the `waitForNextUpdate` function from the React Hooks Testing Library.

Before we can test async Hooks, we need to learn about the new JavaScript construct called `async/await`.

The async/await construct

Normal functions are defined as follows:

```
function doSomething () {
    // ...
}
```

Normal anonymous functions are defined as follows:

```
() => {
    // ...
}
```

Asynchronous functions are defined by adding the `async` keyword:

```
async function doSomething () {
    // ...
}
```

We can also make anonymous functions asynchronous:

```
async () => {
    // ...
}
```

Within `async` functions, we can use the `await` keyword to resolve promises. We do not have to do the following anymore:

```
() => {
    fetchAPITodos ()
        .then(todos => dispatch({ type: FETCH_TODOS, todos }))
}
```

Instead, we can now do this:

```
async () => {
    const todos = await fetchAPITodos()
    dispatch({ type: FETCH_TODOS, todos })
}
```

As we can see, `async` functions make our code much more concise and easier to read! Now that we have learned about the `async`/`await` construct, we can start testing the `useDebouncedUndo` Hook.

Testing the useDebouncedUndo Hook

We are going to use the `waitForNextUpdate` function to test debouncing in our `useDebouncedUndo` Hook by following these steps:

1. Create a new `src/hooks/useDebouncedUndo.test.js` file.

2. Import the `renderHook` and `act` functions as well as the `useDebouncedUndo` Hook:

   ```
   import { renderHook, act } from '@testing-library/react-hooks'
   import useDebouncedUndo from './useDebouncedUndo'
   ```

3. First of all, we `test` whether the Hook returns a proper `result`, including the `content` value, `setter` function, and the `undoRest` object:

   ```
   test('should use debounced undo', () => {
       const { result } = renderHook(() => useDebouncedUndo())
       const [ content, setter, undoRest ] = result.current

       expect(content).toBe('')
       expect(typeof setter).toBe('function')
       expect(typeof undoRest.undo).toBe('function')
       expect(typeof undoRest.redo).toBe('function')
       expect(undoRest.canUndo).toBe(false)
       expect(undoRest.canRedo).toBe(false)
   })
   ```

4. Next, we `test` whether the `content` value gets updated immediately:

```
test('should update content immediately', () => {
    const { result } = renderHook(() => useDebouncedUndo())
    const [ content, setter ] = result.current

    expect(content).toBe('')
    act(() => setter('test'))
    const [ newContent ] = result.current
    expect(newContent).toBe('test')
})
```

Remember that we can give any name to variables we pull out from an array using destructuring. In this case, we first name the `content` variable as `content`, then, later, we name it `newContent`.

5. Finally, we use `waitForNextUpdate` to wait for the debounced effect to trigger. After debouncing, we should now be able to undo our change:

```
test('should debounce undo history update', async () => {
    const { result, waitForNextUpdate } = renderHook(() =>
useDebouncedUndo())
    const [ , setter ] = result.current

    act(() => setter('test'))

    const [ , , undoRest ] = result.current
    expect(undoRest.canUndo).toBe(false)

    await act(async () => await waitForNextUpdate())

    const [ , , newUndoRest ] = result.current
    expect(newUndoRest.canUndo).toBe(true)
})
```

As we can see, we can use `async/await` in combination with the `waitForNextUpdate` function to easily handle testing asynchronous operations in our Hooks.

Running the tests

To run the tests, simply execute the following command:

```
> npm test
```

As we can see from the following screenshot, all our tests are passing successfully:

All Hook tests passing successfully

The test suite actually watches for changes in our files and automatically reruns tests. We can use various commands to manually trigger test reruns and we can press *Q* to quit the test runner.

Example code

The example code can be found in the `Chapter10/chapter10_4` folder.

Just run `npm install` to install all dependencies and `npm start` to start the application, and then visit `http://localhost:3000` in your browser (if it does not open automatically).

Exploring the React Hooks API

The official React library provides certain built-in Hooks, which can be used to create custom Hooks. We have already learned about the three basic Hooks that React provides:

- `useState`
- `useEffect`
- `useContext`

Additionally, React provides more advanced Hooks, which can be very useful in certain use cases:

- `useReducer`
- `useCallback`
- `useMemo`
- `useRef`
- `useImperativeHandle`
- `useLayoutEffect`
- `useDebugValue`

The useState Hook

The `useState` Hook returns a value that will persist across re-renders, and a function to update it. A value for the `initialState` can be passed to it as an argument:

```
const [ state, setState ] = useState(initialState)
```

Calling `setState` updates the value and re-renders the component with the updated value. If the value did not change, React will not re-render the component.

A function can also be passed to the `setState` function, with the first argument being the current value. For example, consider the following code:

```
setState(val => val + 1)
```

Furthermore, a function can be passed to the first argument of the Hook if the initial state is the result of a complex computation. In that case, the function will only be called once during the initialization of the Hook:

```
const [ state, setState ] = useState(() => {
    return computeInitialState()
})
```

The State Hook is the most basic and ubiquitous Hook provided by React.

The useEffect Hook

The `useEffect` Hook accepts a function that contains code with side effects, such as timers and subscriptions. The function passed to the Hook will run after the render is done and the component is on the screen:

```
useEffect(() => {
    // do something
})
```

A cleanup function can be returned from the Hook, which will be called when the component unmounts and is used to, for example, clean up timers or subscriptions:

```
useEffect(() => {
    const interval = setInterval(() => {}, 100)
    return () => {
        clearInterval(interval)
    }
})
```

The cleanup function will also be called before the effect is triggered again, when dependencies of the effect update.

To avoid triggering the effect on every re-render, we can specify an array of values as the second argument to the Hook. Only when any of these values change, the effect will get triggered again:

```
useEffect(() => {
    // do something when state changes
}, [state])
```

This array passed as the second argument is called the dependency array of the effect. If you want the effect to only trigger during mounting, and the cleanup function during unmounting, we can pass an empty array as the second argument.

The useContext Hook

The `useContext` Hook accepts a context object and returns the current `value` for the context. When the context provider updates its `value`, the Hook will trigger a re-render with the latest `value`:

```
const value = useContext(NameOfTheContext)
```

It is important to note that the context object itself needs to be passed to the Hook, not the consumer or provider.

The useReducer Hook

The `useReducer` Hook is an advanced version of the `useState` Hook. It accepts a `reducer` as the first argument, which is a function with two arguments: `state` and `action`. The `reducer` function then returns the updated state computed from the current state and the action. If a reducer returns the same value as the previous state, React will not re-render components or trigger effects:

```
const [ state, dispatch ] = useReducer(reducer, initialState, initFn)
```

We should use the `useReducer` Hook instead of the `useState` Hook when dealing with complex `state` changes. Furthermore, it is easier to deal with global `state` because we can simply pass down the `dispatch` function instead of multiple setter functions.

 The `dispatch` function is stable and will not change on re-renders, so it is safe to omit it from `useEffect` or the `useCallback` dependencies.

We can specify the initial `state` by setting the `initialState` value or specifying an `initFn` function as the third argument. Specifying such a function makes sense when computing the initial `state` takes a long time or when we want to reuse the function to reset `state` through an `action`.

The useMemo Hook

The `useMemo` Hook takes a result of a function and memoizes it. This means that it will not be recomputed every time. This Hook can be used for performance optimizations:

```
const memoizedVal = useMemo(
    () => computeVal(a, b, c),
    [a, b, c]
)
```

In the previous example, `computeVal` is a performance-heavy function that computes a result from a, b, and c.

> `useMemo` runs during rendering, so make sure the computation function does not cause any side effects, such as resource requests. Side effects should be put into a `useEffect` Hook.

The array passed as the second argument specifies the dependencies of the function. If any of these values change, the function will be recomputed; otherwise, the stored result will be used. If no array is provided, a new value will be computed on every render. If an empty array is passed, the value will only be computed once.

> Do not rely on `useMemo` to only compute things once. React may forget some previously memoized values if they are not used for a long time, for example, to free up memory. Use it only for performance optimizations.

The `useMemo` Hook is used for performance optimizations in React components.

The useCallback Hook

The `useCallback` Hook works similarly to the `useMemo` Hook. However, it returns a memoized callback function instead of a value:

```
const memoizedCallback = useCallback(
    () => doSomething(a, b, c),
    [a, b, c]
)
```

The previous code is similar to the following `useMemo` Hook:

```
const memoizedCallback = useMemo(
    () => () => doSomething(a, b, c),
    [a, b, c]
)
```

The function returned will only be redefined if one of the dependency values passed in the array of the second argument changes.

The useRef Hook

The `useRef` Hook returns a ref object that can be assigned to a component or element via the `ref` prop. Refs can be used to deal with references to elements and components in React:

```
const refContainer = useRef(initialValue)
```

After assigning the ref to an element or component, the ref can be accessed via `refContainer.current`. If `InitialValue` is set, `refContainer.current` will be set to this value before assignment.

The following example defines an `input` field that will automatically be focused when rendered:

```
function AutoFocusField () {
    const inputRef = useRef(null)
    useEffect(() => inputRef.current.focus(), [])
    return <input ref={inputRef} type="text" />
}
```

It is important to note that mutating the current value of a ref does not cause a re-render. If this is needed, we should use a `ref` callback using `useCallback` as follows:

```
function WidthMeasure () {
    const [ width, setWidth ] = useState(0)

    const measureRef = useCallback(node => {
        if (node !== null) {
            setWidth(node.getBoundingClientRect().width)
        }
    }, [])

    return <div ref={measureRef}>I am {Math.round(width)}px wide</div>
}
```

Refs can be used to access the DOM, but also to keep mutable values around, such as storing references to intervals:

```
function Timer () {
    const intervalRef = useRef(null)

    useEffect(() => {
        intervalRef.current = setInterval(doSomething, 100)
        return () => clearInterval(intervalRef.current)
    })

    // ...
}
```

Using refs like in the previous example makes them similar to instance variables in classes, such as `this.intervalRef`.

The useImperativeHandle Hook

The `useImperativeHandle` Hook can be used to customize instance values that are exposed to other components when pointing a `ref` to it. Doing this should be avoided as much as possible, however, as it tightly couples components together, which harms reusability.

The `useImperativeHandle` Hook has the following signature:

```
useImperativeHandle(ref, createHandle, [dependencies])
```

We can use this Hook to, for example, expose a `focus` function that other components can trigger via a `ref` to the component. This Hook should be used in combination with `forwardRef` as follows:

```
function FocusableInput (props, ref) {
    const inputRef = useRef()
    useImperativeHandle(ref, () => ({
        focus: () => inputRef.current.focus()
    }))
    return <input {...props} ref={inputRef} />
}
FocusableInput = forwardRef(FocusableInput)
```

Then, we can access the `focus` function as follows:

```
function AutoFocus () {
    const inputRef = useRef()
    useEffect(() => inputRef.current.focus(), [])
    return <FocusableInput ref={inputRef} />
}
```

As we can see, using refs means that we can directly access elements and components.

The useLayoutEffect Hook

The `useLayoutEffect` Hook is identical to the `useEffect` Hook, but it fires synchronously after all DOM mutations are completed and before the component is rendered in the browser. It can be used to read information from the DOM and adjust the appearance of components before rendering. Updates inside this Hook will be processed synchronously before the browser renders the component.

Do not use this Hook unless it is really needed, which is only in certain edge cases. `useLayoutEffect` will block visual updates in the browser, and thus, is slower than `useEffect`.

The rule here is to use `useEffect` first. If your mutation changes the appearance of the DOM node, which can cause it to flicker, you should use `useLayoutEffect` instead.

The useDebugValue Hook

The `useDebugValue` Hook is useful for developing custom Hooks that are part of shared libraries. It can be used to show certain values for debugging in React DevTools.

For example, in our `useDebouncedUndo` custom Hook, we could do the following:

```
export default function useDebouncedUndo (timeout = 200) {
    const [ content, setInput ] = useState('')
    const [ undoContent, { set: setContent, ...undoRest } ] = useUndo('')

    useDebugValue('init')

    const [ setDebounce, cancelDebounce ] = useDebouncedCallback(
        (value) => {
            setContent(value)
            useDebugValue('added to history')
        },
```

```
        timeout
    )
    useEffect(() => {
        cancelDebounce()
        setInput(undoContent.present)
        useDebugValue(`waiting ${timeout}ms`)
    }, [cancelDebounce, undoContent])

    function setter (value) {
        setInput(value)
        setDebounce(value)
    }

    return [ content, setter, undoRest ]
}
```

Adding these `useDebugValue` Hooks will show the following in the React DevTools:

- When the Hook is initialized: **DebouncedUndo: init**
- When a value was entered: **DebouncedUndo: waiting 200 ms**
- After debouncing (after 200 ms): **DebouncedUndo: added to history**

Summary

In this chapter, we first learned how to extract custom Hooks from existing code in our blog app. We extracted various Context Hooks into custom Hooks, then created API Hooks and a more advanced Hook for debounced undo functionality. Next, we learned about interactions between Hooks and how we can use values from other Hooks in custom Hooks. We then created local Hooks for our blog app. Then, we learned about testing various Hooks with Jest and the React Hooks Testing Library. Finally, we learned about all the Hooks provided by the React Hooks API, at the time of writing.

Knowing when and how to extract custom Hooks is a very important skill in React development. In a larger project, we are probably going to define many custom Hooks, specifically tailored to our project's needs. Custom Hooks can also make it easier to maintain our application, as we only need to adjust functionality in one place. Testing custom Hooks is very important, because if we refactor our custom Hooks later on, we want to make sure that they still work properly. Now that we know the full React Hooks API, we can make use of all the Hooks that React provides to create our own custom Hooks.

In the next chapter, we are going to learn how to migrate from React class components to a Hook-based system. We will first create a small project using class components and then we will replace them with function components using Hooks, taking a closer look at the differences between the two solutions.

Questions

To recap what we have learned in this chapter, try answering the following questions:

1. How can we extract a custom Hook from existing code?
2. What is the advantage of creating API Hooks?
3. When should we extract functionality into a custom Hook?
4. How do we use custom Hooks?
5. When should we create local Hooks?
6. Which interactions between Hooks are possible?
7. Which library can we use to test Hooks?
8. How can we test Hook actions?
9. How can we test contexts?
10. How can we test asynchronous code?

Further reading

If you are interested in more information about the concepts we learned in this chapter, take a look at the following reading material:

- Creating custom Hooks: `https://reactjs.org/docs/hooks-custom.html`
- React Hooks Testing Library: `https://react-hooks-testing-library.com/`
- React Testing Library (for testing components): `https://testing-library.com/react`
- React Hooks API Reference: `https://reactjs.org/docs/hooks-reference.html`
- When to use `useCallback`: `https://kentcdodds.com/blog/usememo-and-usecallback`

Section 3: Integration and Migration

In the final part of the book, we will learn how to use existing state management solutions in combination with Hooks. Additionally, we will demonstrate how to migrate React class components, as well as existing Redux and MobX applications to Hooks.

In this section, we will cover the following chapters:

- Chapter 11, *Migrating from React Class Components*
- Chapter 12, *Redux and Hooks*
- Chapter 13, *MobX and Hooks*

11
Migrating from React Class Components

In the previous chapter we learned how to build our own Hooks by extracting custom Hooks from existing code. Then, we used our own Hooks in the blog app and learned about local Hooks and the interactions between Hooks. Finally, we learned how to write tests for Hooks using the React Hooks Testing Library, and implemented tests for our custom Hooks.

In this chapter, we are going to start by implementing a ToDo app using React class components. In the next step, we are going to learn how to migrate an existing React class component application to Hooks. Seeing the differences between function components using Hooks and class components in practice will deepen our understanding about the trade-offs of using either solution. Furthermore, by the end of this chapter we will be able to migrate existing React applications to Hooks.

The following topics will be covered in this chapter:

- Handling state with class components
- Migrating an app from class components to Hooks
- Learning about the trade-offs of class components versus Hooks

Technical requirements

A fairly recent version of Node.js should already be installed (v11.12.0 or higher). The npm package manager for Node.js also needs to be installed.

The code for this chapter can be found on the GitHub repository: https://github.com/ PacktPublishing/Learn-React-Hooks/tree/master/Chapter11.

Check out the following video to see the code in action:

http://bit.ly/2Mm9yoC

 Please note that it is highly recommended that you write the code on your own. Do not simply run the code examples that have been provided. It is important that you write the code yourself in order to be able to learn and understand properly. However, if you run into any issues, you can always refer to the code example.

Now, let's get started with the chapter.

Handling state with class components

Before we start migrating from class components to Hooks, we are going to create a small ToDo list app using React class components. In the next section, we are going to turn these class components into function components using Hooks. Finally, we are going to compare the two solutions.

Designing the app structure

As we did before with the blog app, we are going to start by thinking about the basic structure of our app. For this app, we are going to need the following features:

- A header
- A way to add new todo items
- A way to show all todo items in a list
- A filter for the todo items

It is always a good idea to start with a mock-up. So, let's begin:

1. We start by drawing a mock-up of an interface for our ToDo app:

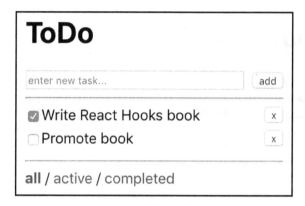

Mock-up of our ToDo app

2. Next, we define the fundamental components, in a similar way to how we did it with the blog app:

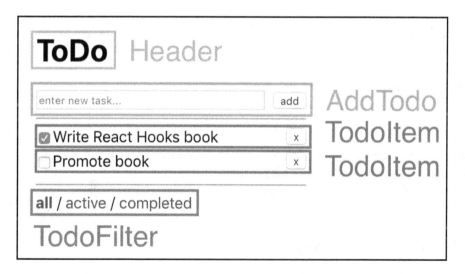

Defining fundamental components in our app mock-up

3. Now we can define the container components:

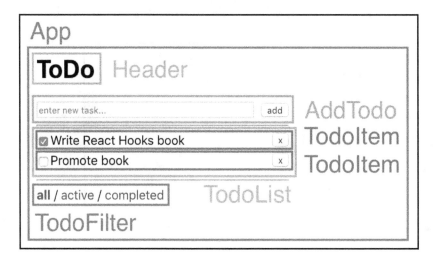

Defining container components in our app mock-up

As we can see, we are going to need the following components:

- App
- Header
- AddTodo
- TodoList
- TodoItem
- TodoFilter (+ TodoFilterItem)

The TodoList component makes use of a TodoItem component, which is used to show an item, with a checkbox to complete and a button to remove it. The TodoFilter component internally uses a TodoFilterItem component to show the various filters.

Initializing the project

We are going to use create-react-app in order to create a new project. Let's initialize the project now:

1. Run the following command:

```
> npx create-react-app chapter11_1
```

2. Then, remove `src/App.css`, as we are not going to need it.

3. Next, edit `src/index.css`, and adjust the margin as follows:

```
margin: 20px;
```

4. Finally, remove the current `src/App.js` file, as we are going to create a new one in the next step.

Now, our project has been initialized, and we can start defining the app structure.

Defining the app structure

We already know what the basic structure of our app is going to be like from the mock-up, so let's start by defining the `App` component:

1. Create a new `src/App.js` file.

2. Import `React` and the `Header`, `AddTodo`, `TodoList`, and `TodoFilter` components:

```
import React from 'react'

import Header from './Header'
import AddTodo from './AddTodo'
import TodoList from './TodoList'
import TodoFilter from './TodoFilter'
```

3. Now define the `App` component as a class component. For now, we are only going to define the `render` method:

```
export default class App extends React.Component {
    render () {
        return (
            <div style={{ width: 400 }}>
                <Header />
                <AddTodo />
                <hr />
                <TodoList />
                <hr />
                <TodoFilter />
            </div>
        )
    }
}
```

The App component defines the basic structure of our app. It will consist of a header, a way to add new todo items, a list of todo items, and a filter.

Defining the components

Now, we are going to define the components as static components. Later in this chapter, we are going to implement dynamic functionality to them. For now, we are going to implement the following static components:

- Header
- AddTodo
- TodoList
- TodoItem
- TodoFilter

Let's get started implementing the components now.

Defining the Header component

We are going to start with the Header component, as it is the most simple out of all the components:

1. Create a new src/Header.js file.
2. Import React and define the class component with a render method:

```
import React from 'react'

export default class Header extends React.Component {
    render () {
        return <h1>ToDo</h1>
    }
}
```

Now, the Header component for our app is defined.

Defining the AddTodo component

Next, we are going to define the `AddTodo` component, which renders an `input` field and a button.

Let's implement the `AddTodo` component now:

1. Create a new `src/AddTodo.js` file.
2. Import `React` and define the class component and a `render` method:

```
import React from 'react'

export default class AddTodo extends React.Component {
    render () {
        return (
```

3. In the `render` method, we return a `form` that contains an `input` field and an **add** button:

```
<form>
    <input type="text" placeholder="enter new task..."
style={{ width: 350, height: 15 }} />
    <input type="submit" style={{ float: 'right',
marginTop: 2 }} value="add" />
    </form>
    )
}
}
```

As we can see, the `AddTodo` component consists of an `input` field and a button.

Defining the TodoList component

Now, we define the `TodoList` component, which is going to make use of the `TodoItem` component. For now, we are going to statically define two todo items in this component.

Let's start defining the `TodoList` component:

1. Create a new `src/TodoList.js` file.
2. Import `React` and the `TodoItem` component:

```
import React from 'react'

import TodoItem from './TodoItem'
```

3. Then, define the class component and a `render` method:

```
export default class TodoList extends React.Component {
    render () {
```

4. In this `render` method, we statically define two todo items:

```
const items = [
    { id: 1, title: 'Write React Hooks book', completed:
true },
    { id: 2, title: 'Promote book', completed: false }
]
```

5. Finally, we are going to render the items using the `map` function:

```
return items.map(item =>
    <TodoItem {...item} key={item.id} />
)
    }
}
```

As we can see, the `TodoList` component renders a list of `TodoItem` components.

Defining the TodoItem component

After defining the `TodoList` component, we are now going to define the `TodoItem` component, in order to render single items.

Let's start defining the `TodoItem` component:

1. Create a new `src/TodoItem.js` component.
2. Import `React`, and define the component, as well as the `render` method:

```
import React from 'react'

export default class TodoItem extends React.Component {
    render () {
```

3. Now, we are going to use destructuring in order to get the `title` and `completed` props:

```
const { title, completed } = this.props
```

4. Finally, we are going to render a `div` element containing a `checkbox`, a `title`, and a `button` to delete the item:

```
return (
    <div style={{ width: 400, height: 25 }}>
        <input type="checkbox" checked={completed} />
        {title}
        <button style={{ float: 'right' }}>x</button>
    </div>
)
    }
}
```

The `TodoItem` component consists of a checkbox, a `title`, and a `button` to delete the item.

Defining the TodoFilter component

Finally, we are going to define the `TodoFilter` component. In the same file, we are going to define another component for the `TodoFilterItem`.

Let's start defining the `TodoFilterItem` and `TodoFilter` components:

1. Create a new `src/TodoFilter.js` file.
2. Define a class component for the `TodoFilterItem`:

```
class TodoFilterItem extends React.Component {
    render () {
```

3. In this `render` method, we use destructuring in order to get the `name` prop:

```
const { name } = this.props
```

4. Next, we are going to define an object for the `style`:

```
const style = {
    color: 'blue',
    cursor: 'pointer'
}
```

5. Then, we return a `span` element with the `name` value of the filter, and use the defined `style` object:

```
return <span style={style}>{name}</span>
    }
}
```

6. Finally, we can define the actual `TodoFilter` component, which is going to render three `TodoFilterItem` components, as follows:

```
export default class TodoFilter extends React.Component {
    render () {
        return (
            <div>
                <TodoFilterItem name="all" />{' / '}
                <TodoFilterItem name="active" />{' / '}
                <TodoFilterItem name="completed" />
            </div>
        )
    }
}
```

Now, we have a component that lists the three different filter possibilities: `all`, `active`, and `completed`.

Implementing dynamic code

Now that we have defined all of the static components, our app should look just like the mock-up. The next step is to implement dynamic code using React state, life cycle, and handler methods.

In this section, we are going to do the following:

- Define a mock API
- Define a `StateContext`
- Make the `App` component dynamic
- Make the `AddTodo` component dynamic
- Make the `TodoList` component dynamic
- Make the `TodoItem` component dynamic
- Make the `TodoFilter` component dynamic

Let's get started.

Defining the API code

First of all, we are going to define an API that will fetch todo items. In our case, we are simply going to return an array of todo items, after a short delay.

Let's start implementing the mock API:

1. Create a new `src/api.js` file.
2. We are going to define a function that will generate a random ID for our todo items based on the **Universally Unique Identifier (UUID)** function:

    ```
    export const generateID = () => {
        const S4 = ()
    =>(((1+Math.random())*0x10000)|0).toString(16).substring(1)
        return (S4()+S4()+"-"+S4()+"-"+S4()+"-"+S4()+"-
    "+S4()+S4()+S4())
    }
    ```

3. Then, we define the `fetchAPITodos` function, which returns a `Promise`, which resolves after a short delay:

    ```
    export const fetchAPITodos = () =>
        new Promise((resolve) =>
            setTimeout(() => resolve([
                { id: generateID(), title: 'Write React Hooks book',
    completed: true },
                { id: generateID(), title: 'Promote book', completed:
    false }
            ]), 100)
        )
    ```

Now, we have a function that simulates fetching todo items from an API, by returning an array after a delay of `100` ms.

Defining the StateContext

Next, we are going to define a context that will keep our current list of todo items. We are going to call this context `StateContext`.

Let's start implementing the `StateContext` now:

1. Create a new `src/StateContext.js` file.
2. Import `React`, as follows:

    ```
    import React from 'react'
    ```

3. Now, define the `StateContext` and set an empty array as the fallback value:

```
const StateContext = React.createContext([])
```

4. Finally, export the `StateContext`:

```
export default StateContext
```

Now, we have a context where we can store our array of todo items.

Making the App component dynamic

We are now going to make the `App` component dynamic by adding functionality to fetch, add, toggle, filter, and remove todo items. Furthermore, we are going to define a `StateContext` provider.

Let's start making the `App` component dynamic:

1. In `src/App.js`, import the `StateContext`, after the other import statements:

```
import StateContext from './StateContext'
```

2. Then, import the `fetchAPITodos` and `generateID` functions from the `src/api.js` file:

```
import { fetchAPITodos, generateID } from './api'
```

3. Next, we are going to modify our `App` class code, implementing a `constructor`, which will set the initial state:

```
export default class App extends React.Component {
    constructor (props) {
```

4. In this `constructor`, we need to first call `super`, to make sure that the parent class (`React.Component`) constructor gets called, and the component gets initialized properly:

```
super (props)
```

5. Now, we can set the initial state by setting `this.state`. Initially, there will be no todo items, and the `filter` value will be set to `'all'`:

```
        this.state = { todos: [], filteredTodos: [], filter: 'all'
    }
  }
```

6. Then, we define the `componentDidMount` life cycle method, which is going to fetch todo items when the component first renders:

```
    componentDidMount () {
        this.fetchTodos()
    }
```

7. Now, we are going to define the actual `fetchTodos` method, which in our case, is simply going to set the state, because we are not going to connect this simple app to a backend. We are also going to call `this.filterTodos()` in order to update the `filteredTodos` array after fetching todos:

```
    fetchTodos () {
        fetchAPITodos().then((todos) => {
            this.setState({ todos })
            this.filterTodos()
        })
    }
```

8. Next, we define the `addTodo` method, which creates a new item, and adds it to the state array, similar to what we did in our blog app using Hooks:

```
    addTodo (title) {
        const { todos } = this.state

        const newTodo = { id: generateID(), title, completed: false
    }

        this.setState({ todos: [ newTodo, ...todos ] })
        this.filterTodos()
    }
```

9. Then, we define the `toggleTodo` method, which uses the `map` function to find and modify a certain todo item:

```
    toggleTodo (id) {
        const { todos } = this.state

        const newTodos = todos.map(t => {
            if (t.id === id) {
```

```
                return { ...t, completed: !t.completed }
            }
            return t
        }, [])

        this.setState({ todos: newTodos })
        this.filterTodos()
    }
```

10. Now, we define the `removeTodo` method, which uses the `filter` function to find and remove a certain todo item:

```
removeTodo (id) {
    const { todos } = this.state
    const newTodos = todos.filter(t => {
        if (t.id === id) {
            return false
        }
        return true
    })

    this.setState({ todos: newTodos })
    this.filterTodos()
}
```

11. Then, we define a method to apply a certain `filter` to our todo items:

```
applyFilter (todos, filter) {
    switch (filter) {
        case 'active':
            return todos.filter(t => t.completed === false)
        case 'completed':
            return todos.filter(t => t.completed === true)
        default:
        case 'all':
            return todos
    }
}
```

12. Now, we can define the `filterTodos` method, which is going to call the `applyFilter` method, and update the `filteredTodos` array and the `filter` value:

```
filterTodos (filterArg) {
    this.setState(({ todos, filter }) => ({
        filter: filterArg || filter,
        filteredTodos: this.applyFilter(todos, filterArg ||
filter)
```

```
        }))
    }
```

 We are using `filterTodos` in order to re-filter todos after adding/removing items, as well as changing the filter. To allow both functionalities to work correctly, we need to check whether the `filter` argument, `filterArg`, was passed. If not, we fall back to the current `filter` argument from the `state`.

13. Then, we adjust the `render` method in order to use state to provide a value for the `StateContext`, and we pass certain methods to the components:

```
render () {
    const { filter, filteredTodos } = this.state
    return (
        <StateContext.Provider value={filteredTodos}>
            <div style={{ width: 400 }}>
                <Header />
                <AddTodo addTodo={this.addTodo} />
                <hr />
                <TodoList toggleTodo={this.toggleTodo}
  removeTodo={this.removeTodo} />
                <hr />
                <TodoFilter filter={filter}
  filterTodos={this.filterTodos} />
            </div>
        </StateContext.Provider>
    )
}
```

14. Finally, we need to re-bind `this` to the class, so that we can pass the methods to our components without the `this` context changing. Adjust the `constructor` as follows:

```
constructor () {
    super(props)
    this.state = { todos: [], filteredTodos: [], filter:
      'all' }

    this.fetchTodos = this.fetchTodos.bind(this)
    this.addTodo = this.addTodo.bind(this)
    this.toggleTodo = this.toggleTodo.bind(this)
    this.removeTodo = this.removeTodo.bind(this)
    this.filterTodos = this.filterTodos.bind(this)
}
```

Now, our `App` component can dynamically fetch, add, toggle, remove, and filter todo items. As we can see, when we use class components, we need to re-bind the `this` context of the handler functions to the class.

Making the AddTodo component dynamic

After making our `App` component dynamic, it is time to make all of our other components dynamic as well. We are going to start from the top, with the `AddTodo` component.

Let's make the `AddTodo` component dynamic now:

1. In `src/AddTodo.js`, we first define a `constructor`, which sets the initial `state` for the `input` field:

```
export default class AddTodo extends React.Component {
    constructor (props) {
        super(props)
        this.state = {
            input: ''
        }
    }
```

2. Then, we define a method for handling changes in the `input` field:

```
handleInput (e) {
    this.setState({ input: e.target.value })
}
```

3. Now, we are going to define a method that can handle a new todo item being added:

```
handleAdd () {
    const { input } = this.state
    const { addTodo } = this.props
    if (input) {
        addTodo(input)
        this.setState({ input: '' })
    }
}
```

4. Next, we can assign the state value and handler methods to the `input` field and button:

```
render () {
    const { input } = this.state
    return (
        <form onSubmit={e => { e.preventDefault();
this.handleAdd() }}>
            <input
                type="text"
                placeholder="enter new task..."
                style={{ width: 350, height: 15 }}
                value={input}
                onChange={this.handleInput}
            />
            <input
                type="submit"
                style={{ float: 'right', marginTop: 2 }}
                disabled={!input}
                value="add"
            />
        </form>
    )
}
```

5. Finally, we need to adjust the `constructor` in order to re-bind the `this` context for all of the handler methods:

```
constructor () {
    super(props)

    this.state = {
        input: ''
    }

    this.handleInput = this.handleInput.bind(this)
    this.handleAdd = this.handleAdd.bind(this)
}
```

Now, our `AddTodo` component will show a disabled button as long as no text is entered. When activated, clicking the button will trigger the `handleAdd` function that has been passed down from the `App` component.

Making the TodoList component dynamic

The next component in our ToDo app is the `TodoList` component. Here, we just need to get the todo items from the `StateContext`.

Let's make the `TodoList` component dynamic now:

1. In `src/TodoList.js`, we first import the `StateContext`, below the `TodoItem` import statement:

   ```
   import StateContext from './StateContext'
   ```

2. Then, we set the `contextType` to the `StateContext`, which will allow us to access the context via `this.context`:

   ```
   export default class TodoList extends React.Component {
       static contextType = StateContext
   ```

   With class components, if we want to use multiple contexts, we have to use the `StateContext.Consumer` component, as follows: `<StateContext.Consumer>{value => <div>State is: {value}</div>}</StateContext.Consumer>`.

   As you can imagine, using multiple contexts like this, will result in a very deep component tree (wrapper hell), and our code will be hard to read and refactor.

3. Now, we can get the items from `this.context` instead of statically defining them:

   ```
   render () {
       const items = this.context
   ```

4. Finally, we pass all props to the `TodoItem` component so that we can use the `removeTodo` and `toggleTodo` methods there:

   ```
   return items.map(item =>
       <TodoItem {...item} {...this.props} key={item.id} />
   )
   }
   ```

Now, our `TodoList` component gets the items from the `StateContext` instead of statically defining them.

Making the TodoItem component dynamic

Now that we have passed on the `removeTodo` and `toggleTodo` methods as props to the `TodoItem` component, we can implement these features there.

Let's make the `TodoItem` component dynamic now:

1. In `src/TodoItem.js`, we start by defining the handler methods for the `toggleTodo` and `removeTodo` functions:

```
handleToggle () {
    const { toggleTodo, id } = this.props
    toggleTodo(id)
}

handleRemove () {
    const { removeTodo, id } = this.props
    removeTodo(id)
}
```

2. Then, we assign the handler methods to the `checkbox` and `button`, respectively:

```
render () {
    const { title, completed } = this.props
    return (
        <div style={{ width: 400, height: 25 }}>
            <input type="checkbox" checked={completed}
onChange={this.handleToggle} />
            {title}
            <button style={{ float: 'right' }}
onClick={this.handleRemove}>x</button>
        </div>
    )
}
```

3. Finally, we need to re-bind the `this` context for the handler methods. Create a new `constructor`, as follows:

```
export default class TodoItem extends React.Component {
    constructor (props) {
        super(props)

        this.handleToggle = this.handleToggle.bind(this)
        this.handleRemove = this.handleRemove.bind(this)
    }
```

Now, the `TodoItem` component triggers the toggle and remove handler functions.

Making the TodoFilter component dynamic

Lastly, we are going to use the `filterTodos` method to dynamically filter our todo item list.

Let's start making the `TodoFilter` component dynamic:

1. In `src/TodoFilter.js`, in the `TodoFilter` class, we pass all props down to the `TodoFilterItem` components:

```
export default class TodoFilter extends React.Component {
    render () {
        return (
            <div>
                <TodoFilterItem {...this.props} name="all" />{' /
' }
                <TodoFilterItem {...this.props} name="active" />{'
/ '}
                <TodoFilterItem {...this.props} name="completed" />
            </div>
        )
    }
}
```

2. In `src/TodoFilter.js`, in the `TodoFilterItem` class, we first define a handler method for setting the filter:

```
handleFilter () {
    const { name, filterTodos } = this.props
    filterTodos(name)
}
```

3. We then get the `filter` prop from `TodoFilter`:

```
render () {
    const { name, filter = 'all' } = this.props
```

4. Next, we use the `filter` prop to display the currently selected filter in bold:

```
const style = {
    color: 'blue',
    cursor: 'pointer',
    fontWeight: (filter === name) ? 'bold' : 'normal'
}
```

5. Then, we bind the handler method—via `onClick`—to the filter item:

```
        return <span style={style}
    onClick={this.handleFilter}>{name}</span>
        }
```

6. Finally, we create a new `constructor` for the `TodoFilterItem` class, and re-bind the `this` context of the handler method:

```
    class TodoFilterItem extends React.Component {
        constructor (props) {
            super(props)
            this.handleFilter = this.handleFilter.bind(this)
        }
```

Now, our `TodoFilter` component triggers the `handleFilter` method in order to change the filter. Our whole app is dynamic now, and we can use all of its functionalities.

Example code

The example code can be found in the `Chapter11/chapter11_1` folder.

Just run `npm install` in order to install all dependencies, and `npm start` to start the application, then visit `http://localhost:3000` in your browser (if it did not open automatically).

Migrating from React class components

After setting up our example project with React class components, we are now going to migrate this project to React Hooks. We are going to show how to migrate side effects, such as fetching todos when the component mounts, as well as state management, which we used for the inputs.

In this section, we are going to migrate the following components:

- `TodoItem`
- `TodoList`
- `TodoFilterItem`
- `TodoFilter`

- AddTodo
- App

Migrating the TodoItem component

One of the simplest components to migrate is the `TodoItem` component. It does not use any state or side effects so we can simply convert it to a function component.

Let's start migrating the `TodoItem` component:

1. Edit `src/TodoItem.js` and remove the class component code. We are going to define a function component instead now.
2. We start by defining the function, which accepts five props—the `title` value, the `completed` boolean, the `id` value, the `toggleTodo` function, and the `removeTodo` function:

   ```
   export default function TodoItem ({ title, completed, id,
   toggleTodo, removeTodo }) {
   ```

3. Next, we define our two handler functions:

   ```
   function handleToggle () {
       toggleTodo(id)
   }

   function handleRemove () {
       removeTodo(id)
   }
   ```

4. Finally, we return JSX code in order to render our component:

   ```
   return (
       <div style={{ width: 400, height: 25 }}>
           <input type="checkbox" checked={completed}
   onChange={handleToggle} />
           {title}
           <button style={{ float: 'right' }}
   onClick={handleRemove}>x</button>
       </div>
   )
   }
   ```

Try to keep your function components small, and combine them by creating new function components that wrap them. It is always a good idea to have many small components, rather than one large component. They are much easier to maintain, reuse, and refactor.

As we can see, function components do not require us to re-bind `this`, or to define constructors at all. Furthermore, we do not need to destructure from `this.props` multiple times. We can simply define all props in the header of our function.

Migrating the TodoList component

Next, we are going to migrate the `TodoList` component, which wraps the `TodoItem` component. Here, we use a context, which means that we can now use a Context Hook.

Let's migrate the `TodoList` component now:

1. Edit `src/TodoList.js` and import the `useContext` Hook from React:

   ```
   import React, { useContext } from 'react'
   ```

2. Remove the class component code. We are going to define a function component instead now.

3. We start by defining the header of our function. In this case, we do not destructure props, but simply store them in a `props` object:

   ```
   export default function TodoList (props) {
   ```

4. Now we define the Context Hook:

   ```
   const items = useContext(StateContext)
   ```

5. Finally, we return the list of rendered `items`, passing the `item` and `props` objects to it using destructuring:

   ```
   return items.map(item =>
       <TodoItem {...item} {...props} key={item.id} />
   )
   }
   ```

We define the `key` prop last, in order to avoid overwriting it with the destructuring of the `item` and `props` objects.

As we can see, using contexts with Hooks is much more straightforward. We can simply call a function, and use the return value. No magical assignment of `this.context` or wrapper hell when using multiple contexts!

Furthermore, we can see that we can gradually migrate components to React Hooks, and our app will still work. There is no need to migrate all components to Hooks at once. React class components can work well together with function React components that use Hooks. The only limitation is that we cannot use Hooks in class components. Therefore, we need to migrate a whole component at a time.

Migrating the TodoFilter component

Next up is the `TodoFilter` component, which is not going to use any Hooks. However, we are going to replace the `TodoFilterItem` and `TodoFilter` components with two function components: one for the `TodoFilterItem`, and one for the `TodoFilter` component.

Migrating TodoFilterItem

First of all, we are going to migrate the `TodoFilterItem` component. Let's start migrating the component now:

1. Edit `src/TodoFilter.js` and remove the class component code. We are going to define a function component instead now.

2. Define a function for the `TodoFilterItem` component, which is going to accept three props—the `name` value, the `filterTodos` function, and the `filter` value:

   ```
   function TodoFilterItem ({ name, filterTodos, filter = 'all' }) {
   ```

3. In this function, we define a handler function for changing the filter:

   ```
   function handleFilter () {
       filterTodos(name)
   }
   ```

4. Next, we define a `style` object for our `span` element:

   ```
   const style = {
       color: 'blue',
       cursor: 'pointer',
       fontWeight: (filter === name) ? 'bold' : 'normal'
   }
   ```

5. Finally, we return and render the `span` element:

```
        return <span style={style} onClick={handleFilter}>{name}</span>
    }
```

As we can see, a function component requires much less boilerplate code than the corresponding class component.

Migrating TodoFilter

Now that we have migrated the `TodoFilterItem` component, we can migrate the `TodoFilter` component. Let's migrate it now:

1. Edit `src/TodoFilter.js` and remove the class component code. We are going to define a function component instead now.

2. Define a function for the `TodoFilter` component. We are not going to use destructuring on the props here:

```
    export default function TodoFilter (props) {
```

3. In this component, we only return and render three `TodoFilterItem` components—passing the `props` down to them:

```
        return (
            <div>
                <TodoFilterItem {...props} name="all" />{' / '}
                <TodoFilterItem {...props} name="active" />{' / '}
                <TodoFilterItem {...props} name="completed" />
            </div>
        )
    }
```

Now, our `TodoFilter` component has been successfully migrated.

Migrating the AddTodo component

Next, we are going to migrate the `AddTodo` component. Here, we are going to use a State Hook to handle the `input` field state.

Let's migrate the `AddTodo` component now:

1. Edit `src/AddTodo.js` and adjust the import statement to import the `useState` Hook from React:

   ```
   import React, { useState } from 'react'
   ```

2. Remove the class component code. We are going to define a function component instead now.

3. First, we define the function, which accepts only one prop—the `addTodo` function:

   ```
   export default function AddTodo ({ addTodo }) {
   ```

4. Next, we define a State Hook for the `input` field state:

   ```
   const [ input, setInput ] = useState('')
   ```

5. Now we can define the handler functions for the `input` field and the **add** button:

   ```
   function handleInput (e) {
       setInput(e.target.value)
   }

   function handleAdd () {
       if (input) {
           addTodo(input)
           setInput('')
       }
   }
   ```

6. Finally, we return and render the `input` field and the **add** button:

   ```
   return (
       <form onSubmit={e => { e.preventDefault(); handleAdd() }}>
           <input
               type="text"
               placeholder="enter new task..."
               style={{ width: 350, height: 15 }}
               value={input}
               onChange={handleInput}
           />
           <input
               type="submit"
               style={{ float: 'right', marginTop: 2 }}
               disabled={!input}
               value="add"
   ```

```
                        />
                </form>
            )
        }
```

As we can see, using the State Hook makes state management much simpler. We can define a separate value and setter function for each state value, instead of having to deal with a state object. Furthermore, we do not need to destructure from `this.state` all the time. As a result, our code is much more clean and concise.

Migrating the App component

Lastly, all that is left to do is migrating the `App` component. Then, our whole ToDo app will have been migrated to React Hooks. Here, we are going to use a Reducer Hook to manage the state, an Effect Hook to fetch todos when the component mounts, and a Memo Hook to store the filtered todos list.

In this section, we are going to do the following:

- Define the actions
- Define the reducers
- Migrate the `App` component

Defining the actions

Our app is going to accept five actions:

- `FETCH_TODOS`: To fetch a new list of todo items—`{ type: 'FETCH_TODOS', todos: [] }`
- `ADD_TODO`: To insert a new todo item—`{ type: 'ADD_TODO', title: 'Test ToDo app' }`
- `TOGGLE_TODO`: To toggle the `completed` value of a todo item—`{ type: 'TOGGLE_TODO', id: 'xxx' }`
- `REMOVE_TODO`: To remove a todo item—`{ type: 'REMOVE_TODO', id: 'xxx' }`
- `FILTER_TODOS`: To filter todo items—`{ type: 'FILTER_TODOS', filter: 'completed' }`

After defining the actions, we can move on to defining the reducers.

Defining the reducers

We are now going to define the reducers for our state. We are going to need one app reducer and two sub-reducers: one for the todos and one for the filter.

The filtered todos list is going to be computed on the fly by the App component. We can later use a Memo Hook to cache the result and avoid unnecessary re-computation of the filtered todos list.

Defining the filter reducer

We are going to start by defining the reducer for the `filter` value. Let's define the filter reducer now:

1. Create a new `src/reducers.js` file and import the `generateID` function from the `src/api.js` file:

   ```
   import { generateID } from './api'
   ```

2. In the `src/reducers.js` file, define a new function, which is going to handle the `FILTER_TODOS` action, and set the value accordingly:

   ```
   function filterReducer (state, action) {
       if (action.type === 'FILTER_TODOS') {
           return action.filter
       } else {
           return state
       }
   }
   ```

Now, the `filterReducer` function is defined, and we can handle the `FILTER_TODOS` action properly.

Defining the todos reducer

Next, we are going to define a function for the todo items. Here, we are going to handle the `FETCH_TODOS`, `ADD_TODO`, `TOGGLE_TODO` and `REMOVE_TODO` actions.

Let's define the `todosReducer` function now:

1. In the `src/reducers.js` file, define a new function, which is going to handle these actions:

   ```
   function todosReducer (state, action) {
       switch (action.type) {
   ```

2. For the `FETCH_TODOS` action, we simply replace the current state with the new `todos` array:

```
case 'FETCH_TODOS':
    return action.todos
```

3. For the `ADD_TODO` action, we are going to insert a new item at the beginning of the current state array:

```
case 'ADD_TODO':
    const newTodo = {
        id: generateID(),
        title: action.title,
        completed: false
    }
    return [ newTodo, ...state ]
```

4. For the `TOGGLE_TODO` action, we are going to use the `map` function to update a single todo item:

```
case 'TOGGLE_TODO':
    return state.map(t => {
        if (t.id === action.id) {
            return { ...t, completed: !t.completed }
        }
        return t
    }, [])
```

5. For the `REMOVE_TODO` action, we are going to use the `filter` function to remove a single todo item:

```
case 'REMOVE_TODO':
    return state.filter(t => {
        if (t.id === action.id) {
            return false
        }
        return true
    })
```

6. By default (for all other actions), we simply return the current `state`:

```
default:
    return state
    }
}
```

Now, the todos reducer is defined, and we can handle the FETCH_TODOS, ADD_TODO, TOGGLE_TODO and REMOVE_TODO actions.

Defining the app reducer

Finally, we need to combine our other reducers into a single reducer for our app state. Let's define the appReducer function now:

1. In the src/reducers.js file, define a new function for the appReducer:

```
export default function appReducer (state, action) {
```

2. In this function, we return an object with the values from the other reducers. We simply pass the sub-state and action down to the other reducers:

```
return {
    todos: todosReducer(state.todos, action),
    filter: filterReducer(state.filter, action)
}
}
```

Now, our reducers are grouped together. So, we only have one state object and one dispatch function.

Migrating the component

Now that we have defined our reducers, we can start migrating the App component. Let's migrate it now:

1. Edit src/App.js and adjust the import statement to import useReducer, useEffect, and useMemo from React:

```
import React, { useReducer, useEffect, useMemo } from 'react'
```

2. Import the appReducer function from src/reducers.js:

```
import appReducer from './reducers'
```

3. Remove the class component code. We are going to define a function component instead now.

4. First, we define the function, which is not going to accept any props:

```
export default function App () {
```

5. Now, we define a Reducer Hook using the `appReducer` function:

```
const [ state, dispatch ] = useReducer(appReducer, { todos: [],
filter: 'all' })
```

6. Next, we define an Effect Hook, which is going to fetch `todos` via the API function, and then a `FETCH_TODOS` action will be dispatched:

```
useEffect(() => {
    fetchAPITodos().then((todos) =>
        dispatch({ type: 'FETCH_TODOS', todos })
    )
}, [])
```

7. Then, we implement the filter mechanism using a Memo Hook, in order to optimize performance and avoid re-computing the filtered todos list when nothing changes:

```
const filteredTodos = useMemo(() => {
    const { filter, todos } = state
    switch (filter) {
        case 'active':
            return todos.filter(t => t.completed === false)
        case 'completed':
            return todos.filter(t => t.completed === true)

        default:
        case 'all':
            return todos
    }
}, [ state ])
```

8. Now, we define various functions that are going to dispatch actions and change the state:

```
function addTodo (title) {
    dispatch({ type: 'ADD_TODO', title })
}

function toggleTodo (id) {
    dispatch({ type: 'TOGGLE_TODO', id })
}

function removeTodo (id) {
```

```
                    dispatch({ type: 'REMOVE_TODO', id })
                }

                function filterTodos (filter) {
                    dispatch({ type: 'FILTER_TODOS', filter })
                }
```

9. Finally, we return and render all the components that are needed for our ToDo app:

```
        return (
            <StateContext.Provider value={filteredTodos}>
                <div style={{ width: 400 }}>
                    <Header />
                    <AddTodo addTodo={addTodo} />
                    <hr />
                    <TodoList toggleTodo={toggleTodo}
        removeTodo={removeTodo} />
                    <hr />
                    <TodoFilter filter={state.filter}
        filterTodos={filterTodos} />
                </div>
            </StateContext.Provider>
        )
    }
```

As we can see, using a reducer to handle complex state changes makes our code much more concise and easier to maintain. Our app is now fully migrated to Hooks!

Example code

The example code can be found in the `Chapter11/chapter11_2` folder.

Just run `npm install` in order to install all dependencies and run `npm start` to start the application, then visit `http://localhost:3000` in your browser (if it did not open automatically).

Trade-offs of class components

Now that we have finished our migration from class components to Hooks, let's revise and sum up what we have learned.

Counting the lines of code, we can see that with 392 total lines of JavaScript code, function components with Hooks are more concise than class components, which required 430 total lines of JavaScript code. Additionally, the function components with Hooks are easier to understand and test since they simply use JavaScript functions instead of complex React constructs. Furthermore, we were able to refactor all of the state-changing logic into a separate `reducers.js` file, thus decoupling it from the `App` component and making it easier to refactor and test. This reduced the file size of `App.js` from 109 lines to 64 lines, with an additional 50 lines in the `reducers.js` file.

We can see the reduced lines of code in the following table:

Comparison: lines of JavaScript code	
Class components	**Function components with Hooks**
36 ./TodoFilter.js 15 ./TodoList.js 59 ./AddTodo.js 12 ./index.js 7 ./Header.js 5 ./StateContext.js 9 ./App.test.js 135 ./serviceWorker.js 12 ./api.js 109 ./App.js 31 ./TodoItem.js	25 ./TodoFilter.js 12 ./TodoList.js 42 ./AddTodo.js 12 ./index.js 7 ./Header.js 50 ./reducers.js 5 ./StateContext.js 9 ./App.test.js 135 ./serviceWorker.js 12 ./api.js 64 ./App.js 19 ./TodoItem.js
430 total	392 total

With function components and Hooks, the following points do not need to be taken into consideration:

- No need to deal with constructors
- No confusing `this` context (`this` re-binding)
- No need to destructure the same values over and over again
- No magic when dealing with contexts, props, and state
- No need to define `componentDidMount` and `componentDidUpdate` if we want to re-fetch data when the props change

Furthermore, function components have the following advantages:

- Encourage making small and simple components
- Are easier to refactor
- Are easier to test
- Require less code
- Are easier to understand for beginners
- Are more declarative

However, class components can be fine in the following situations:

- When sticking to certain conventions.
- When using the latest JavaScript features to avoid `this` re-binding.
- Are possibly easier to understand for the team because of existing knowledge.
- Many projects still use classes. For libraries, this is not such a problem, because they can work well together with function components. At work, you might need to use classes, though.
- Are not going to be removed from React anytime soon (according to the React team).

In the end, it is a matter of preference, but Hooks do have many advantages over classes! If you are starting a new project, definitely go for Hooks. If you are working on an existing project, consider whether it might make sense to refactor certain components to Hook-based components in order to make them simpler. However, you should not immediately port all your projects to Hooks, as refactoring can always introduce new bugs. The best way to adopt Hooks is to slowly but surely replace old class components with Hook-based function components when appropriate. For example, if you are already refactoring a component, you can refactor it to use Hooks!

Summary

In this chapter, we first built a ToDo app using React class components. We started by designing the app structure, then implemented static components, and finally, we made them dynamic. In the next section, we learned how to migrate an existing project using class components, to function components using Hooks. Finally, we learned about the trade-offs of class components, when class components or Hooks should be used, and how one should go about migrating an existing project to Hooks.

We have now seen in practice how React class components differ to function components with Hooks. Hooks make our code much more concise and easier to read and maintain. We have also learned that we should gradually migrate our components from class components to function components with Hooks—there is no need to immediately migrate the whole application.

In the next chapter, we are going to learn about handling state with Redux, the trade-offs of using Redux versus just function components with Hooks, how to use Redux with Hooks, and how to migrate an existing Redux application to a Hook-based setup.

Questions

In order to recap what we have learned in this chapter, try to answer the following questions:

1. How are React class components defined?
2. What do we need to call when using a `constructor` with class components? Why?
3. How do we set the initial state with class components?
4. How do we change the state with class components?
5. Why do we need to re-bind the `this` context with class component methods?
6. How can we re-bind the `this` context?
7. How can we use React context with class components?
8. What can we replace state management with when migrating to Hooks?
9. What are the trade-offs of using Hooks versus class components?
10. When and how should an existing project be migrated to Hooks?

Further reading

If you are interested in more information about the concepts that we have learned in this chapter, take a look at the following reading material:

- ES6 classes: `https://developer.mozilla.org/en/docs/Web/JavaScript/Reference/Classes`
- React class components: `https://www.robinwieruch.de/react-component-types/#react-class-components`

12
Redux and Hooks

In the previous chapter we learned about React class components, and how to migrate from an existing class component-based project to a Hook-based one. Then, we learned about the trade-offs between the two solutions, and we discussed when and how existing projects should be migrated.

In this chapter, we are going to turn the ToDo application that we created in the previous chapter into a Redux application. First, we are going to learn what Redux is, including the three principles of Redux. We are also going to learn when it makes sense to use Redux in an app, and that it is not appropriate for every app. Furthermore, we are going to learn how to handle state with Redux. Afterward, we are going to learn how to use Redux with Hooks, and how to migrate an existing Redux application to Hooks. Finally, we are going to learn the trade-offs of Redux, in order to be able to decide which solution would be best for a certain use case. By the end of this chapter, you will fully understand how to write Redux applications using Hooks.

The following topics will be covered in this chapter:

- What Redux is and when and why it should be used
- Handling state with Redux
- Using Redux with Hooks
- Migrating a Redux application
- Learning the trade-offs of Redux

Technical requirements

A fairly recent version of Node.js should already be installed (v11.12.0 or higher). The npm package manager for Node.js also needs to be installed.

The code for this chapter can be found on the GitHub repository: `https://github.com/ PacktPublishing/Learn-React-Hooks/tree/master/Chapter12`.

Check out the following video to see the code in action:

`http://bit.ly/2Mm9yoC`

 Please note that it is highly recommended that you write the code on your own. Do not simply run the code examples that have been provided. It is important that write the code yourself in order for you to be able to learn and understand properly. However, if you run into any issues, you can always refer to the code example.

Now, let's get started with the chapter.

What is Redux?

As we have previously learned, there are two kinds of state in an application:

- **Local state**: For example, to handle input field data
- **Global state**: For example, to store the currently logged-in user

Previously in this book, we handled local state by using a State Hook, and more complex state (often global state) using a Reducer Hook.

Redux is a solution that can be used to handle all kinds of state in React applications. It provides a single state tree object, which contains all application state. This is similar to what we did with the Reducer Hook in our blog application. Traditionally, Redux was also often used to store local state, which makes the state tree very complex.

Redux essentially consists of five elements:

- **Store**: Contains state, which is an object that describes the full state of our application—`{ todos: [], filter: 'all' }`
- **Actions**: Objects that describe a state modification—`{ type: 'FILTER_TODOS', filter: 'completed' }`

- **Action creators**: Functions that create action objects—`(filter) => ({ type: 'FILTER_TODOS', filter })`
- **Reducers**: Functions that take the current `state` value and an `action` object, and return a new state—`(state, action) => { ... }`
- **Connectors**: Higher-order components that connect an existing component to Redux, by injecting the Redux state and action creators as props—`connect(mapStateToProps, mapDispatchToProps)(Component)`

In the Redux life cycle, the **Store** contains state, which defines the UI. The UI is connected to the Redux store, via **Connectors**. User interactions with the UI then trigger **Actions**, which are sent to the **Reducer**. The **Reducer** then updates the state in the **Store**.

We can see a visualization of the Redux life cycle in the following diagram:

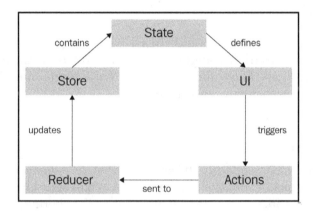

Visualization of the Redux life cycle

As you can see, we have already learned about three of these components: the store (state tree), actions, and reducers. Redux is like a more advanced version of the Reducer Hook. The difference is that with Redux, we always dispatch state to a single reducer, therefore changing a single state. There should not be more than one instance of Redux. Through this restriction, we can be sure that our whole application state is contained in a single object, which allows us to reconstruct the whole application state, just from the Redux store.

As a result of having a single store containing all state, we can easily debug faulty states by saving the Redux store in a crash report, or we can automatically replay certain actions during debugging so that we do not need to manually enter text and click on buttons, over and over again. Additionally, Redux offers middleware that simplifies how we deal with asynchronous requests, such as fetching data from a server. Now that we understand what Redux is, in the next section, we will learn the three fundamental principles of Redux.

The three principles of Redux

The Redux API is very small, and actually only consists of a handful of functions. What makes Redux so powerful is a certain set of rules that are applied to your code when using the library. These rules allow for the writing of scalable applications that are easy to extend, test, and debug.

Redux is based on three fundamental principles:

- Single source of truth
- Read-only state
- State changes are processed with pure functions

Single source of truth

This Redux principle states that data should always have a single source of truth. This means that global data comes from a single Redux store, and local data comes from, for example, a certain State Hook. Each kind of data only has a single source. As a result, applications become easier to debug, and are less prone to errors.

Read-only state

With Redux, it is not possible to modify the application state directly. It is only possible to change the state by dispatching actions. This principle makes state changes predictable: if no action happened, the application state will not change. Furthermore, actions are processed one at a time, so we do not have to deal with race conditions. Finally, actions are plain JavaScript objects, which makes them easy to serialize, log, store, or replay. As a result, debugging and testing a Redux application becomes very easy to do.

State changes are processed with pure functions

Pure functions are functions that, given the same input, will always return the same output. Reducer functions in Redux are pure, so, given the same state and action, they will always return the same new state.

For example, the following reducer is an impure function, because calling the function multiple times with the same input results in a different output:

```
let i = 0
function counterReducer (state, action) {
    if (action.type === 'INCREMENT') {
```

```
        i++
    }
    return i
}

console.log(counterReducer(0, { type: 'INCREMENT' })) // prints 1
console.log(counterReducer(0, { type: 'INCREMENT' })) // prints 2
```

To turn this reducer into a pure function, we have to make sure it does not depend on an outside state, and only uses its arguments for the computation:

```
function counterReducer (state, action) {
    if (action.type === 'INCREMENT') {
        return state + 1
    }
    return state
}

console.log(counterReducer(0, { type: 'INCREMENT' })) // prints 1
console.log(counterReducer(0, { type: 'INCREMENT' })) // prints 1
```

Using pure functions for reducers makes them predictable, and easy to test and debug. With Redux, we need to be careful to always return a new state, and not modify the existing one. So, for example, we cannot use `Array.push()` on an array state, as it would modify the existing array; we have to use `Array.concat()` in order to create a new array. The same goes for objects, where we have to use rest/spread syntax to create new objects, instead of modifying existing ones. For example, `{ ...state, completed: true }`.

Now that we have learned about the three fundamental principles of Redux, we can move on to using Redux in practice, by implementing state handling with Redux in our ToDo application.

Handling state with Redux

State management with Redux is actually really similar to using a Reducer Hook. We first define the state object, then actions, and finally, our reducers. An additional pattern in Redux is to create functions that return action objects, so-called action creators. Furthermore, we need to wrap our whole app with a `Provider` component, and connect components to the Redux store in order to be able to use Redux state and action creators.

Installing Redux

First of all, we have to install Redux, React Redux, and Redux Thunk. Let us look at what each one does individually:

- Redux itself just deals with JavaScript objects, so it provides the store, deals with actions and action creators, and handles reducers.
- React Redux provides connectors in order to connect Redux to our React components.
- Redux Thunk is a middleware that allows us to deal with asynchronous requests in Redux.

Using **Redux** in combination with **React** offloads global state management to **Redux**, while **React** deals with rendering the application and local state:

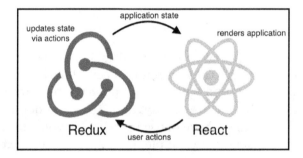

Illustration of how React and Redux work together

To install Redux and React Redux, we are going to use npm. Execute the following command:

```
> npm install --save redux react-redux redux-thunk
```

Now that all of the required libraries are installed, we can start setting up our Redux store.

Defining state, actions, and reducers

The first step in developing a Redux application is defining the state, then the actions that are going to change the state, and finally, the reducer functions, which carry out the state modification. In our ToDo application, we have already defined the state, the actions, and the reducers, in order to use the Reducer Hook. Here, we simply recap what we defined in the previous chapter.

State

The full state object of our ToDo app consists of two keys: an array of todo items, and a string, which specifies the currently selected `filter` value. The initial state looks as follows:

```
{
    "todos": [
        { "id": 1, "title": "Write React Hooks book", "completed": true },
        { "id": 2, "title": "Promote book", "completed": false }
    ],
    "filter": "all"
}
```

As we can see, in Redux, the state object contains all of the state that is important to our app. In this case, the application state consists of an array of `todos` and a `filter`.

Actions

Our app accepts the following five actions:

- `FETCH_TODOS`: To fetch a new list of todo items—`{ type: 'FETCH_TODOS', todos: [] }`

- `ADD_TODO`: To insert a new todo item—`{ type: 'ADD_TODO', title: 'Test ToDo app' }`

- `TOGGLE_TODO`: To toggle the `completed` value of a todo item—`{ type: 'TOGGLE_TODO', id: 'xxx' }`

- `REMOVE_TODO`: To remove a todo item—`{ type: 'REMOVE_TODO', id: 'xxx' }`

- `FILTER_TODOS`: To filter todo items—`{ type: 'FILTER_TODOS', filter: 'completed' }`

Reducers

We defined three reducers—one for each part of our state—and an app reducer to combine the other two reducers. The filter reducer waits for a `FILTER_TODOS` action, and then sets the new filter accordingly. The todos reducer listens to the other todo-related actions, and adjusts the todos array by adding, removing, or modifying elements. The app reducer then combines both reducers, and passes actions down to them. After defining all the elements that are needed to create a Redux application, we can now set up the Redux store.

Setting up the Redux store

In order to keep things simple initially, and to show how Redux works, we are not going to use connectors for now. We are simply going to replace the `state` object, and the `dispatch` function that was previously provided by a Reducer Hook, with Redux.

Let's set up the Redux store now:

1. Edit `src/App.js`, and import the `useState` Hook, as well as the `createStore` function from the Redux library:

    ```
    import React, { useState, useEffect, useMemo } from 'react'
    import { createStore } from 'redux'
    ```

2. Below the import statements and before the `App` function definition, we are going to initialize the Redux store. We start by defining the initial state:

    ```
    const initialState = { todos: [], filter: 'all' }
    ```

3. Next, we are going to use the `createStore` function in order to define the Redux store, by using the existing `appReducer` function and passing the `initialState` object:

    ```
    const store = createStore(appReducer, initialState)
    ```

     Please note that in Redux, it is not best practice to initialize the state by passing it to `createStore`. However, with a Reducer Hook, we need to do it this way. In Redux, we usually initialize state by setting default values in the reducer functions. We are going to learn more about initializing state via Redux reducers later in this chapter.

4. Now, we can get the `dispatch` function from the store:

    ```
    const { dispatch } = store
    ```

5. The next step is removing the following Reducer Hook definition within the `App` function:

    ```
    const [ state, dispatch ] = useReducer(appReducer, { todos: [],
    filter: 'all' })
    ```

    It is replaced with a simple State Hook, which is going to store our Redux state:

    ```
    const [ state, setState ] = useState(initialState)
    ```

6. Finally, we define an Effect Hook, in order to keep the State Hook in sync with the Redux store state:

```
useEffect(() => {
    const unsubscribe = store.subscribe(() =>
setState(store.getState()))
    return unsubscribe
}, [])
```

As we can see, the app still runs in exactly the same way as before. Redux works very similarly to the Reducer Hook, but with more functionality. However, there are slight differences in how actions and reducers should be defined, which we are going to learn about in the following sections.

Example code

The example code can be found in the `Chapter12/chapter12_1` folder.

Just run `npm install` in order to install all dependencies and `npm start` to start the application, then visit `http://localhost:3000` in your browser (if it did not open automatically).

Defining action types

The first step when creating a full Redux application is to define so-called action types. They will be used to create actions in action creators and to handle actions in reducers. The idea here is to avoid making typos when defining, or comparing, the `type` property of actions.

Let's define the action types now:

1. Create a new `src/actionTypes.js` file.
2. Define and export the following constants in the newly created file:

```
export const FETCH_TODOS = 'FETCH_TODOS'
export const ADD_TODO = 'ADD_TODO'
export const TOGGLE_TODO = 'TOGGLE_TODO'
export const REMOVE_TODO = 'REMOVE_TODO'
export const FILTER_TODOS = 'FILTER_TODOS'
```

Now that we have defined our action types, we can start using them in action creators and reducers.

Defining action creators

After defining the action types, we need to define the actions themselves. In doing so, we are going to define the functions that will return the action objects. These functions are called action creators, of which there are two types:

- **Synchronous action creators**: These simply return an action object
- **Asynchronous action creators**: These return an `async` function, which will later dispatch an action

We are going to start by defining synchronous action creators, then we are going to learn how to define asynchronous action creators.

Defining synchronous action creators

We have already defined the action creator functions earlier, in `src/App.js`. We can now copy them from our `App` component, making sure that we adjust the `type` property in order to use the action type constants, instead of a static string.

Let's define the synchronous action creators now:

1. Create a new `src/actions.js` file.
2. Import all action types, which we are going to need to create our actions:

```
import {
    ADD_TODO, TOGGLE_TODO, REMOVE_TODO, FILTER_TODOS
} from './actionTypes'
```

3. Now, we can define and export our action creator functions:

```
export function addTodo (title) {
    return { type: ADD_TODO, title }
}

export function toggleTodo (id) {
    return { type: TOGGLE_TODO, id }
}

export function removeTodo (id) {
    return { type: REMOVE_TODO, id }
```

```
    }

    export function filterTodos (filter) {
        return { type: FILTER_TODOS, filter }
    }
```

As we can see, synchronous action creators simply create and return action objects.

Defining asynchronous action creators

The next step is defining an asynchronous action creator for the fetchTodos action. Here, we are going to use the async/await construct.

We are now going to use an async function to define the fetchTodos action creator:

1. In src/actions.js, first import the FETCH_TODOS action type and the fetchAPITodos function:

```
import {
    FETCH_TODOS, ADD_TODO, TOGGLE_TODO, REMOVE_TODO, FILTER_TODOS
} from './actionTypes'
import { fetchAPITodos } from './api'
```

2. Then, define a new action creator function, which will return an async function that is going to get the dispatch function as an argument:

```
export function fetchTodos () {
    return async (dispatch) => {
```

3. In this async function, we are now going to call the API function, and dispatch our action:

```
        const todos = await fetchAPITodos()
        dispatch({ type: FETCH_TODOS, todos })
    }
}
```

As we can see, asynchronous action creators return a function that will dispatch actions at a later time.

Adjusting the store

In order for us to be able to use asynchronous action creator functions in Redux, we are going to need to load the `redux-thunk` middleware. This middleware checks if an action creator returned a function, rather than a plain object, and if that is the case, it executes that function, while passing the `dispatch` function to it as an argument.

Let's adjust the store to allow for asynchronous action creators now:

1. Create a new `src/configureStore.js` file.
2. Import the `createStore` and `applyMiddleware` functions from Redux:

   ```
   import { createStore, applyMiddleware } from 'redux'
   ```

3. Next, import the `thunk` middleware and `appReducer` function:

   ```
   import thunk from 'redux-thunk'

   import appReducer from './reducers'
   ```

4. Now, we can define the store and apply the `thunk` middleware to it:

   ```
   const store = createStore(appReducer, applyMiddleware(thunk))
   ```

5. Finally, we export the `store`:

   ```
   export default store
   ```

Using the `redux-thunk` middleware, we can now dispatch functions that will later dispatch actions, which means that our asynchronous action creator is going to work fine now.

Adjusting reducers

As previously mentioned, Redux reducers differ from Reducer Hooks in that they have certain conventions:

- Each reducer needs to set its initial state by defining a default value in the function definition
- Each reducer needs to return the current state for unhandled actions

We are now going to adjust our existing reducers so that they follow these conventions. The second convention is already implemented, because we defined a single app reducer earlier, in order to avoid having multiple dispatch functions.

Setting the initial state in Redux reducers

So, we are going to focus on the first convention—to set the initial state by defining a default value in the function arguments, as follows:

1. Edit `src/reducers.js` and import the `combineReducers` function from Redux:

    ```
    import { combineReducers } from 'redux'
    ```

2. Then, rename `filterReducer` to `filter`, and set a default value:

    ```
    function filter (state = 'all', action) {
    ```

3. Next, edit `todosReducer` and repeat the same process there:

    ```
    function todos (state = [], action) {
    ```

4. Finally, we are going to use the `combineReducers` function to create our `appReducer` function. Instead of creating the function manually, we can now do the following:

    ```
    const appReducer = combineReducers({ todos, filter })
    export default appReducer
    ```

As we can see, Redux reducers are very similar to Reducer Hooks. Redux even provides a function that allows us to combine multiple reducer functions into a single app reducer!

Connecting components

Now, it is time to introduce connectors and container components. In Redux we can use the `connect` higher-order component to connect existing components to Redux, through injecting state and action creators as props into them.

Redux defines two different kinds of components:

- **Presentational components**: React components, as we have been defining them until now
- **Container components**: React components that connect presentational components to Redux

Container components use a connector to connect Redux to a presentational component. This connector accepts two functions:

- `mapStateToProps(state)`: Takes the current Redux state, and returns an object of props to be passed to the component; used to pass state to the component
- `mapDispatchToProps(dispatch)`: Takes the `dispatch` function from the Redux store, and returns an object of props to be passed to the component; used to pass action creators to the component

We are now going to define container components for our existing presentational components:

1. First, we create a new `src/components/` folder for all our presentational components.
2. Then, we copy all of the existing component files to the `src/components/` folder, and adjust the import statements for the following files: `AddTodo.js`, `App.js`, `Header.js`, `TodoFilter.js`, `TodoItem.js`, and `TodoList.js`.

Connecting the AddTodo component

We are now going to start connecting our components to the Redux store. The presentational components can stay the same as before. We only create new components—container components—that wrap the presentational components, and pass certain props to them.

Let's connect the `AddTodo` component now:

1. Create a new `src/containers/` folder for all our container components.
2. Create a new `src/containers/ConnectedAddTodo.js` file.
3. In this file, we import the `connect` function from `react-redux`, and the `bindActionCreators` function from `redux`:

   ```
   import { connect } from 'react-redux'
   import { bindActionCreators } from 'redux'
   ```

4. Next, we import the `addTodo` action creator and the `AddTodo` component:

   ```
   import { addTodo } from '../actions'
   import AddTodo from '../components/AddTodo'
   ```

5. Now, we are going to define the `mapStateToProps` function. Since this component does not deal with any state from Redux, we can simply return an empty object here:

```
function mapStateToProps (state) {
    return {}
}
```

6. Then, we define the `mapDispatchToProps` function. Here we use `bindActionCreators` to wrap the action creator with the `dispatch` function:

```
function mapDispatchToProps (dispatch) {
    return bindActionCreators({ addTodo }, dispatch)
}
```

This code is essentially the same as manually wrapping the action creators, as follows:

```
function mapDispatchToProps (dispatch) {
    return {
        addTodo: (...args) => dispatch(addTodo(...args))
    }
}
```

7. Finally, we use the `connect` function to connect the `AddTodo` component to Redux:

```
export default connect(mapStateToProps,
mapDispatchToProps)(AddTodo)
```

Now, our `AddTodo` component is successfully connected to the Redux store.

Connecting the TodoItem component

Next, we are going to connect the `TodoItem` component, so that we can use it in the `TodoList` component in the next step.

Let's connect the `TodoItem` component now:

1. Create a new `src/containers/ConnectedTodoItem.js` file.
2. In this file, we import the `connect` function from `react-redux`, and the `bindActionCreators` function from `redux`:

```
import { connect } from 'react-redux'
import { bindActionCreators } from 'redux'
```

3. Next, we import the `toggleTodo` and `removeTodo` action creators, and the `TodoItem` component:

```
import { toggleTodo, removeTodo } from '../actions'
import TodoItem from '../components/TodoItem'
```

4. Again, we only return an empty object from `mapStateToProps`:

```
function mapStateToProps (state) {
    return {}
}
```

5. This time, we bind two action creators to the `dispatch` function:

```
function mapDispatchToProps (dispatch) {
    return bindActionCreators({ toggleTodo, removeTodo }, dispatch)
}
```

6. Finally, we connect the component, and export it:

```
export default connect(mapStateToProps,
mapDispatchToProps)(TodoItem)
```

Now, our `TodoItem` component is successfully connected to the Redux store.

Connecting the TodoList component

After connecting the `TodoItem` component, we can now use the `ConnectedTodoItem` component in the `TodoList` component.

Let's connect the `TodoList` component now:

1. Edit `src/components/TodoList.js`, and adjust the import statement as follows:

```
import ConnectedTodoItem from '../containers/ConnectedTodoItem'
```

2. Then, rename the component that is returned from the function to `ConnectedTodoItem`:

```
return filteredTodos.map(item =>
    <ConnectedTodoItem {...item} key={item.id} />
)
```

3. Now, create a new `src/containers/ConnectedTodoList.js` file.

4. In this file, we import only the `connect` function from `react-redux`, as we are not going to bind the action creators this time:

```
import { connect } from 'react-redux'
```

5. Next, we import the `TodoList` component:

```
import TodoList from '../components/TodoList'
```

6. Now, we define the `mapStateToProps` function. This time, we use destructuring to get `todos` and `filter` from the `state` object, and return them:

```
function mapStateToProps (state) {
    const { filter, todos } = state
    return { filter, todos }
}
```

7. Next, we define the `mapDispatchToProps` function, where we only return an empty object, since we are not going to pass any action creators to the `TodoList` component:

```
function mapDispatchToProps (dispatch) {
    return {}
}
```

8. Finally, we connect and export the connected `TodoList` component:

```
export default connect(mapStateToProps,
mapDispatchToProps)(TodoList)
```

Now, our `TodoList` component is successfully connected to the Redux store.

Adjusting the TodoList component

Now that we have connected the `TodoList` component, we can move the filter logic from the `App` component to the `TodoList` component, as follows:

1. Import the `useMemo` Hook in `src/components/TodoList.js`:

```
import React, { useMemo } from 'react'
```

2. Edit `src/components/App.js`, and remove the following code:

```
const filteredTodos = useMemo(() => {
    const { filter, todos } = state
    switch (filter) {
        case 'active':
            return todos.filter(t => t.completed === false)

        case 'completed':
            return todos.filter(t => t.completed === true)

        default:
        case 'all':
            return todos
    }
}, [ state ])
```

3. Now, edit `src/components/TodoList.js`, and add the `filteredTodos` code here. Please note that we removed the destructuring from the state object, as the component already receives the `filter` and `todos` values as props. We also adjusted the dependency array accordingly:

```
const filteredTodos = useMemo(() => {
    switch (filter) {
        case 'active':
            return todos.filter(t => t.completed === false)

        case 'completed':
            return todos.filter(t => t.completed === true)

        default:
        case 'all':
            return todos
    }
}, [ filter, todos ])
```

Now, our filtering logic is in the `TodoList` component, instead of the `App` component. Let's move on to connecting the rest of our components.

Connecting the TodoFilter component

Next up is the `TodoFilter` component. Here, we are going to use both `mapStateToProps` and `mapDispatchToProps`.

Let's connect the `TodoFilter` component now:

1. Create a new `src/containers/ConnectedTodoFilter.js` file.

2. In this file, we import the `connect` function from `react-redux` and the `bindActionCreators` function from `redux`:

   ```
   import { connect } from 'react-redux'
   import { bindActionCreators } from 'redux'
   ```

3. Next, we import the `filterTodos` action creator and the `TodoFilter` component:

   ```
   import { filterTodos } from '../actions'
   import TodoFilter from '../components/TodoFilter'
   ```

4. We use destructuring to get the `filter` from our `state` object, and then we return it:

   ```
   function mapStateToProps (state) {
       const { filter } = state
       return { filter }
   }
   ```

5. Next, we bind and return the `filterTodos` action creator:

   ```
   function mapDispatchToProps (dispatch) {
       return bindActionCreators({ filterTodos }, dispatch)
   }
   ```

6. Finally, we connect the component and export it:

   ```
   export default connect(mapStateToProps,
   mapDispatchToProps)(TodoFilter)
   ```

Now, our `TodoFilter` component is successfully connected to the Redux store.

Connecting the App component

The only component that still needs to be connected now, is the App component. Here, we are going to inject the fetchTodos action creator, and update the component so that it uses the connected versions of all the other components.

Let's connect the App component now:

1. Edit src/components/App.js, and adjust the following import statements:

```
import ConnectedAddTodo from '../containers/ConnectedAddTodo'
import ConnectedTodoList from '../containers/ConnectedTodoList'
import ConnectedTodoFilter from '../containers/ConnectedTodoFilter'
```

2. Also, adjust the following components that are returned from the function:

```
return (
    <div style={{ width: 400 }}>
        <Header />
        <ConnectedAddTodo />
        <hr />
        <ConnectedTodoList />
        <hr />
        <ConnectedTodoFilter />
    </div>
)
```

3. Now, we can create the connected component. Create a new src/containers/ConnectedApp.js file.

4. In this newly created file, we import the connect function from react-redux, and the bindActionCreators function from redux:

```
import { connect } from 'react-redux'
import { bindActionCreators } from 'redux'
```

5. Next, we import the fetchTodos action creator, and the App component:

```
import { fetchTodos } from '../actions'
import App from '../components/App'
```

6. We already deal with the various parts of our state in other components, so there is no need to inject any state into our App component:

```
function mapStateToProps (state) {
    return {}
}
```

7. Then, we bind and return the `fetchTodos` action creator:

```
function mapDispatchToProps (dispatch) {
    return bindActionCreators({ fetchTodos }, dispatch)
}
```

8. Finally, we connect the `App` component and export it:

```
export default connect(mapStateToProps, mapDispatchToProps)(App)
```

Now, our `App` component is successfully connected to the Redux store.

Setting up the Provider component

Finally, we have to set up a `Provider` component, which is going to provide a context for the Redux store, which will be used by the connectors.

Let's set up the `Provider` component now:

1. Edit `src/index.js`, and import the `Provider` component from `react-redux`:

```
import { Provider } from 'react-redux'
```

2. Now, import the `ConnectedApp` component from the `containers` folder and import the Redux store that was created by `configureStore.js`:

```
import ConnectedApp from './containers/ConnectedApp'
import store from './configureStore'
```

3. Finally, adjust the first argument to `ReactDOM.render`, by wrapping the `ConnectedApp` component with the `Provider` component, as follows:

```
ReactDOM.render(
    <Provider store={store}>
        <ConnectedApp />
    </Provider>,
    document.getElementById('root')
)
```

Now, our application will work in the same way as before, but everything is connected to the Redux store! As we can see, Redux requires a bit more boilerplate code than simply using React, but it comes with a lot of advantages:

- Easier handling of asynchronous actions (using the `redux-thunk` middleware)
- Centralized action handling (no need to define action creators in the components)
- Useful functions for binding action creators and combining reducers
- Reduced possibilities for errors (for example, by using action types, we can ensure that we did not make a typo)

However, there are also disadvantages, which are as follows:

- A lot of boilerplate code is required (action types, action creators, and connected components)
- Mapping of state/action creators in separate files (not in the components, where they are needed)

The first point is an advantage and disadvantage at the same time; action types and action creators do require more boilerplate code, but they also make it easier to update action-related code at a later stage. The second point, and the boilerplate code that is required for the connected components, can be solved by using Hooks to connect our components to Redux. We are going to use Hooks with Redux in the next section of this chapter.

Example code

The example code can be found in the `Chapter12/chapter12_2` folder.

Just run `npm install` in order to install all dependencies and `npm start` to start the application, then visit `http://localhost:3000` in your browser (if it did not open automatically).

Using Redux with Hooks

After turning our todo application into a Redux-based application, we are now using higher-order components, instead of Hooks, in order to get access to the Redux state and action creators. This is the traditional way to develop a Redux application. However, in the latest versions of Redux, it is possible to use Hooks instead of higher-order components! We are now going to replace the existing connectors with Hooks.

Even with Hooks, the `Provider` component is still required in order to provide the Redux store to other components. The definition of the store and the provider can stay the same when refactoring from `connect()` to Hooks.

The latest version of React Redux offers various Hooks as an alternative to the `connect()` higher-order component. With these Hooks, you can subscribe to the Redux store, and dispatch actions without having to wrap your components.

Using the dispatch Hook

The `useDispatch` Hook returns a reference to the `dispatch` function that is provided by the Redux store. It can be used to dispatch actions that are returned from action creators. Its API looks as follows:

```
const dispatch = useDispatch()
```

We are now going to use the Dispatch Hook to replace the existing container components with Hooks.

 You do not need to migrate your whole Redux application at once in order to use Hooks. It is possible to selectively refactor certain components—meaning that they will use Hooks—while still using `connect()` for other components.

After learning how to use the Dispatch Hook, let's move on to migrating our existing components so that they use the Dispatch Hook.

Using Hooks for the AddTodo component

Now that we have learned about the Dispatch Hook, let's see it in action by implementing it in our `AddTodo` component.

Let's migrate the `AddTodo` component to Hooks now:

1. First delete the `src/containers/ConnectedAddTodo.js` file.
2. Now, edit the `src/components/AddTodo.js` file and import the `useDispatch` Hook from `react-redux`:

```
import { useDispatch } from 'react-redux'
```

3. Additionally, import the `addTodo` action creator:

```
import { addTodo } from '../actions'
```

4. Now, we can remove the props from the function definition:

```
export default function AddTodo () {
```

5. Then, define the Dispatch Hook:

```
const dispatch = useDispatch()
```

6. Finally, adjust the handler function and call `dispatch()`:

```
function handleAdd () {
    if (input) {
        dispatch(addTodo(input))
        setInput('')
    }
}
```

7. Now, all that is left to do is to replace the `ConnectedAddTodo` component with the `AddTodo` component in `src/components/App.js`. First, adjust the import statement:

```
import AddTodo from './AddTodo'
```

8. Then, adjust the rendered component:

```
return (
    <div style={{ width: 400 }}>
        <Header />
        <AddTodo />
```

As you can see, our app still works in the same way as before, but we are now using Hooks in order to connect the component to Redux!

Using Hooks for the App component

Next, we are going to update our `App` component so that it directly dispatches the `fetchTodos` action. Let's migrate the `App` component to Hooks now:

1. First delete the `src/containers/ConnectedApp.js` file.

2. Now, edit the `src/components/App.js` file and import the `useDispatch` Hook from `react-redux`:

```
import { useDispatch } from 'react-redux'
```

3. Additionally, import the `fetchTodos` action creator:

```
import { fetchTodos } from '../actions'
```

4. Now, we can remove the props from the function definition:

```
export default function App () {
```

5. Then, define the Dispatch Hook:

```
const dispatch = useDispatch()
```

6. Finally, adjust the Effect Hook and call `dispatch()`:

```
useEffect(() => {
    dispatch(fetchTodos())
}, [ dispatch ])
```

7. Now, all that is left to do is to replace the `ConnectedApp` component with the `App` component in `src/index.js`. First, adjust the import statement:

```
import App from './components/App'
```

8. Then, adjust the rendered component:

```
ReactDOM.render(
    <Provider store={store}>
        <App />
    </Provider>,
    document.getElementById('root')
)
```

As we can see, using Hooks is much simpler and more concise than defining a separate container component.

Using Hooks for the TodoItem component

Now, we are going to upgrade the `TodoItem` component to use Hooks. Let's migrate it now:

1. First delete the `src/containers/ConnectedTodoItem.js` file.

2. Now, edit the `src/components/TodoItem.js` file, and import the `useDispatch` Hook from `react-redux`:

   ```
   import { useDispatch } from 'react-redux'
   ```

3. Additionally, import the `toggleTodo` and `removeTodo` action creators:

   ```
   import { toggleTodo, removeTodo } from '../actions'
   ```

4. Now, we can remove the action creator-related props from the function definition. The new code should look as follows:

   ```
   export default function TodoItem ({ title, completed, id }) {
   ```

5. Then, define the Dispatch Hook:

   ```
   const dispatch = useDispatch()
   ```

6. Finally, adjust the handler functions to call `dispatch()`:

   ```
   function handleToggle () {
       dispatch(toggleTodo(id))
   }

   function handleRemove () {
       dispatch(removeTodo(id))
   }
   ```

7. Now, all that is left to do is to replace the `ConnectedTodoItem` component with the `TodoItem` component in `src/components/TodoList.js`. First, adjust the import statement:

   ```
   import TodoItem from './TodoItem'
   ```

8. Then, adjust the rendered component:

   ```
   return filteredTodos.map(item =>
       <TodoItem {...item} key={item.id} />
   )
   ```

Now the `TodoItem` component uses Hooks instead of a container component. Next, we are going to learn about the Selector Hook.

Using the Selector Hook

Another very important Hook that is provided by Redux is the Selector Hook. It allows us to get data from the Redux store state, by defining a selector function. The API for this Hook is as follows:

```
const result = useSelector(selectorFn, equalityFn)
```

`selectorFn` is a function that works similarly to the `mapStateToProps` function. It will get the full state object as its only argument. The selector function gets executed whenever the component renders, and whenever an action is dispatched (and the state is different than the previous state).

It is important to note that returning an object with multiple parts of the state from one Selector Hook will force a re-render every time an action is dispatched. If multiple values from the store need to be requested, we can do the following:

- Use multiple Selector Hooks, each one returning a single field from the state object
- Use `reselect`, or a similar library, to create a memoized selector (we are going to cover this in the next section)
- Use the `shallowEqual` function from `react-redux` as `equalityFn`

We are now going to implement the Selector Hook in our ToDo application, specifically in the `TodoList` and `TodoFilter` components.

Using Hooks for the TodoList component

First, we are going to implement a Selector Hook to get all `todos` for the `TodoList` component, as follows:

1. First delete the `src/containers/ConnectedTodoList.js` file.
2. Now, edit the `src/components/TodoList.js` file, and import the `useSelector` Hook from `react-redux`:

    ```
    import { useSelector } from 'react-redux'
    ```

3. Now, we can remove all the props from the function definition:

```
export default function TodoList () {
```

4. Then, we define two Selector Hooks, one for the `filter` value, and one for the `todos` value:

```
const filter = useSelector(state => state.filter)
const todos = useSelector(state => state.todos)
```

5. Now, all that is left to do is to replace the `ConnectedTodoList` component with the `TodoList` component in `src/components/App.js`. First, adjust the import statement:

```
import TodoList from './TodoList'
```

6. Then, adjust the rendered component:

```
return (
    <div style={{ width: 400 }}>
        <Header />
        <AddTodo />
        <hr />
        <TodoList />
```

The rest of the component can stay the same, because the values where we store the parts of the state have the same names as before.

Using Hooks for the TodoFilter component

Finally, we are going to implement both the Selector and Dispatch Hooks in the `TodoFilter` component, because we need to highlight the current filter (state from the Selector Hook) and dispatch an action to change the filter (the Dispatch Hook).

Let's implement Hooks for the `TodoFilter` component now:

1. First, delete the `src/containers/ConnectedTodoFilter.js` file.
2. We can also delete the `src/containers/` folder, as it is empty now.
3. Now, edit the `src/components/TodoFilter.js` file, and import the `useSelector` and `useDispatch` Hooks from `react-redux`:

```
import { useSelector, useDispatch } from 'react-redux'
```

4. Additionally, import the `filterTodos` action creator:

```
import { filterTodos } from '../actions'
```

5. Now, we can remove all the props from the function definition:

```
export default function TodoFilter () {
```

6. Then, define the Dispatch and Selector Hooks:

```
const dispatch = useDispatch()
const filter = useSelector(state => state.filter)
```

7. Finally, adjust the handler function to call `dispatch()`:

```
function handleFilter () {
    dispatch(filterTodos(name))
}
```

8. Now, all that is left to do is to replace the `ConnectedTodoFilter` component with the `TodoFilter` component in `src/components/App.js`. First, adjust the import statement:

```
import TodoFilter from './TodoFilter'
```

9. Then, adjust the rendered component:

```
return (
    <div style={{ width: 400 }}>
        <Header />
        <AddTodo />
        <hr />
        <TodoList />
        <hr />
        <TodoFilter />
    </div>
)
```

Now, our Redux application makes full use of Hooks instead of container components!

Example code

The example code can be found in the `Chapter12/chapter12_3` folder.

Just run `npm install` in order to install all dependencies and `npm start` to start the application, then visit `http://localhost:3000` in your browser (if it did not open automatically).

Creating reusable selectors

When defining selectors as we have done until now, a new instance of the selector is created every time the component is rendered. This is fine, if the selector function does not do any complex operations and does not maintain internal state. Otherwise, we need to use reusable selectors, which we are going to learn about now.

Setting up reselect

In order to create reusable selectors, we can use the `createSelector` function from the `reselect` library. First, we have to install the library via `npm`. Execute the following command:

```
> npm install --save reselect
```

Now, the `reselect` library has been installed, and we can use it to create reusable selectors.

Memoizing selectors that only depend on state

If we want to memoize selectors, and the selector only depends on the state (not props), we can declare the selector outside of the component, as follows:

1. Edit the `src/components/TodoList.js` file, and import the `createSelector` function from `reselect`:

   ```
   import { createSelector } from 'reselect'
   ```

2. Then, we define selectors for the `todos` and `filter` parts of the state, before the component definition:

    ```
    const todosSelector = state => state.todos
    const filterSelector = state => state.filter
    ```

> If selectors are used by many components, it might make sense to put them in a separate `selectors.js` file, and import them from there. For example, we could put the `filterSelector` in a separate file, and then import it in `TodoList.js`, as well as `TodoFilter.js`.

3. Now, we define a selector for the filtered todos, before the component is defined, as follows:

    ```
    const selectFilteredTodos = createSelector(
    ```

4. First, we specify the other two selectors that we want to reuse:

    ```
    todosSelector,
    filterSelector,
    ```

5. Now, we specify a filtering selector, copying the code from the `useMemo` Hook:

    ```
    (todos, filter) => {
        switch (filter) {
            case 'active':
                return todos.filter(t => t.completed === false)
            case 'completed':
                return todos.filter(t => t.completed === true)
            default:
            case 'all':
                return todos
        }
    }
    )
    ```

6. Finally, we use our defined selector in the Selector Hook:

    ```
    export default function TodoList () {
        const filteredTodos = useSelector(selectFilteredTodos)
    ```

Now that we have defined a reusable selector for the filtered todos, the result of filtering the todos will be memoized, and will not be re-computed if the state did not change.

Example code

The example code can be found in the `Chapter12/chapter12_4` folder.

Just run `npm install` in order to install all dependencies and `npm start` to start the application, then visit `http://localhost:3000` in your browser (if it did not open automatically).

Using the store Hook

React Redux also provides a `useStore` Hook, which returns a reference to the Redux store itself. This is the same `store` object that was passed to the `Provider` component. Its API looks like this:

```
const store = useStore()
```

It is best practice to avoid using the Store Hook directly. It usually makes more sense to use Dispatch or Selector Hooks instead. However, there are special use cases, such as replacing reducers, where using this Hook may be required.

In this section, we have learned how to replace connectors with Hooks in existing Redux applications. Now, we are going to learn a strategy that will allow us to effectively migrate existing Redux applications to Hooks.

Migrating a Redux application

In some Redux applications, local state was also stored in the Redux state tree. In others, React class component state was used to store local state. In either case, the way to migrate an existing Redux application is as follows:

- Replace **simple local state**, such as input field values, with State Hooks
- Replace **complex local state** with Reducer Hooks
- Keep **global state** (state that is used across multiple components) in the Redux store

We have already learned how to migrate React class components in the previous chapter. In the previous section, we learned how to migrate from Redux connectors to using Selector and Dispatch Hooks. We are now going to show an example of migrating Redux local state to a Hook-based approach.

Let us assume that our existing todo application stores the input field state in Redux, as follows:

```
{
    "todos": [],
    "filter": "all",
    "newTodo": ""
}
```

Right now, whenever text is entered, we need to dispatch an action, compute the new state by calling all reducers, and then update the Redux store state. As you can imagine, this can get quite performance heavy if we have many input fields. Instead of storing the `newTodo` field in Redux, we should use a State Hook to store this local state, as it is only used internally by one component. We have already done this correctly during the implementation of the `AddTodo` component in our example app.

Now that we have learned how to migrate existing Redux applications to Hooks, we can move on to discussing the trade-offs of Redux.

Trade-offs of Redux

To wrap up, let us summarize the pros and cons of using Redux in a web application. First, let us start with the positives:

- Provides a certain project structure that allows us to easily extend and modify code later on
- Fewer possibilities for errors in our code
- Better performance than using React Context for state
- Makes the `App` component much simpler (offloads state management and action creators to Redux)

Redux is a perfect fit for larger projects that deal with complex state changes, and state that is used across many components.

However, there are also downsides to using Redux:

- Writing boilerplate code required
- Project structure becomes more complicated
- Redux requires a wrapper component (`Provider`) to connect the app to the store

As a result, Redux should not be used for simple projects. In these cases, a Reducer Hook might be enough. With a Reducer Hook, there is no need for wrapper components in order to connect our app to the state store. Furthermore, if we use multiple Reducer Hooks, it is slightly more performant to send actions to a specific reducer, instead of a global app reducer. However, the downside lies in having to deal with multiple dispatch functions, and keeping the various states synchronized. We also cannot use middleware, including support for asynchronous actions, with a Reducer Hook. If state changes are complex but only local to a certain component, it might make sense to use a Reducer Hook, but if the state is used throughout multiple components, or it is relevant for the whole app, we should definitely store it in Redux.

You might not need Redux if your component does not do the following:

- Use the network
- Save or load state
- Share state with other non-child components

In that case, it makes sense to use a State or Reducer Hook, instead of Redux.

Summary

In this chapter we first learned what Redux is, as well as when and why it should be used. Then, we learned about the three principles of Redux. Next, we used Redux in practice to handle state in our ToDo application. We also learned about synchronous and asynchronous action creators. Then, we learned how to use Redux with Hooks, and how to migrate an existing Redux application to a Hook-based solution. Finally, we learned about the trade-offs of using Redux and Reducer Hooks.

In the next and final chapter, we are going to learn about handling state with MobX. We are going to learn what MobX is and how to use it the traditional way with React. Then, we are going to learn how to use MobX with Hooks, and we will also understand how to migrate an existing MobX application to a Hook-based solution.

Questions

In order to recap what we have learned in this chapter, try to answer the following questions:

1. What kind of state should Redux be used for?
2. Which elements does Redux consist of?
3. What are the three principles of Redux?
4. Why do we define action types?
5. How can we connect components to Redux?
6. Which Hooks can we use with Redux?
7. Why should we create reusable selectors?
8. How can we migrate a Redux application?
9. What are the trade-offs of Redux?
10. When should we use Redux?

Further reading

If you are interested in more information about the concepts that we have learned in this chapter, take a look at the following reading material:

- *Learning Redux*, published by *Packt:* https://www.packtpub.com/web-development/learning-redux
- Official Redux docs: https://redux.js.org
- Official React-Redux docs: https://react-redux.js.org/
- Information about Hooks and Redux: https://react-redux.js.org/next/api/hooks
- Reselect library on GitHub: https://github.com/reduxjs/reselect

13
MobX and Hooks

In the previous chapter, we learned about Redux and how to use Redux in combination with Hooks. We also learned how to migrate existing Redux applications to a Hook-based solution. Furthermore, we learned about the trade-offs of using Reducer Hooks versus Redux, and when to use either one of them.

In this chapter, we are going to learn how to use MobX in combination with Hooks. We are going to start by learning how to handle state with MobX, then move on to using MobX with Hooks. Furthermore, we will learn how to migrate an existing MobX application to Hooks. Finally, we are going to discuss the pros and cons of using MobX. By the end of this chapter, you will fully understand how to write MobX applications using Hooks.

The following topics will be covered in this chapter:

- Learning what MobX is and how it works
- Handling state with MobX
- Using MobX with Hooks
- Migrating a MobX application
- Learning about the trade-offs of MobX

Technical requirements

A fairly recent version of Node.js should already be installed (v11.12.0 or higher). The `npm` package manager for Node.js also needs to be installed.

The code for this chapter can be found in the GitHub repository: `https://github.com/PacktPublishing/Learn-React-Hooks/tree/master/Chapter13`.

Check out the following video to see the code in action:

`http://bit.ly/2Mm9yoC`

 Please note that it is highly recommended that you write the code on your own. Do not simply run the code examples that have been provided. It is important that you write the code yourself in order to be able to learn and understand it properly. However, if you run into any issues, you can always refer to the code example.

Now, let's get started with the chapter.

What is MobX?

MobX takes a different approach than Redux. Rather than applying restrictions to make state changes predictable, it aims to automatically update anything that is derived from the application state. Rather than dispatching actions, in MobX we can directly modify the state object and MobX will take care of updating anything that uses the state.

The MobX life cycle works as follows:

1. Events (such as `onClick`) invoke actions, which are the only things that can modify state:

```
@action onClick = () => {
    this.props.todo.completed = true
}
```

2. State is observable, and should not contain redundant or derivable data. State is very flexible—it can contain classes, arrays, references, or it can even be a graph:

```
@observable todos = [
    { title: 'Learn MobX', completed: false }
]
```

3. Computed values are derived from state through a pure function. These will be automatically updated by MobX:

```
@computed get activeTodos () {
    return this.todos.filter(todo => !todo.completed)
}
```

4. Reactions are like computed values, but they can also produce a side effect instead of a value, such as updating the user interface in React:

```
const TodoList = observer(({ todos }) => (
    <div>
        {todos.map(todo => <TodoItem {...todo} />)}
    </div>
)
```

We can see a visualization of the MobX life cycle in the following diagram:

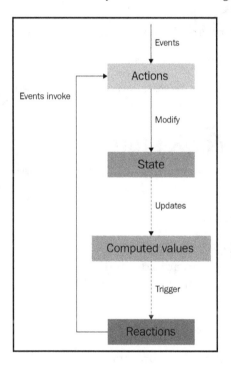

Visualization of the MobX life cycle

MobX and React work very well together. Whenever MobX detects that state has changed, it will cause a re-render of the appropriate components.

Unlike Redux, there are not many restrictions to learn about in order to use MobX. We only need to learn about a handful of core concepts, such as observables, computed values, and reactions.

Now that we know about the MobX life cycle, let's move on to handling state with MobX in practice.

Handling state with MobX

The best way to learn about MobX is by using it in practice and seeing how it works. So, let's start by porting our ToDo application from Chapter 11, *Migrating from React Class Components*, to MobX. We start by copying the code example from Chapter11/chapter11_2/.

Installing MobX

The first step is to install MobX and MobX React, via npm. Execute the following command:

```
> npm install --save mobx mobx-react
```

Now that MobX and MobX React are installed, we can start setting up the store.

Setting up the MobX store

After installing MobX, it is time to set up our MobX store. The store will store all state, and the related computed values and actions. It is usually defined with a class.

Let's define the MobX store now:

1. Create a new src/store.js file.
2. Import the observable, action, and computed decorators, as well as the decorate function from MobX. These will be used to tag various functions and values in our store:

    ```
    import { observable, action, computed, decorate } from 'mobx'
    ```

3. Also import the fetchAPITodos and generateID functions from our API code:

    ```
    import { fetchAPITodos, generateID } from './api'
    ```

4. Now, we define the store by using a class:

    ```
    export default class TodoStore {
    ```

5. In this store, we store a todos array, and the filter string value. These two values are observables. We are going to tag them as such later on:

    ```
    todos = []
    filter = 'all'
    ```

With a special project setup, we could use an experimental JavaScript feature, known as **decorators**, to tag our values as observables by writing `@observable todos = []`. However, this syntax is not supported by `create-react-app`, since it is not part of the JavaScript standard yet.

6. Next, we define a computed value in order to get all of the filtered `todos` from our store. The function will be similar to the one that we had in `src/App.js`, but now we will use `this.filter` and `this.todos`. Again, we have to tag the function as `computed` later on. MobX will automatically trigger this function when needed, and store the result until the state that it depends on changes:

```
get filteredTodos () {
    switch (this.filter) {
        case 'active':
            return this.todos.filter(t => t.completed ===
false)
        case 'completed':
            return this.todos.filter(t => t.completed === true)

        default:
        case 'all':
            return this.todos
    }
}
```

7. Now, we define our actions. We start with the `fetch` action. As before, we have to tag our action functions with the `action` decorator at a later point. In MobX, we can directly modify our state by setting `this.todos`. Because the `todos` value is observable, any changes to it will be automatically tracked by MobX:

```
fetch () {
    fetchAPITodos().then((fetchedTodos) => {
        this.todos = fetchedTodos
    })
}
```

8. Then, we define our `addTodo` action. In MobX, we do not use immutable values, so we should not create a new array. Instead, we always modify the existing `this.todos` value:

```
addTodo (title) {
    this.todos.push({ id: generateID(), title, completed: false
})
}
```

As you can see, MobX takes a more imperative approach, where values are directly modified, and MobX automatically keeps track of the changes. We do not need to use the rest/spread syntax to create new arrays; instead, we modify the existing state array directly.

9. Next up is the `toggleTodo` action. Here, we loop through all of the `todos` and modify the item with a matching `id`. Note how we can modify items within an array, and the change will still be tracked by MobX. In fact, MobX will even notice that only one value of the array has changed. In combination with React, this means that the list component will not re-render; only the item component of the item that changed is going to re-render. Please note that for this to be possible, we have to split up our components appropriately, such as making separate list and item components:

```
toggleTodo (id) {
    for (let todo of this.todos) {
        if (todo.id === id) {
            todo.completed = !todo.completed
            break
        }
    }
}
```

The `for (let .. of ..) {` construct will loop through all items of an array, or any other iterable value.

10. Now, we define the `removeTodo` action. First, we find the `index` of the `todo` item that we want to remove:

```
removeTodo (id) {
    let index = 0
    for (let todo of this.todos) {
        if (todo.id === id) {
            break
        } else {
            index++
        }
    }
}
```

11. Then, we use `splice` to remove one element—starting from the `index` of the found element. This means that we cut out the item with the given `id` from our array:

```
this.todos.splice(index, 1)
    }
```

12. The last action that we define, is the `filterTodos` action. Here, we simply set the `this.filter` value to the new filter:

```
filterTodos (filterName) {
    this.filter = filterName
    }
}
```

13. Finally, we have to decorate our store with the various decorators that we mentioned earlier. We do this by calling the `decorate` function on our store class and passing an object mapping values and methods to decorators:

```
decorate(TodoStore, {
```

14. We start with the `todos` and `filter` values, which are observables:

```
todos: observable,
filter: observable,
```

15. Then, we decorate the `computed` value—`filteredTodos`:

```
filteredTodos: computed,
```

16. Last but not least, we decorate our actions:

```
fetch: action,
addTodo: action,
toggleTodo: action,
removeTodo: action,
filterTodos: action
})
```

Now, our MobX store is decorated properly and ready to be used!

Defining the Provider component

We could now initialize the store in our `App` component, and pass it down to all of the other components. However, it is a better idea to use React Context. That way, we can access the store from anywhere in our app. MobX React offers a `Provider` component, which provides the store in a context.

Let's get started using the `Provider` component now:

1. Edit `src/index.js`, and import the `Provider` component from `mobx-react`:

   ```
   import { Provider } from 'mobx-react'
   ```

2. Then, import the `TodoStore` from our `store.js` file:

   ```
   import TodoStore from './store'
   ```

3. Now, we create a new instance of the `TodoStore` class:

   ```
   const store = new TodoStore()
   ```

4. Finally, we have to adjust the first argument to `ReactDOM.render()`, in order to wrap the `App` component with the `Provider` component:

   ```
   ReactDOM.render(
       <Provider todoStore={store}>
           <App />
       </Provider>,
       document.getElementById('root')
   )
   ```

> Unlike Redux, with MobX, it is possible to provide multiple stores in our app. However, here, we only provide one store, and we call it `todoStore`.

Now, our store is initialized and ready to be used in all other components.

Connecting components

Now that our MobX store is available as a context, we can start connecting our components to it. To do so, MobX React provides the `inject` higher-order component, which we can use to inject the store into our components.

In this section, we are going to connect the following components to our MobX store:

- App
- TodoList
- TodoItem
- AddTodo
- TodoFilter

Connecting the App component

We are going to start by connecting our App component, where we will use the fetch action to fetch all todos from our API, when the app initializes.

Let's connect the App component now:

1. Edit src/App.js, and import the inject function from mobx-react:

   ```
   import { inject } from 'mobx-react'
   ```

2. Then, wrap the App component with inject. The inject function is used to inject the store (or multiple stores) as props to the component:

   ```
   export default inject('todoStore')(function App ({ todoStore }) {
   ```

    It is possible to specify multiple stores in the inject function, as follows: inject('todoStore', 'otherStore'). Then, two props will be injected: todoStore and otherStore.

3. Now that we have the todoStore available, we can use it to call the fetch action within our Effect Hook:

   ```
   useEffect(() => {
       todoStore.fetch()
   }, [ todoStore ])
   ```

4. We can now remove the filteredTodos Memo Hook, the handler functions, the StateContext.Provider component, and all of the props that we passed down to the other components:

   ```
   return (
       <div style={{ width: 400 }}>
           <Header />
   ```

```
                    <AddTodo />
                    <hr />
                    <TodoList />
                    <hr />
                    <TodoFilter />
            </div>
        )
    })
```

Now, our `App` component will fetch `todos` from the API, and then they will be stored in the `TodoStore`.

Connecting the TodoList component

After storing the `todos` in our store, we can get them from the store, and then we can list all of the todo items in the `TodoList` component.

Let's connect the `TodoList` component now:

1. Edit `src/TodoList.js` and import the `inject` and `observer` functions:

   ```
   import { inject, observer } from 'mobx-react'
   ```

2. Remove all context-related imports and Hooks.
3. As before, we use the `inject` function to wrap the component. Additionally, we now wrap our component with the `observer` function. The `observer` function tells MobX that this component should re-render when the store updates:

   ```
   export default inject('todoStore')(observer(function TodoList ({
   todoStore }) {
   ```

4. We can now use the `filteredTodos` computed value from our store, to list all todo items with the filter applied. To make sure that MobX can still track when changes to the `item` object occur, we *do not* use the spread syntax here. If we used the spread syntax, all of the todo items would re-render, even if only one changed:

   ```
       return todoStore.filteredTodos.map(item =>
           <TodoItem key={item.id} item={item} />
       )
   })))
   ```

Now, our app will already list all of the todo items. However, we cannot toggle or remove the todo items yet.

Connecting the TodoItem component

To be able to toggle or remove todo items, we have to connect the `TodoItem` component. We also define the `TodoItem` component as an observer, so that MobX knows it will have to re-render the component when the `item` object changes.

Let's connect the `TodoItem` component now:

1. Edit `src/TodoItem.js`, and import the `inject` and `observer` functions from `mobx-react`:

   ```
   import { inject, observer } from 'mobx-react'
   ```

2. Then, wrap the `TodoItem` component with `inject` and `observer`:

   ```
   export default inject('todoStore')(observer(function TodoItem ({
   item, todoStore }) {
   ```

3. We can now use destructuring of the `item` object within the component. As it is defined as an observer, MobX will be able to track changes to the `item` object, even after destructuring:

   ```
   const { title, completed, id } = item
   ```

4. Now that we have the `todoStore` available, we can use it to adjust our handler functions, and to call the corresponding actions:

   ```
   function handleToggle () {
       todoStore.toggleTodo(id)
   }

   function handleRemove () {
       todoStore.removeTodo(id)
   }
   ```

Now, our `TodoItem` component will call the `toggleTodo` and `removeTodo` actions from our `todoStore`, so we can now toggle and remove the todo items!

Connecting the AddTodo component

To be able to add new todo items, we have to connect the `AddTodo` component.

Let's connect the `AddTodo` component now:

1. Edit `src/AddTodo.js` and import the `inject` function from `mobx-react`:

    ```
    import { inject } from 'mobx-react'
    ```

2. Then, wrap the `AddTodo` component with `inject`:

    ```
    export default inject('todoStore')(function AddTodo ({ todoStore })
    {
    ```

3. Now that we have the `todoStore` available, we can use it to adjust our handler function, and to call the `addTodo` action:

    ```
    function handleAdd () {
        if (input) {
            todoStore.addTodo(input)
            setInput('')
        }
    }
    ```

Now, our `AddTodo` component will call the `addTodo` action from our `todoStore`, so we can now add new todo items!

Connecting the TodoFilter component

Lastly, we have to connect the `TodoFilter` component in order to be able to select different filters. We also want to show the currently selected filter, so this component needs to be an `observer`.

Let's connect the `TodoFilter` component now:

1. Edit `src/TodoFilter.js` and import the `inject` and `observer` functions:

    ```
    import { inject, observer } from 'mobx-react'
    ```

2. We use the `inject` and `observer` functions to wrap the component:

    ```
    const TodoFilterItem = inject('todoStore')(observer(function
    TodoFilterItemWrapped ({ name, todoStore }) {
    ```

3. We now adjust our handler function to call the `filterTodos` action from the store:

```
function handleFilter () {
    todoStore.filterTodos(name)
}
```

4. Finally, we adjust the `style` object to use the `filter` value from `todoStore`, in order to check whether the filter is currently selected:

```
const style = {
    color: 'blue',
    cursor: 'pointer',
    fontWeight: (todoStore.filter === name) ? 'bold': 'normal'
}
```

5. Furthermore, we can now get rid of passing down the props in the `FilterItem` component. Remove the following parts that are marked in bold:

```
export default function TodoFilter (props) {
    return (
        <div>
            <TodoFilterItem {...props} name="all" />{' / '}
            <TodoFilterItem {...props} name="active" />{' / '}
            <TodoFilterItem {...props} name="completed" />
        </div>
    )
}
```

Now, we can select new filters, which will be marked as selected, in bold. The todo list will also automatically be filtered, because MobX detects a change in the `filter` value, which causes the `filteredTodos` computed value to update, and the `TodoList` observer component to re-render.

Example code

The example code can be found in the `Chapter13/chapter13_1` folder.

Just run `npm install` in order to install all dependencies, and `npm start` to start the application, then visit `http://localhost:3000` in your browser (if it did not open automatically).

Using MobX with Hooks

In the previous section, we learned how to use MobX with React. As we have seen, to be able to connect our components to the MobX store, we need to wrap them with the `inject` function, and in some cases, also with the `observer` function. Instead of using these higher-order components to wrap our components, since the release of v6 of `mobx-react`, we can also use Hooks to connect our components to the MobX store. We are now going to use MobX with Hooks!

Defining a store Hook

First of all, we have to define a Hook in order to access our own store. As we have learned before, MobX uses React Context to provide, and inject, state into various components. We can get the `MobXProviderContext` from `mobx-react` and create our own custom context Hook in order to access all stores. Then, we can create another Hook, to specifically access our `TodoStore`.

So, let's begin defining a store Hook:

1. Create a new `src/hooks.js` file.
2. Import the `useContext` Hook from `react`, and the `MobXProviderContext` from `mobx-react`:

   ```
   import { useContext } from 'react'
   import { MobXProviderContext } from 'mobx-react'
   ```

3. Now, we define and export a `useStores` Hook, which returns a Context Hook for the `MobXProviderContext`:

   ```
   export function useStores () {
       return useContext(MobXProviderContext)
   }
   ```

4. Finally, we define a `useTodoStore` Hook, which gets the `todoStore` from our previous Hook, and then returns it:

   ```
   export function useTodoStore () {
       const { todoStore } = useStores()
       return todoStore
   }
   ```

Now, we have a general Hook, to access all stores from MobX, and a specific Hook to access the `TodoStore`. If we need to, we can also define more Hooks for other stores at a later point.

Upgrading components to Hooks

After creating a Hook to access our store, we can use it instead of wrapping our components with the `inject` higher-order component function. In the upcoming sections, we will see how we can use Hooks to upgrade our various components.

Using Hooks for the App component

We are going to start by upgrading our `App` component. It is possible to gradually refactor components so that they use Hooks instead. We do not need to refactor every component at once.

Let's use Hooks for the `App` component now:

1. Edit `src/App.js` and remove the following `import` statement:

   ```
   import { inject } from 'mobx-react'
   ```

2. Then, import the `useTodoStore` Hook from our `hooks.js` file:

   ```
   import { useTodoStore } from './hooks'
   ```

3. Now, remove the `inject` function that is wrapping the `App` component, and remove all props. The `App` function definition should now look as follows:

   ```
   export default function App () {
   ```

4. Finally, use our Todo Store Hook to get the `todoStore` object:

   ```
   const todoStore = useTodoStore()
   ```

As you can see, our app still works in the same way as before! However, we are now using Hooks in the `App` component, which makes the code much more clean and concise.

Using Hooks for the TodoList component

Next, we are going to upgrade our `TodoList` component. Additionally, we are also going to use the `useObserver` Hook, which replaces the `observer` higher-order component.

Let's use Hooks for the `TodoList` component now:

1. Edit `src/TodoList.js`, and remove the following import statement:

   ```
   import { inject, observer } from 'mobx-react'
   ```

2. Then, import the `useObserver` Hook from `mobx-react` and the `useTodoStore` Hook from our `hooks.js` file:

   ```
   import { useObserver } from 'mobx-react'
   import { useTodoStore } from './hooks'
   ```

3. Now, remove the `inject` and `observer` functions that are wrapping the `TodoList` component, and also remove all props. The `TodoList` function definition should now look as follows:

   ```
   export default function TodoList () {
   ```

4. Again, we use the Todo Store Hook to get the `todoStore` object:

   ```
   const todoStore = useTodoStore()
   ```

5. Finally, we wrap the returned elements with the `useObserver` Hook. Everything within the Observer Hook will be recomputed when the state that is used within the Hook changes:

   ```
   return useObserver(() =>
       todoStore.filteredTodos.map(item =>
           <TodoItem key={item.id} item={item} />
       )
   )
   }
   ```

In our case, MobX will detect that the observer that was defined via the `useObserver` Hook depends on `todoStore.filteredTodos`, and `filteredTodos` depends on the `filter` and `todos` values. As a result, the list will be re-rendered whenever either the `filter` value or the `todos` array changes.

Using Hooks for the TodoItem component

Next, we are going to upgrade the `TodoItem` component, which will be a similar process to what we did with the `TodoList` component.

Let's use Hooks for the `TodoItem` component now:

1. Edit `src/TodoItem.js` and remove the following `import` statement:

   ```
   import { inject, observer } from 'mobx-react'
   ```

2. Then, import the `useObserver` Hook from `mobx-react`, and the `useTodoStore` Hook from our `hooks.js` file:

   ```
   import { useObserver } from 'mobx-react'

   import { useTodoStore } from './hooks'
   ```

3. Now, remove the `inject` and `observer` functions that are wrapping the `TodoItem` component, and also remove the `todoStore` prop. The `TodoItem` function definition should now look as follows:

   ```
   export default function TodoItem ({ item }) {
   ```

4. Next, we have to remove the destructuring (the code in bold) because our whole component is not defined as observable anymore, so MobX will not be able to track the changes to the `item` object:

   `const { title, completed, id } = item`

5. Then, use the Todo Store Hook to get the `todoStore` object:

   ```
   const todoStore = useTodoStore()
   ```

6. Now, we have to adjust the handler functions so that they use `item.id` instead of `id` directly. Please note that we assume that the `id` does not change, therefore, it is not wrapped within an Observer Hook:

   ```
   function handleToggle () {
       todoStore.toggleTodo(item.id)
   }

   function handleRemove () {
       todoStore.removeTodo(item.id)
   }
   ```

7. Finally, we wrap the `return` statement with an Observer Hook and do the destructuring there. This ensures that changes to the `item` object are tracked by MobX, and that the component will re-render accordingly when the properties of the object change:

```
return useObserver(() => {
    const { title, completed } = item
    return (
        <div style={{ width: 400, height: 25 }}>
            <input type="checkbox" checked={completed}
onChange={handleToggle} />
            {title}
            <button style={{ float: 'right' }}
onClick={handleRemove}>x</button>
        </div>
    )
})
}
```

Now, our `TodoItem` component is properly connected to the MobX store.

If the `item.id` property changes, we would have to wrap the handler functions, and the `return` function, within a single `useObserver` Hook, as follows:

```
return useObserver(() => {
    const { title, completed, id } = item

    function handleToggle () {
        todoStore.toggleTodo(id)
    }

    function handleRemove () {
        todoStore.removeTodo(id)
    }

    return (
        <div style={{ width: 400, height: 25 }}>
            <input type="checkbox" checked={completed}
onChange={handleToggle} />
            {title}
            <button style={{ float: 'right' }}
onClick={handleRemove}>x</button>
        </div>
    )
})
```

Note that we cannot wrap the handler functions and the `return` statement in separate Observer Hooks, because then the handler functions would only be defined within the closure of the first Observer Hook. This would mean that we would not be able to access the handler functions from within the second Observer Hook.

Next, we are going to continue to upgrade our components by using Hooks for the `AddTodo` component.

Using Hooks for the AddTodo component

We repeat the same upgrade process as we did in the `App` component for the `AddTodo` component, as follows:

1. Edit `src/AddTodo.js` and remove the following `import` statement:

   ```
   import { inject } from 'mobx-react'
   ```

2. Then, import the `useTodoStore` Hook from our `hooks.js` file:

   ```
   import { useTodoStore } from './hooks'
   ```

3. Now, remove the `inject` function that is wrapping the `AddTodo` component, and also remove all props. The `AddTodo` function definition should now look as follows:

   ```
   export default function AddTodo () {
   ```

4. Finally, use the Todo Store Hook to get the `todoStore` object:

   ```
   const todoStore = useTodoStore()
   ```

Now, our `AddTodo` component is connected to the MobX store and we can move on to upgrading the `TodoFilter` component.

Using Hooks for the TodoFilter component

For the `TodoFilter` component, we are going to use a similar process to the one that we used for the `TodoList` component. We are going to use our `useTodoStore` Hook and the `useObserver` Hook.

Let's use Hooks for the `TodoFilter` component now:

1. Edit `src/TodoFilter.js` and remove the following `import` statement:

```
import { inject, observer } from 'mobx-react'
```

2. Then, import the `useObserver` Hook from `mobx-react`, and the `useTodoStore` Hook from our `hooks.js` file:

```
import { useObserver } from 'mobx-react'
import { useTodoStore } from './hooks'
```

3. Now, remove the `inject` and `observer` functions that are wrapping the `TodoFilterItem` component, and also remove the `todoStore` prop. The `TodoFilterItem` function definition should now look as follows:

```
function TodoFilterItem ({ name }) {
```

4. Again, we use the Todo Store Hook to get the `todoStore` object:

```
const todoStore = useTodoStore()
```

5. Finally, we wrap the `style` object with the `useObserver` Hook. Remember, everything within the Observer Hook will be re-computed when the state that is used within the Hook changes:

```
const style = useObserver(() => ({
    color: 'blue',
    cursor: 'pointer',
    fontWeight: (todoStore.filter === name) ? 'bold' : 'normal'
}))
```

In this case, the `style` object will be re-computed whenever the `todoStore.filter` value changes, which will cause the element to re-render, and change the font weight when a different filter is selected.

Example code

The example code can be found in the `Chapter13/chapter13_2` folder.

Just run `npm install` in order to install all dependencies, and `npm start` to start the application, then visit `http://localhost:3000` in your browser (if it did not open automatically).

Using the local store Hook

In addition to providing global stores to store application-wide state, MobX also provides local stores to store local state. To create a local store, we can use the `useLocalStore` Hook.

We are now going to implement the Local Store Hook in the `AddTodo` component:

1. Edit `src/AddTodo.js` and import the `useLocalStore` Hook, as well as the `useObserver` Hook from `mobx-react`:

   ```
   import { useLocalStore, useObserver } from 'mobx-react'
   ```

2. Then, remove the following State Hook:

   ```
   const [ input, setInput ] = useState('')
   ```

   Replace it with a Local Store Hook:

   ```
   const inputStore = useLocalStore(() => ({
   ```

   In this local store, we can define state values, computed values, and actions. The `useLocalStore` Hook will automatically decorate values as observable, getter functions (the `get` prefix) as computed values, and normal functions as actions.

3. We start with a `value` state for the `input` field:

   ```
   value: '',
   ```

4. Then, we define a computed value, which will tell us whether the **add** button should be `disabled` or not:

   ```
   get disabled () {
       return !this.value
   },
   ```

5. Next, we define the actions. The first action updates the `value` from an input event:

   ```
   updateFromInput (e) {
       this.value = e.target.value
   },
   ```

6. Then, we define another action to update the `value` from a simple string:

```
update (val) {
    this.value = val
}
})) 
```

7. Now, we can adjust the input handler function, and call the `updateFromInput` action:

```
function handleInput (e) {
    inputStore.updateFromInput (e)
}
```

8. We also have to adjust the `handleAdd` function:

```
function handleAdd () {
    if (inputStore.value) {
        todoStore.addTodo (inputStore.value)
        inputStore.update ('')
    }
}
```

9. Finally, we wrap the elements with a `useObserver` Hook, in order to make sure that the `input` field value gets updated when it changes, and we adjust the `disabled` and `value` props:

```
return useObserver (() => (
    <form onSubmit={e => { e.preventDefault(); handleAdd() }}>
        <input
            type="text"
            placeholder="enter new task..."
            style={{ width: 350, height: 15 }}
            value={inputStore.value}
            onChange={handleInput}
        />
        <input
            type="submit"
            style={{ float: 'right', marginTop: 2 }}
            disabled={inputStore.disabled}
            value="add"
        />
    </form>
))
}
```

Now, our `AddTodo` component uses a local MobX store in order to handle its input value, and to disable/enable the button. As you can see, with MobX, it is possible to use multiple stores, for local as well as global states. The hard part is deciding how to split up and group your stores in a way that makes sense for the given application.

Example code

The example code can be found in the `Chapter13/chapter13_3` folder.

Just run `npm install` in order to install all dependencies, and `npm start` to start the application, then visit `http://localhost:3000` in your browser (if it did not open automatically).

Migrating a MobX application

In the previous section, we learned how to replace MobX higher-order components, such as `inject` and `observer` in existing MobX applications with Hooks. Now, we are going to learn how to migrate local state to Hooks in existing MobX applications.

An existing MobX application can be migrated to a Hook-based solution by following three steps:

- Using a State Hook for simple local state
- Using the `useLocalState` Hook for complex local state
- Keeping global state in separate MobX stores

We have already learned how to use a State Hook in the early chapters of this book. State Hooks make sense for simple state, such as the current state of a checkbox.

We have already learned how to use the `useLocalState` Hook in this chapter. We can use the Local State Hook for complex local state, such as complex forms where multiple fields interact with each other. Then, we can replace multiple State and Effect Hooks with a single Local State Hook and computed values and actions.

Lastly, global state should be stored in separate MobX stores, such as the `TodoStore`, which we defined in this chapter. In MobX, multiple stores can be created and passed down to components using the `Provider` component. We can then create a separate custom Hook for each of the stores.

The trade-offs of MobX

To wrap up, let's summarize the pros and cons of using MobX in a web application. First, let's start with the positives:

- It provides a simple way of dealing with state changes
- Less boilerplate code is required
- It offers flexibility in how our application code is structured
- Multiple global and local stores can be used
- It makes the App component much simpler (it offloads state management and actions to MobX)

MobX is perfect for small—and large projects—that deal with complex state changes, and state that is used across many components.

However, there are also downsides to using MobX:

- State changes could happen anywhere, not just in a single store
- Its flexibility means that it is possible to structure the project in a bad way, which could cause errors or bugs
- MobX requires a wrapper component (Provider) in order to connect the app to the store, if we want to get all the features (we could directly import and use the MobX store, but it would break features such as server-side rendering)

If state changes are simple, and only local state within components is needed, MobX should not be used. In that case, a State or a Reducer Hook might be enough. With Reducer and State Hooks, there is no need for wrapper components in order to connect our app to the store.

Flexibility is a good thing, but it can also cause us to structure a project badly. However, MobX provides a project called mobx-state-tree, which allows us to make our MobX applications more structured and enforce a certain kind of architecture. More information can be found on the project page in the following GitHub repository: https://github.com/mobxjs/mobx-state-tree.

Summary

In this chapter, we first learned what MobX is, which elements it consists of, and how they work together. Then, we learned how to use MobX for state management in practice. We also learned how to connect a MobX store to React components, by using the `inject` and `observer` higher-order components. Next, we replaced the higher-order components with Hooks, which made our code much more clean and concise. We also learned how to use a Local Store Hook to deal with complex local state in MobX. Finally, we learned how to migrate an existing MobX application to Hooks, and we recapped what the trade-offs of using MobX are.

This chapter marks the end of this book. In this book, we started out with a motivation to use Hooks. We learned that there are common problems in React apps that cannot be easily solved without Hooks. Then, we created our first component using Hooks and compared it to a class-component-based solution. Next, we learned about various Hooks in depth, starting with the State Hook, which is the most ubiquitous of them all. We also learned about solving common problems with Hooks, such as conditional Hooks and Hooks in loops.

After learning about the State Hook in depth, we developed a small blog app using Hooks. We then learned about Reducer Hooks, Effect Hooks, and Context Hooks, in order to be able to implement more features in our app. Next, we learned how to request resources efficiently using Hooks. Furthermore, we learned how to prevent unnecessary re-rendering with `React.memo`, and how to implement lazy-loading with React Suspense. Then, we implemented routes in our blog app, and we learned how Hooks can make dynamic routing much easier.

We also learned about various Hooks that are provided by the community, which make dealing with input fields, various data structures, responsive design, and undo/redo functionality so much easier. Furthermore, we learned about the rules of Hooks, how to create our own custom Hooks, and how interactions between Hooks work. Toward the end, we learned how to effectively migrate from existing class-component-based apps, to a Hook-based solution. Finally, we learned how to use Hooks with Redux and MobX, and how to migrate existing Redux and MobX applications to Hooks.

Now that we have learned about Hooks in depth, we are ready to use them in our applications! We have also learned how to migrate existing projects to Hooks, so we can start doing that now. I hope you enjoyed learning about React Hooks, and that you are looking forward to implementing Hooks in your applications! I am sure that using Hooks will make coding much more enjoyable for you, just like they did for me.

Questions

In order to recap what we have learned in this chapter, try to answer the following questions:

1. Which elements form the MobX life cycle?
2. Which decorators does MobX provide?
3. How can we connect components to MobX?
4. Which Hooks does MobX provide?
5. How can we access the MobX store using Hooks?
6. Can we store local state using MobX?
7. How should we go about migrating an existing MobX application to Hooks?
8. What are the advantages of using MobX?
9. What are the disadvantages of using MobX?
10. When should MobX not be used?

Further reading

If you are interested in more information about the concepts that we have learned in this chapter, take a look at the following reading material:

- An introduction to MobX from the official MobX docs: `https://mobx.js.org/getting-started.html`
- The official MobX docs: `https://mobx.js.org`
- A video course on the basics of MobX: `https://egghead.io/lessons/react-sync-the-ui-with-the-app-state-using-mobx-observable-and-observer-in-react`
- The official MobX React docs: `https://mobx-react.js.org/`
- The `mobx` project on GitHub: `https://github.com/mobxjs/mobx`
- The `mobx-react` project on GitHub: `https://github.com/mobxjs/mobx-react`
- The `mobx-state-tree` project on GitHub: `https://github.com/mobxjs/mobx-state-tree`

Assessments

Answers to questions

Here, we answer all the questions asked at the end of each chapter. You can use these questions to review what you have learned throughout the book.

Chapter 1: Introducing React and React Hooks

1. What are React's three fundamental principles?
    - **Declarative**: Instead of telling React how to do things, we tell it what we want. As a result, we can easily design our applications and React will efficiently update and render just the right components when data changes.
    - **Component-based**: React encapsulates components that manage their own state and views, then allows us to compose them to create complex user interfaces.
    - **Learn once, write anywhere:** React does not make assumptions about your technology stack and tries to ensure you can develop without rewriting existing code as much as possible.

2. What are the two types of components in React?
    - **Function components**: JavaScript functions that take the props as an argument and return the user interface (usually via JSX)
    - **Class components**: JavaScript classes that provide a `render` method, which returns the user interface (usually via JSX)

3. What are the problems with class components in React?
    - JavaScript classes are hard to understand for developers: The `this` context can be confusing, and we sometimes have to write code in multiple places at once
    - They are also hard to understand for machines: It is hard to tell which methods will be called and, as such, performance optimizations are not really possible

- They are not declarative and thus go against React's fundamental principles: To use React features, we have to write code that tells React what to do, not how to do it

4. What is the problem of using higher-order components in React?
    - Using higher-order components introduces components to our view tree that do not actually matter in terms of view structure. Having many higher-order components causes the so-called **wrapper hell**.

5. Which tool can we use to set up a React project, and what is the command that we need to run to use it?
    - We can use `create-react-app`. To create a new project, we have to run `npx create-react-app <app-name>` or `yarn create react-app <app-name>`.

6. What do we need to do if we get the following error with class components: *TypeError: undefined is not an object (evaluating 'this.setState')*?
    - We forgot to re-bind the `this` context of the method in the `constructor` of our class. As a result, `this` is not pointing to the class but, instead, to the context of the input field.

7. How do we access and set React state using Hooks?
    - We make use of the `useState()` Hook as follows: `const [ name, setName ] = useState('')`

8. What are the advantages of using function components with Hooks, in comparison to class components?
    - Function components with Hooks do not suffer from the same problems as classes. They are declarative and thus fit React's fundamental principles better. Hooks also make our code more concise and easier to understand.

9. Do we need to replace all class components with function components using Hooks when updating React?
    - No, we do not need to replace all class components. Function components with Hooks can work side-by-side with existing class components and are 100% backward-compatible. We can simply write new components using Hooks or upgrade existing components at our own pace.

10. What are the three basic hooks provided by React?
  - The `useState`, `useEffect`, and `useContext` Hooks are the basic Hooks provided by React and used very frequently in projects. However, React also provides some more advanced Hooks out of the box.

Chapter 2: Using the State Hook

1. What problems did we run into while developing our own reimplementation of the `useState` hook? How did we solve these problems?
  - One problem was the initialization of the value every time the component gets rendered. We solved this problem by using a global variable to store the value.
  - Then, we had the problem that multiple Hooks write to the same global variable. To solve this problem, we stored the values in an array and kept track of the current Hook by assigning an index to each Hook.

2. Why are conditional Hooks not possible in the React implementation of Hooks?
  - Conditional Hooks are not possible, because React uses the order of Hook definitions to keep track of the values. If we change the order of Hooks later on, the values will be assigned to different Hooks.

3. What are Hooks and what do they deal with?
  - Hooks are functions that deal with state and effects in a React application

4. What do we need to watch out for when using Hooks?
  - We need to ensure that the order of Hooks always stays the same, so we cannot use Hooks in loops or conditionals

5. What are the common problems of alternative API ideas for Hooks?
  - Named Hooks have the problem of name collisions. Each Hook would have to have a unique name, even when using Hooks within libraries.
  - Hook factories require more boilerplate code, mainly instantiating each Hook twice, once outside of the component and once inside. Furthermore, they make it much harder to create custom Hooks.

6. How do we implement conditional Hooks?
  - In simple cases, we can always define the Hook. Otherwise, we have to split up the components and conditionally render a separate component instead of conditionally rendering the Hook.

7. How do we implement Hooks in loops?
    - In simple cases, we can store an array in the State Hook. Otherwise, we have to split up the components and render a separate component in a loop.

Chapter 3: Writing Your First Application with React Hooks

1. What is the best practice for folder structures in React?
    - Start with a simple structure at first and nest more deeply when needed. Do not spend too much time thinking about the file structure when starting a project.

2. Which principle should we use when splitting up React components?
    - The single responsibility principle, which states that every component should have responsibility over a single encapsulated part of the functionality

3. What does the map function do?
    - The map function applies a given function to all elements of an array and returns a new array with the results

4. How does destructuring work, and when do we use it?
    - With destructuring, we can get properties from an object or elements from an array by specifying the structure and variable names on the left side of the assignment. We can use destructuring to get certain props in React components.

5. How does the spread operator work, and when do we use it?
    - The spread operator inserts all properties of an object or all elements of an array at a certain point in another object/array. It can be used to create new arrays or objects or to pass on all properties of an object as props to a React component.

6. How do we deal with input fields using React Hooks?
    - We create a State Hook for the input field value and define a handler function that sets the value

7. Where should local State Hooks be defined?
    - Local State Hooks should always be defined in the component where they are used

8. What is global state?
   - Global state is state that is used across multiple components throughout the whole application

9. Where should global State Hooks be defined?
   - Global State Hooks should be defined as high up in the component tree as possible. In our case, we defined them in the `App` component.

Chapter 4: Using the Reducer and Effect Hooks

1. What are common problems with State Hooks?
   - Complex state changes are hard to do with State Hooks

2. What are actions?
   - Actions are objects that describe a state change, for example, `{ type: 'CHANGE_FILTER', byAuthor: 'Daniel Bugl' }`

3. What are reducers?
   - Reducers are functions that process state changes. They accept the current state and an action object and return a new state.

4. When should we use a Reducer Hook instead of a State Hook?
   - Reducer Hooks should be used when complex state changes are needed. Usually, this is the case for global state.
   - When setter functions of multiple State Hooks are called together, this is a good indicator for using a Reducer Hook instead.

5. Which steps are needed in order to turn a State Hook into a Reducer Hook?
   - We first need to define actions, then the reducer function, and finally a Reducer Hook

6. How can we create actions more easily?
   - We could define functions that return action objects, so called **action creators**

7. When should we merge Reducer Hooks?
   - When we want to avoid having two separate dispatch functions or when the same action modifies state in multiple reducers

8. What do we need to watch out for when merging Reducer Hooks?
   - We need to make sure that each reducer returns the current state for unhandled actions

9. What is the equivalent of an Effect Hook in class components?
    - In React class components we would use `componentDidMount` and `componentDidUpdate` to deal with effects

10. What are the advantages of using an Effect Hook versus class components?
    - With Effect Hooks we do not need to define both `componentDidMount` and `componentDidUpdate`. Furthermore, Effect Hooks are much easier to understand, and we do not need to know how React works internally to be able to use them.

Chapter 5: Implementing React Context

1. Which problem do contexts avoid?
    - Contexts avoid having to pass down props through multiple levels of components

2. What are the two parts that contexts consist of?
    - React contexts consist of a provider and a consumer

3. Are both parts required to be defined in order to use contexts?
    - The provider is not required, as contexts will use the default value passed to `React.createContext` when no provider is defined

4. What is the advantage of using Hooks instead of traditional context consumers?
    - Hooks do not require using a component and render props for the consumer. Using multiple contexts with consumer components makes our component tree very deep and our app harder to debug and maintain. Hooks avoid this problem by allowing us to consume contexts by simply calling a Hook function.

5. What is an alternative to contexts, and when should we use it?
    - Contexts make reusing components more difficult. Contexts should only be used when we need to access data in multiple components at different nesting levels. Otherwise, we can either pass down props or pass down the rendered component, using a technique called inversion of control.

6. How can we implement dynamically changing contexts?
    - We need to use a State Hook to provide the value for the context provider

7. When does it make sense to use contexts for state?
   - Usually, it makes sense to use contexts for global state, which is used across multiple components at different nesting levels

Chapter 6: Implementing Requests and React Suspense

1. How can we easily create a full REST API from a simple JSON file?
   - We can use the `json-server` tool to create a full REST API from a JSON file for development and testing

2. What are the advantages of using a proxy to access our backend server during development?
   - When using a proxy, we do not need to deal with cross-site restrictions during development

3. Which combinations of Hooks can we use to implement requests?
   - We can implement requests using an Effect and a State or Reducer Hook

4. Which libraries can we use to implement requests?
   - We can also use the `axios` and `react-request-hook` libraries to implement requests

5. How can we deal with loading states using `react-request-hook`?
   - We can use the `result.isLoading` flag returned from the `useResource` Hook and conditionally display a loading message

6. How can we deal with errors using `react-request-hook`?
   - We can use the `result.error` object returned from the `useResource` Hook and dispatch an error action

7. How can we prevent unnecessary re-rendering of components?
   - Using `React.memo`, we can prevent unnecessary re-rendering, similarly to `shouldComponentUpdate`

8. How can we reduce the bundle size of our app?
   - We can use `React.Suspense` to lazily load certain components, which means that they will only be requested from the server when needed

Chapter 7: Using Hooks for Routing

1. Why do we need to define separate pages?
    - Most large apps consist of multiple pages. For example, a separate page for each blog post
2. How do we define routes using the Navi library?
    - We use the `mount` function and pass an object mapping path to `route` functions
3. How do we define routes with URL parameters?
    - We can use the `:parameter` syntax to specify URL parameters within the path

4. How are static links defined with Navi?
    - Static links can be defined using the `Link` component from `react-navi`
5. How can we implement dynamic navigation?
    - Dynamic navigation can be implemented using the `useNavigation` Hook and calling `navigation.navigate()`
6. Which Hook is used to access route information of the current route?
    - The `useCurrentRoute` Hook gives us all information about the current route
7. Which Hook is used to access route information of the currently loading route?
    - The `useLoadingRoute` Hook gives us all information about the route that is currently being loaded

Chapter 8: Using Community Hooks

1. Which Hook can we use to simplify input field handling?
    - We can use the `useInput` Hook from the `react-hookedup` library
2. How are the `componentDidMount` and `componentWillUnmount` life cycles implemented using Effect Hooks?
    - `componentDidMount` can be implemented by using an Effect Hook with an empty array passed as the second argument. For example, `useEffect(() => console.log('did mount'), [])`.

- `componentWillUnmount` can be implemented by returning a function from an Effect Hook with an empty array passed as the second argument, for example, `useEffect(() => { return () => console.log('will unmount') }, [])`.

3. How can we use Hooks to get the behavior of `this.setState()`?
   - `this.setState()` merges the existing state object with the given state object. We can get the same behavior by using the `useMergeState` Hook instead of a simple State Hook.

4. Why should we use timer Hooks instead of calling `setTimeout` and `setInterval` directly?
   - When defining simple timeouts or intervals they are going to reset when the component re-renders. To prevent this resetting from happening, we have to use the `useTimeout` and `useInterval` Hooks from `react-hookedup` instead.

5. Which Hooks can we use to simplify dealing with common data structures?
   - We can use the `useBoolean`, `useArray`, and `useCounter` Hooks from `react-hookedup`

6. When should we use responsive design with Hooks versus simply using CSS media queries?
   - We should use Hooks for responsive design when rendering elements within a canvas or WebGL, or when we dynamically want to decide whether to load components based on the window size

7. Which Hook can we use to implement undo/redo functionality?
   - We can use the `useUndo` Hook from the `use-undo` library to implement simple undo/redo functionality in our app

8. What is debouncing? Why do we need to do it?
   - Debouncing means that a function will only be called after a certain amount of time, not every time an event triggers it. Using debouncing, we can store a value entered in a text field in the undo history only after each second, not after every typed character.

9. Which Hook can we use for debouncing?
   - We can use the `useDebounce` or the `useDebouncedCallback` Hook from the `use-debounce` library

Chapter 9: Rules of Hooks

1. Where can Hooks be called?
   - Hooks can only be called at the beginning of React function components or custom Hooks

2. Can we use Hooks in React class components?
   - No, it is not possible to use Hooks in React class components

3. What do we need to watch out for regarding the order of Hooks?
   - The order of Hooks should never change, as it is used to track the values of various Hooks

4. Can hooks be called inside conditions, loops, or nested functions?
   - No, Hooks cannot be called inside conditionals, loops, or nested functions, because that would change the order of Hooks

5. What is the naming convention for Hooks?
   - Hook function names should always start with a `use` prefix and then a name in `CamelCase`. For example: `useSomeHookName`.

6. How can we automatically enforce the rules of Hooks?
   - We can use `eslint` with `eslint-plugin-react-hooks` to enforce the rules of Hooks

7. What is the exhaustive dependencies rule?
   - The exhaustive dependencies rule ensures that in an Effect Hook all variables that are used are listed as dependencies via the second argument

8. How can we automatically fix linter warnings?
   - We can run the `npm run lint -- --fix` command to automatically fix linter warnings. Running this command will, for example, automatically enter all variables used in an Effect Hook as dependencies.

Chapter 10: Building Your Own Hooks

1. How can we extract a custom Hook from existing code?
   - We can simply put our code into a separate function. In custom Hook functions other Hook functions can be used, but we need to make sure not to violate the rules of Hooks.

2. What is the advantage of creating API Hooks?
   - When defining separate functions for the various API calls, we can easily adjust them if the API changes later on, because we have all the API-related code in one place

3. When should we extract functionality into a custom Hook?
   - We should create a custom Hook when a certain functionality is used in multiple places or when it could be re-used later on

4. How do we use custom Hooks?
   - We can simply call custom Hooks just like we would call official React Hooks or Hooks from libraries

5. When should we create local Hooks?
   - Local Hooks can be used when we want to encapsulate a certain functionality in a separate function, but it will only be used in a single component

6. Which interactions between Hooks are possible?
   - We can use other Hooks in Hook functions and we can pass values from other Hooks to Hooks

7. Which library can we use to test Hooks?
   - We can use the `jest` test runner in combination with the React Hooks Testing Library (`@testing-library/react-hooks`) and the `react-test-renderer` to test Hooks

8. How can we test Hook actions?
   - Hook actions can be tested by using the `act` function. For example, `act(() => result.current.increment())`.

9. How can we test contexts?
   - Contexts can be tested by writing a context wrapper function, which returns the provider. The wrapper function can then be passed to the `renderHook` function. For example, `const { result } = renderHook(() => useTheme(), { wrapper: ThemeContextWrapper })`.

10. How can we test asynchronous code?
    - We can use the async/await construct in combination with the `waitForNextUpdate` function returned from `renderHook` to wait for asynchronous code to finish running

Chapter 11: Migrating from React Class Components

1. How are React class components defined?
    - React class components are defined by using `class ComponentName extends React.Component {`

2. What do we need to call when using a `constructor` with class components? Why?
    - We first need to call `super(props)` to ensure that the props get passed on to the `React.Component` class

3. How do we set the initial state with class components?
    - We can set the initial state in class components by defining the `this.state` object in the `constructor`

4. How do we change the state with class components?
    - In class components, we use `this.setState()` to change the state

5. Why do we need to re-bind the `this` context with class component methods?
    - When passing a method to an element as event handler, the `this` context changes to the element that triggered the event. We need to re-bind the `this` context to the class to prevent this from happening.

6. How can we re-bind the `this` context?
    - We need to use `.bind(this)` on the method in the constructor. For example, `this.handleInput = this.handleInput.bind(this)`.

7. How can we use React context with class components?
    - We can set the `contextType` and then access `this.context`. For example, `static contextType = StateContext`.
    - If we want to use multiple contexts, we can use context consumers. For example, `<StateContext.Consumer>{value => <div>State is: {value}</div>}</StateContext.Consumer>`.

8. What can we replace state management with when migrating to Hooks?
    - We can replace `this.state` and `this.setState` with a State Hook

9. What are the trade-offs of using Hooks versus class components?
    - Function components with Hooks are simpler (no need to deal with constructors, `this`, or destructuring the same values multiple times, no magic when dealing with contexts, props, and state, no need to define both `componentDidMount` and `componentDidUpdate`). Function components also encourage making small and simple components, are easier to refactor and test, require less code, are easier to understand for beginners, and are more declarative.
    - However, class components can be fine when sticking to certain conventions and using the latest JavaScript features to avoid `this` re-binding. Furthermore, class components might be easier to understand for the team, because of existing knowledge.

10. When and how should an existing project be migrated to Hooks?
    - Slowly replace old class components with Hook-based function components when appropriate. For example, when you are already refactoring a component.

Chapter 12: Redux and Hooks

1. What kind of state should Redux be used for?
    - Redux should be used for global state, which is state that is used in multiple components across our app

2. Which elements does Redux consist of?
    - Redux consists of the **store** (an object that describes the full state of our application), **actions** (objects that describe state modifications), **action creators** (functions that create action objects), **reducers** (functions that take the current state and an action object and return a new state), and **connectors** (higher-order components that connect an existing component to Redux)

3. What are the three principles of Redux?
    - Single source of truth (data should always have a single source)
    - Read-only state (it is not possible to modify state directly, only through dispatching actions)
    - State changes are processed with pure functions (given the same state and action, reducers will always return the same new state)

4. Why do we define action types?
    - Action types avoid making typos when defining or comparing the `type` property of actions

5. How can we connect components to Redux?
    - We can either use the `connect` higher-order component, or Dispatch and Selector Hooks

6. Which Hooks can we use with Redux?
    - `useDispatch` to get the dispatch function, `useSelector` to get a certain part of the state, and `useStore` to get the Redux store (for special use cases, such as replacing reducers)

7. Why should we create reusable selectors?
    - Reusable selectors can be used in multiple components. Furthermore, they memoize the result and only recompute it when the state changes.

8. How can we migrate a Redux application?
    - We should first replace simple local state, such as input field values, with State Hooks. Then replace complex local state with Reducer Hooks. We keep global state, which is used across multiple components, in the Redux store. Finally, we use the Selector and Dispatch Hooks instead of the `connect` higher-order component.

9. What are the trade-offs of Redux?
    - The pros of using Redux are: It provides a certain project structure that allows us to easily extend and modify code later on, there are fewer possibilities for errors in our code, it has better performance than simply using React context for state, and it makes our `App` component much simpler by offloading state management and action creators to Redux
    - The downsides of using Redux are: It requires a lot of boilerplate code, the project structure becomes more complicated, and it requires a wrapper component (`Provider`) to connect the app to the store

10. When should we use Redux?
    - We should use Redux only for applications that require complex state changes. For simple projects, Reducer Hooks or even just State Hooks might be enough.

Chapter 13: MobX and Hooks

1. Which elements form the MobX life cycle?
    - Events invoke **actions**, which modify state. **State** is observable and should not contain redundant or derivable data. **Computed values** are derived from the state through pure functions. **Reactions** are like computed values, but they can also produce a side-effect, such as updating the user interface in React.

2. Which decorators does MobX provide?
    - MobX provides decorators for the various elements: `observer`, `observable`, `computed`, and `action`

3. How can we connect components to MobX?
    - We can connect our app to the MobX store by using the `Provider` component and then connect components via the `inject` higher-order component. If we want a component to automatically re-render on state changes, we also need to wrap it with the `observer` decorator function.

4. Which Hooks does MobX provide?
    - We can use the `useObserver` Hook to define parts of our component that should re-compute when the state changes

5. How can we access the MobX store using Hooks?
    - MobX provides a context, which can be used to create custom Hooks that access the MobX stores. We can use a normal Context Hook to access the `MobXProviderContext` from `mobx-react`.

6. Can we store local state using MobX?
    - Yes, with MobX we can create as many stores as we want. MobX even provides a `useLocalStore` Hook to create local stores.

7. How should we go about migrating an existing MobX application to Hooks?
    - We can slowly upgrade certain parts of our MobX applications. Instead of the `inject` higher-order component, we can use a custom Hook that accesses a part of the context. Instead of the `observer` higher-order component, we can use the `useObserver` Hook.
    - We should first use a State Hook for simple local state, then a `useLocalState` Hook for complex local state, and finally keep global state in separate MobX stores.

8. What are the advantages of using MobX?
    - It provides a simple way of dealing with state changes, requires less boilerplate code, provides more flexibility in how our application code is structured, allows using multiple global and local stores, and makes the App component much simpler by offloading state management and actions to MobX

9. What are the disadvantages of using MobX?
    - It allows state changes to happen anywhere, not just in a single store, which could make our app more unpredictable. More flexibility also means it is possible to structure the project in a bad way and cause errors or bugs. Furthermore, MobX requires a wrapper component to connect the app to the store if we want to get all features (we could directly import and use the MobX store, but it would break features such as server-side rendering).

10. When should MobX not be used?
    - MobX should not be used if state changes are simple and only local state within components is used. In that case, State and Reducer Hooks might be enough.

Other Books You May Enjoy

If you enjoyed this book, you may be interested in these other books by Packt:

React Design Patterns and Best Practices - Second Edition
Carlos Santana Roldán

ISBN: 978-1-78953-017-9

- Get familiar with the new React features, like context API and React Hooks
- Learn the techniques of styling and optimizing React components
- Make components communicate with each other by applying consolidate patterns
- Use server-side rendering to make applications load faster
- Write a comprehensive set of tests to create robust and maintainable code
- Build high-performing applications by optimizing components

Mastering React Test-Driven Development
Daniel Irvine

ISBN: 978-1-78913-341-7

- Build test-driven applications using React 16.9+ and Jest
- Build complete web applications using a variety of HTML input elements
- Understand the different types of test double and when to apply them
- Test-drive the Integration of libraries such as React Router, Redux, and Relay (GraphQL)
- Learn when to be pragmatic and how to apply TDD shortcuts
- Test-drive interaction with browser APIs including fetch and WebSockets
- Use Cucumber.js and Puppeteer to build BDD-style acceptance tests for your applications
- Build and test async Redux code using redux-saga and expect-redux

Leave a review - let other readers know what you think

Please share your thoughts on this book with others by leaving a review on the site that you bought it from. If you purchased the book from Amazon, please leave us an honest review on this book's Amazon page. This is vital so that other potential readers can see and use your unbiased opinion to make purchasing decisions, we can understand what our customers think about our products, and our authors can see your feedback on the title that they have worked with Packt to create. It will only take a few minutes of your time, but is valuable to other potential customers, our authors, and Packt. Thank you!

Index

R

CPSIA information can be obtained
at www.ICGtesting.com
Printed in the USA
FSHW011724090820
72821FS